The Grammar of Society
The Nature and Dynamics of Social Norms

In *The Grammar of Society*, Cristina Bicchieri examines social norms, such as fairness, cooperation, and reciprocity, in an effort to understand their nature and dynamics, the expectations that they generate, and how they evolve and change. Drawing on several intellectual traditions and methods, including those of social psychology, experimental economics, and evolutionary game theory, Bicchieri provides an integrated account of how social norms emerge, why and when we follow them, and the situations in which we are most likely to focus on relevant norms. Examining the existence and survival of inefficient norms, she demonstrates how norms evolve in ways that depend on the psychological dispositions of the individual and how such dispositions may impair collective welfare. By contrast, she also shows how certain psychological propensities may naturally lead individuals to evolve fairness norms that closely resemble those we follow in modern societies.

Cristina Bicchieri is the Carol and Michael Lowenstein Term Chair and Professor of philosophy at the University of Pennsylvania, where she is also the Director of the Philosophy, Politics, and Economics Program. The author of many articles and books, including *Rationality and Coordination, The Logic of Strategy, The Dynamics of Norms*, and *Knowledge, Belief and Strategic Interaction*, she has been a Fellow at the Wissenschaftskolleg zu Berlin, the Swedish Collegium for Advanced Study in the Social Sciences, the London School of Economics (Leverhulme Trust), and the Institute for Advanced Studies at the University of Jerusalem.

The Grammar of Society

The Nature and Dynamics of Social Norms

CRISTINA BICCHIERI

University of Pennsylvania

CAMBRIDGE
UNIVERSITY PRESS

CAMBRIDGE UNIVERSITY PRESS
Cambridge, New York, Melbourne, Madrid, Cape Town, Singapore,
São Paulo, Delhi, Dubai, Tokyo, Mexico City

Cambridge University Press
The Edinburgh Building, Cambridge CB2 8RU, UK

Published in the United States of America by Cambridge University Press, New York

www.cambridge.org
Information on this title: www.cambridge.org/9780521574907

First published 2006

A catalogue record for this publication is available from the British Library

Library of Congress Cataloguing in Publication Data

Bicchieri, Cristina.
The grammar of society : the nature and dynamics of social norms /
Cristina Bicchieri.
p. cm.
Includes bibliographical references and index.
ISBN 0-521-57372-6 (hardcover : alk. paper) – ISBN 0-521-57490-0 (pbk. : alk. paper)
1. Social norms. I. Title.
HM676.B53   2006
306–dc22   2005006200

ISBN 978-0-521-57372-6 Hardback
ISBN 978-0-521-57490-7 Paperback

To my parents Vanna and Ettore
and my daughter Tatiana, who
taught me much about
following and breaking rules

Contents

Preface

I do not remember when my interest in social norms began, but the subject has been a long-standing source of curiosity and frustration for me. As a stranger living for many years in foreign countries, I have had to constantly negotiate the meaning of rules and practices that more often than not I did not fully understand, the subtleties of a social language that was not my mother tongue. Norms are the language a society speaks, the embodiment of its values and collective desires, the secure guide in the uncertain lands we all traverse, the common practices that hold human groups together. The norms I am talking about are not written and codified; you cannot find them in books or be explicitly told about them at the outset of your immersion in a foreign culture. We learn such rules and practices by observing others and solidify our grasp through a long process of trial and error. I call social norms *the grammar of society* because, like a collection of linguistic rules that are implicit in a language and define it, social norms are implicit in the operations of a society and make it what it is. Like a grammar, a system of norms specifies what is acceptable and what is not in a social group. And analogously to a grammar, a system of norms is not the product of human design and planning.

My fascination with norms has thus been both personal and intellectual. I am always surprised to realize that norms are supported by and in some sense consist of a cluster of self-fulfilling expectations. If people believe that a sufficiently large number of others uphold a given norm, then, under the right conditions, they will conform to it. A norm's destiny is strictly connected to the dynamics of such expectations; a change in expectations may lead to a dramatic decline in norm compliance and to the eventual demise of the norm itself. How such expectations are formed, where they come from, is one of the themes I address in this book. My frustration has similarly had both very personal and intellectual facets – personal because learning a society's norms as an adult is far less natural and effortless than when you are born into a given culture, and intellectual because much of what is written about norms does not seem to capture what I consider to be their essential features. This book is an answer to my deep-rooted questions about the nature of norms, how they can emerge and thrive or decay, and what compels people to follow them.

The social norms I am talking about are not the formal, prescriptive or proscriptive rules designed, imposed, and enforced by an exogenous authority through the administration of selective incentives. I rather discuss informal norms that emerge through the decentralized interaction of agents within a collective and are not imposed or designed by an authority. Social norms can spontaneously develop from the interactions of individuals who did not plan or design them, as can conventions and descriptive norms. All three are social constructs that have a life simply because enough people believe they exist and act accordingly. To distinguish between these three very different social constructs, I focus in Chapter 1 on the kinds of situations in which they are likely to emerge, as well as on the types of expectations and preferences that support them. Descriptive norms such as fashions and fads, for example, arise in contexts in which people desire to coordinate with (or imitate) others and prefer to do what others do on the condition that they expect a sufficient number of people to act in a certain way. A 'sufficient number' may be just one person, as in the case of a celebrity we want to imitate, or the number may vary from person to person, depending on how cautious one is in assessing the threshold at which to take action. Conventions are descriptive norms that have endured the test of time. If one's main objective is to coordinate with others, and the right mutual expectations are present, people will follow whatever convention is in place. Social norms, on the contrary, are not there to solve a coordination problem. The kinds of situations to which social norms most often apply are those in which there is a tension between individual and collective gains. Pro-social norms of fairness, reciprocity, cooperation, and the like exist precisely because it might not be in the individual's immediate self-interest to behave in a socially beneficial way. This does not mean we follow such norms only when coerced to do so. Granted, some people need incentives in the form of the expectation of rewards and punishments to be induced to comply.

Others instead obey a norm just because they recognize the legitimacy of others' expectations that they will follow the norm. My definition of what it takes for a social norm to exist and be followed takes into account the fact that there are different types of people. All have conditional preferences for conformity, and all need to believe that enough people are obeying the norm to make it worthwhile to conform. What makes people different is the nature of their normative expectations: Some just need to believe that enough other people expect them to conform, whereas others need to believe that others are also prepared to punish their transgressions. In both cases, I stress that preference for conformity is *conditional.* If expectations change, so does conforming behavior. I maintain that norms are never the solution of an original coordination game. However, once a norm is in place, it will *transform* the original game into a new coordination game, at least for those who believe that the norm is in fact followed. In the new game the choice is to follow the standing norm or 'defect' and thus revert to the original game. This choice depends on what we expect others to do. These expectations may be grounded in our knowledge of past behavior of the people we interact with, but more often than not we do not have such personal knowledge of our parties. Where our expectations come from and what grounds them is the theme of Chapter 2.

Because the important question is not whether norms affect behavior, but when, how, and to what degree, in Chapter 2 I show under which conditions the beliefs and preferences that support a norm are activated as the result of the interpretation of specific cues, the categorization of the situation based on those cues, and the consequent activation of appropriate scripts. A situation can be interpreted and categorized in several ways, with very different consequences for norm compliance. An observed exchange, for example, can be perceived as a market interaction, an instance of gift giving, or an act of bribing. Depending on how we categorize it, our expectations, predictions, and emotional responses will be very different. Categorizing an exchange as an instance of gift giving will activate a script that specifies, among other things, roles and possible action sequences. Norms, I argue, are embedded into scripts, the rudimentary theories about social roles and situations that guide us in interpreting social interactions, forming expectations and predictions, assessing intentions, and making causal attributions. Once a script has been activated, the corresponding beliefs, preferences, and behavioral rules (norms) are prompted. The expectations and preferences that determine our choices are thus the result of the activation of collectively shared scripts that are general enough to subsume a wide variety of situations.

The only systematic evidence presently available about which cues make people focus on particular norms are the results of experiments on Ultimatum, Dictator, Trust, and Social Dilemma games. Though the experiments I discuss in Chapters 3 and 4 were not meant to test hypotheses about norms, their results are consistent with a theory of script activation. Furthermore, I show that some behavioral inconsistencies that have baffled investigators can become comprehensible in light of the view of norms I am proposing. In Chapter 3, I consider experimental Ultimatum and Dictator games and contrast the social preference models that have been proposed to explain the results with my own norm-based utility function. I hope to convince the reader that such a utility function is more general than many of those that have been proposed, and that it makes interesting, testable predictions about how manipulating subjects' expectations may induce, or eliminate, conformity to a norm. Chapter 4 examines social dilemma experiments and the surprising results obtained by allowing pre-play communication among the players. When subjects are permitted to communicate about the experiment, even if for a very brief time, we observe almost universal cooperation. A favored explanation is that communication creates a social identity, an *esprit de corps* that would induce a deep change in preferences. I examine the merits of the social identity hypothesis but argue that the available data do not support it. Instead, they support an explanation in terms of social norms. Communication is particularly successful when people make promises to each other, and even if the one-shot nature of the interaction should make such promises no more than cheap talk, it is sufficient to yield scripts (and norms) that support cooperative behavior.

In the last two chapters I look at how a norm might emerge in a situation in which there is none – individuals may, nonetheless, believe a norm exists and actively try to conform to it. A common assumption many people tend to make is that if a norm emerges, then it must be socially advantageous or efficient. In Chapter 5, I show that the dynamics of norm formation may be such that a bad descriptive norm or a bad convention can easily come about if certain conditions are present. And the transformation of such a bad convention into a poor social norm is always possible. The most common condition in which a bad norm is likely to occur is one in which individuals are in a state of *pluralistic ignorance*. When there is an incentive to conform to what other people do, there is no transparent communication, and individuals have a tendency to believe that what they observe others doing reflects their true preferences, then it is likely that the collective outcome will be something most participants did not want and may even keenly dislike. Again, this is a particularly powerful example of the role collective beliefs play in generating social institutions that may turn out to be far from efficient or socially beneficial.

In Chapter 6, I look at how a social norm, a norm of fair division in this case, can evolve from the interactions of agents who believe a norm exists but have no idea what it is. I assume that agents care in varying degrees about norms, and that they are trying to learn what the shared norm is, because they wrongly believe there must be one. This model is quite different from the traditional evolutionary models we find in the literature on the evolution of norms, especially because it starts from specific psychological assumptions about individual dispositions, assumptions that are in fact well supported by psychological research. The interesting result is that individuals endowed with such dispositions who interact with each other and are capable of learning and revising their strategies according to a best-reponse dynamics will indeed generate a norm of fair division. Such a norm is very close to the modal and median offers we observe in experimental Ultimatum games. Much work remains to be done about how certain dispositions to recognize and follow norms have evolved, and why. What I want to show is that norms can endogenously emerge from the interactions of individuals who share such dispositions, and I hope I have convinced my readers that this is a real possibility.

Acknowledgments

This book took a very long time to write, and I cannot hope to recall all the colleagues and students with whom, at various times, I have discussed some of the topics it addresses. Brian Skyrms offered constant encouragement and intellectually stimulating exchanges over the years. Robyn Dawes's friendship and intellectual companionship has given me more than I will ever be able to acknowledge. His criticism was always constructive, and he guided my first steps in the maze of experimental research. Colleagues at Carnegie Mellon, the Center for Rationality and Interactive Decision Theory at the University of Jerusalem, and the Swedish Collegium for Advanced Study in the Social Sciences in Uppsala have read earlier versions of many chapters and have provided advice, encouragement, and constructive criticism. Part of the book was written during the year I spent at the Wissenschaftskolleg in Berlin. The norms seminar we had every week was a fun, stimulating, and challenging arena in which to test some of my ideas: Ernst Fehr, Robert Boyd, Joe Heinrich, Alex Kacelnik, Michael Kosfeld, and (too briefly) Shlomo Shwartz and Catherine Eckel were wonderful partners in the quest for understanding why we (and animals) behave as we do.

My students had an important role to play, because many of them were exposed to several versions of the manuscript, and their thoughtful comments helped make it what it is. Erin Krupka edited some of the chapters and always offered intelligent advice, as did Giacomo Sillari and Ryan Muldoon, who read and reread the whole manuscript and gave me precious suggestions. Daniel Neill and Jiji Zhang were wonderful helpers, always ready to pick a formal challenge. Jason Dana's knowledge of the experimental literature was a boon, especially with respect to the work done on fairness. Finally, several friends and colleagues read and commented on different versions of specific chapters of the book. A special thanks goes to Jason Alexander, Peter Vandershraaf, Rachel Croson, John Duffy, Yoshi Fukui, Massimo Bigliardo, Matteo Motterlini, Bill Keech, Roberto Weber, and Peyton Young.

Chapters 4 and 5 are based on previous articles. Chapter 4 draws from "Covenants Without Swords: Group Identity, Norms, and Communication in Social Dilemmas," *Rationality and Society* 14(2): 192–228, 2002. Chapter 5 contains part of the material that appeared in "The Great Illusion: Ignorance, Informational Cascades and the Persistence of Unpopular Norms" (with Y. Fukui), *Business Ethics Quarterly* 9: 127–155, 1999. I wish to thank those journals for allowing me to publish some of the material. Some of the material of Chapter 6 will appear in "The Evolution of Fairness," an article jointly written with Jason Alexander.

1

The Rules We Live By

Introduction

Despite the ubiquitous reference to the concept of social norms in the social sciences, there is no consensus about the power of social norms to direct human action. For some, norms have a central and regular influence on human behavior, while for others, the concept is too vague, and the evidence we have about norm compliance is too contradictory to support the claim that they appreciably affect behavior. Those who doubt that norms have a behavior-guiding force argue that human behavior only occasionally conforms with the dominant social norms. If the same norms are in place when behavior is norm-consistent as when it is norm inconsistent, why should we believe that norms mediated any of it?

Much of the discussion about the power norms have to affect behavior arises from a confusion about what is meant by 'norm.' A norm can be formal or informal, personal or collective, descriptive of what most people do, or prescriptive of behavior. In the same social setting, conformity to these different kinds of norms stems from a variety of motivations and produces distinct, sometimes even opposing, behavioral patterns. Take for example a culture in which many individuals have strong personal norms that prohibit corrupt practices and in which there are legal norms against bribing public officers, yet bribing is widespread and tolerated. Suppose we were able to independently assess whether an individual has a personal norm against corruption. Can we predict whether a person, who we know condemns corruption, will bribe a public officer when given a chance? Probably not, but we could come closer to a good prediction if we knew certain factors and cues are present in this situation and have an influence on the decision. The theories of norms we have inherited, mainly from sociology, offer little help, because they did not develop an understanding of the conditions under which individuals are likely to follow a norm or, when several norms may apply, what makes one of them focal.

A first step in the direction of a deeper understanding of what motivates us to follow a norm is to clarify what we mean by a social norm. 'Norm' is a term used to refer to a variety of behaviors, and accompanying expectations. These should not be lumped together, on pain of missing some important features that are of great help in understanding phenomena such as variance in norm compliance. Inconsistent conformity, for example, is to be expected with certain types of norms, but not with others. In this chapter I put forth a 'constructivist' theory of norms, one that explains norms in terms of the expectations and preferences of those who follow them. My view is that the very existence of a social norm depends on a sufficient number of people believing that it exists and pertains to a given type of situation, and expecting that enough other people are following it in those kinds of situations. Given the right kind of expectations, people will have conditional preferences for obeying a norm, meaning that preferences will be conditional on having expectations about other people's conformity. Such expectations and preferences will result in collective behaviors that further confirm the existence of the norm in the eyes of its followers.

Expectations and conditional preferences are the building blocks of several social constructs, though, not just social norms. *Descriptive norms* such as fashions and fads are also based on expectations of conformity and conditional preferences, and so are *conventions*, such as signaling systems, rules of etiquette, and traffic rules. In both cases, the preference for conformity does not clash with self-interest, especially if we define it in purely material terms.[1] One can model descriptive norms and conventions as solutions to coordination games. Such games capture the structure of situations where there exist several possible equilibria and, although we might like one of them best, what we most want is to coordinate with others on *any* equilibrium; hence we act in conformity to what we expect others to do. Descriptive norms and conventions are thus representable as equilibria of original coordination games. *Social norms*, on the contrary, often go against narrow self-interest, as when we are

---

[1] What one most prefers in these cases is to 'do as others do,' or to coordinate with others' choices.

required to cooperate, reciprocate, act fairly, or do anything that may involve some material cost or the forgoing of some benefit. The kinds of problems that social norms are meant to solve differ from the coordination problems that conventions and descriptive norms 'solve.' We need social norms in all those situations in which there is conflict of interest but also a potential for joint gain. The games that social norms solve are called mixed-motive games.[2] Such mixed-motive games are not games of coordination to start with, but social norms, as I shall argue, *transform* mixed-motive games into coordination ones. This transformation, however, hinges on each individual expecting enough other people to follow the norm, too. If this expectation is violated, an individual will revert to playing the original game and to behaving 'selfishly.' This chapter thus starts with a precise definition of social norms and only later considers what differentiates such norms from descriptive norms and conventions. Because all three are based on expectations and conditional preferences, I pay special attention to the nature of expectations (empirical and/or normative) that support each construct.

The definition of social norm I am proposing should be taken as a *rational reconstruction* of what a social norm is, not a faithful descriptive account of the real beliefs and preferences people have or of the way in which they in fact deliberate. Such a reconstruction, however, will have to be reliable in that it must be possible to extract meaningful, testable predictions from it. This is one of the tasks I undertake in Chapters 3 and 4. An important claim I make in this chapter is that the belief/desire model of choice that is the core of my rational reconstruction of social norms does not commit us to avow that we always engage in conscious deliberation to decide whether to follow a norm. We may follow a norm automatically and thoughtlessly and yet still be able to explain our action in terms of beliefs and desires.

The simplistic, common view that we conform to norms either because of external sanctions or because they have been internalized flies in the face of much evidence that people sometimes obey norms even in the absence of any obvious incentive structure or personal commitment to what the norm stands for (Cialdini et al. 1990). Many who postulate internal or external incentives as the sole reasons for compliance also maintain compliance is the result of a conscious process of balancing costs

---

[2] Well-known examples of mixed-motive games that can be 'solved' (or better, 'transformed') by norms of fairness, reciprocity, promise-keeping, etc., are the Prisoner's Dilemma, the Trust game, and Ultimatum games.

and benefits, culminating in a decision to conform or to transgress. Yet personal experience tells us that compliance is often automatic and unreflective: Even important social norms like those that regulate fair exchanges and reciprocation are often acted on without much thought to (or awareness of) their personal or social consequences. Whereas the literature on social norms has traditionally stressed the deliberational side of conformity, in this book I want to emphasize its automatic component. Both aspects are important, but too much emphasis on conscious deliberation may miss crucial links between decision heuristics and norms, as I explain in this chapter and the next.

Whenever we enter any environment, we have to decide how to behave. There are two ways to reach a decision. One is somewhat ideally depicted by the traditional rational choice model: We may systematically assess the situation, gather information, list and evaluate the possible consequences of different actions, assess the probability of each consequence occurring, and then calculate the expected utility of the alternative courses of action and choose one that maximizes our expected utility. I dub this the *deliberational* route to behavior. The process of rational deliberation ending in the choice of a course of action is likely to be costly in time, resources, and effort and to require considerable skill. The deliberational way to behavior is likely to be chosen when one is held accountable for one's choice; when the consequences may be particularly important and long-lasting; or when one has the time, knowledge, and disposition to ponder over alternative choices. But even in these cases deliberation may fall short of the ideal. Behavioral decision theorists have gathered compelling evidence that actors systematically violate the assumptions of rational choice theory (Camerer 2003). Thus the deliberational way need not assume perfect rationality. It only requires conscious deliberation and balancing of what one perceives (or misperceives) as the costs and benefits of alternative courses of action. On occasion we do engage in conscious deliberation, even if the process is marred by mistakes of judgment and calculation.

A second way to reach a decision relies on following behavioral rules that prescribe a particular course of action for the situation (or a class of similar situations). These guides to behavior include habits, roles, and, of course, norms. Once one adopts a behavioral rule, one follows it without the conscious and systematic assessment of the situation performed in deliberation. The question of how a particular behavioral rule is primed is of great interest. The answer is likely to lie in the interplay of (external) situational cues and (internal) categorization processes. These processes lie beyond awareness and probably occur in split seconds. Models of mental processes (Lamberts and Shanks 1997) suggest that, when faced with a new situation, we immediately search for cues about how to interpret it or what is appropriate behavior for that situation. It is conjectured that we compare the situation we face with others we remember that possess similar characteristics, and that this comparison activates behavior that is considered most "normal" for this type of situation. The comparison process is one of 'categorization,' of finding relevant similarities between the current context and other ones we have experienced in the past. To efficiently search our memory and group a new event with previously encountered ones, we use cognitive shortcuts. Cognitive shortcuts play a crucial role in categorization and the subsequent activation of scripts and schemata.[3] Consequently, they are responsible for some norms rather than others being activated in different situations. Let us call this route to behavior the *heuristic* route. In the heuristic route, behavior is guided by *default rules* stored in memory that are cued by contextual stimuli. Norms are one class of default rules. According to the heuristic route, norm compliance is an automatic response to situational cues that focus our attention on a particular norm, rather than a conscious decision to give priority to normative considerations. On the heuristic view, norms are context-dependent, meaning that different social norms will be activated, or appear appropriate, depending on how a situation is understood. In turn, our understanding of a situation is influenced by which previous contexts we view as similar to the present one, and this process of assessing similarities and 'fitting' a situation into a pre-existing category will make specific norms salient. I spell out in detail the process of drawing social inferences and categorizing in the next chapter.

The distinction between deliberational and heuristic routes to behavior is a useful simplification, and it should be taken as such. The truth is that we often combine the two routes, and what is a staple of the heuristic process can also be an object of deliberation. Conformity to a norm, for example, is not always an automatic, nondeliberational affair. Especially when we are tempted to shirk an obligation, the thought of the personal and social consequences of alternative courses of action is often present and important in determining our choice. I want to stress, again, that deliberation is not synonymous with 'rational deliberation', in part

---

[3] Schemata are cognitive structures that contain knowledge about people, events, roles, etc. Schemata for events (e.g., a lecture, going to a restaurant, playing a chess game) are also called scripts. Chapter 2 further elaborates on the roles of scripts and schemata.

because the list of possible mistakes and cognitive impairments with which our decision processes are fraught is potentially very long. *Rational deliberation* is better conceived of as an ideal type, against which we measure the amplitude of our deviations. What is important in deliberation is the *conscious* processing of information and evaluation of options. Whether ideally or less than ideally rational, deliberation refers to beliefs and desires of which we are *aware.* Deliberation is the process of consciously choosing what we most desire according to our beliefs. In the deliberational view, beliefs and desires (preferences) are treated as mental states of which we are conscious, at least in the course of deciding which action to take.

The problem with taking beliefs and desires to be conscious mental states is that they can then play no role in the heuristic route to behavior. There is, however, a long and reputable philosophical tradition that takes beliefs and desires to be *dispositions* to act in a certain way in the appropriate circumstance. According to the dispositional account, to say that someone has a belief or a preference implies that we expect such motives to manifest themselves in the relevant circumstances. Thus, for example, one might automatically obey a norm of truth-telling without thinking of the beliefs and preferences that underlie one's behavior. These beliefs and preferences might become manifest only when they happen to be unfulfilled. To assess the nature of such beliefs and desires, all we need is a simple counterfactual exercise. Suppose we ask someone if he would keep telling the truth (as he normally and almost automatically does) in a world where he came to realize that people systematically lie. Our subject may answer in a variety of ways, but whatever course of action he claims he would choose, it is likely that he never thought of it before. *He did not know,* for example, that he would be ready to become a liar until he was put in the condition to reflect on it. Our subject may reason that it would be stupid on his part to keep telling the truth, as it would put him at an obvious disadvantage. Evidently his preference for sincerity is conditional on expecting reciprocity. If these expectations were not met, his preference would be different. Note that dispositions need not be stable: Preferences, for example, can be context-dependent, in the sense that even a small change of context may elicit different, even opposite, preferences. The research on framing effects shows just that (Tversky and Kahneman 1981). The heuristic way to behavior seems perfectly compatible with a dispositional account of beliefs and desires. Namely, the default rules that we tend to automatically follow are accompanied and supported by beliefs and desires that we become aware of only when they are challenged. Surprise in this case breeds awareness of our underlying motives. Moreover, whenever a norm is 'cued' or made salient in a particular environment, the mechanism that primes it elicits the beliefs and preferences that support that particular norm. The remainder of this chapter presents a taxonomy of norms that relies on preferences and beliefs as 'building blocks.'

The idea that social norms may be cued, and hence manipulated, is attractive. It suggests that we may be able to induce pro-social behavior and maintain social order at low cost. Norms differ in different cultures, and what cues a Westerner into cooperation will probably differ from what cues a Mapuche Indian (Henrich 2000). In both cases, however, it may be possible to structure the environment in a way that produces desirable behavior. If you sail along the Italian coast, you will notice large beach posters that invite sailors not to litter and pollute "your" sea. In Sweden, instead, environmentalist appeals always refer to "our" environment. The individualistic Italians are seemingly thought to be more responsive to an invitation to protect a "private" good, whereas Swedes are expected to be sensitive to pleas for the common good. Knowing what makes people focus on the environment in a positive way can be a powerful tool in the hands of shrewd policymakers. Still, developing successful policies that rely on social norms presents several difficulties. To successfully manipulate social settings, we need to predict how people will interpret a given context, which cues will 'stand out' as salient, and how particular cues relate to certain norms. When multiple conflicting norms could apply, we should be able to tell which cues will favor one of them. Many norms are not socially beneficial, and once established they are difficult to eliminate. If we know what induces people to conform to "anti-social" norms, we may have a chance to curb destructive behavior. Without a better understanding of the mechanisms through which norms control our actions, however, there is little hope of predicting and thus influencing behavior. The mechanisms that induce conformity are very different for different kinds of norms. Consequently, a good understanding of their diversity will prevent us from focusing on the wrong type of norm in our efforts to induce pro-social behavior.

In the remainder of this chapter I will introduce the reader to my definition of social norms, descriptive norms, conventions, and the conditions under which one might see individuals following any of these. I shall especially focus on the four (individually) necessary and (jointly) sufficient conditions for a social norm to exist that I develop in the following pages: contingency, empirical expectations, normative expectations, and conditional preferences.

Social Norms

Social norms are frequently confused with codified rules, normative expectations, or recurrent, observable behavior. However, there are significant problems with such definitions of social norms. By the term *social norm*, I shall always refer to informal norms, as opposed to formal, codified norms such as legal rules. Social norms are, like legal ones, public and shared, but, unlike legal rules, which are supported by formal sanctions, social norms may not be enforced at all. When they are enforced, the sanctions are informal, as when the violation of a group norm brings about responses that range from gossip to open censure, ostracism, or dishonor for the transgressor. Some such norms may become part of our system of values, and we may feel a strong obligation to obey them. Guilt and remorse will accompany transgression, as much as the breach of a moral rule elicits painfully negative feelings in the offender. Social norms should also be distinguished from moral rules: As I shall argue in the following, expectations are crucial in sustaining the former but not necessarily the latter. In particular, conformity to a social norm is conditional on expectations about other people's behavior and/or beliefs. The feelings of shame and guilt that may accompany a transgression merely reinforce one's tendency to conform, but they are never the sole or the ultimate determinants of conformity. I will come back to this point later.

A norm cannot be simply identified with a recurrent, collective behavioral pattern. For one, norms can be either prescriptive or proscriptive: In the latter case, we usually do not observe the proscribed behavior. As anyone who has lived in a foreign country knows, learning proscriptive norms can be difficult and the learning process slow and fraught with misunderstandings and false steps. Often the legal system helps, in that many proscriptive norms are made explicit and supported by laws, but a host of socially relevant proscriptions such as "do not stare at someone you pass by" or "do not touch people you are not intimate with when you talk to them" are not codified and can only be learned by trial and error. In most cases in which a proscriptive norm is in place, we *do not* observe the behavior proscribed by the norm, and it is impossible to determine whether the absence of certain behaviors is due to a proscription or to something else, unless we assess people's beliefs and expectations. Furthermore, if we were to adopt a purely behavioral account of norms, nothing would distinguish shared fairness criteria from, say, the collective morning habit of brushing one's teeth. It would also be difficult to deal with those cases in which people pay lip service to the norm in public and deviate in private. Avoiding a purely behavioral account means focusing on the role expectations play in supporting those kinds of collective behaviors that we take to be norm-driven. After all, I brush my teeth whether or not I expect others to do the same, but I would not even try to ask for a salary proportionate to my education if I expected my co-workers to go by the rule of giving to each in proportion to seniority. There are also behaviors that can be explained only by the existence of norms, even if the behavior prescribed by the norm in question is never observed. In his study of the Ik, Turnbull (1972) reports that these starved hunter-gatherers tried hard to elude situations where their compliance with norms of reciprocity was expected. Thus they would go out of their way to avoid being in the role of gift-taker. A leaking roof would be repaired at night, so as to ward off offers to help and future obligations to repay the favor. Hunting was a solitary and furtive activity, so as to escape the obligation to share one's bounty with anyone encountered along the way. Much of the Ik's behavior can be explained as a successful attempt at *eluding* existing reciprocity norms. The Ik seemed to have collective beliefs about what sort of behavior was prescribed/proscribed in a given social context but acted in ways that prevented the underlying norms from being activated. Their practices demonstrate that it is not necessary to observe compliance to argue that a norm exists and affects behavior.

As Turnbull's example shows, having normative beliefs and expecting others to conform to a norm do not always result in a norm being activated. Nobody is violating the norm, but everybody is trying to avoid situations where they would have to follow it. Thus, simply focusing on norms as clusters of expectations might be as misleading as focusing only on the behavioral dimension, because there are many examples of discrepancies between normative expectations and behavior. Take the widely acknowledged norm of self-interest (Miller and Ratner 1998): It is remarkable to observe how often people (especially in the United States) expect others to act selfishly, even when they are prepared to act altruistically themselves. Studies show that people's willingness to give blood is not altered by monetary incentives, but typically those very people who are willing to donate blood for free expect others to donate blood only in the presence of a sufficient monetary reward (Wuthnow 1991). Similarly, when asked whether they would rent an apartment to an unmarried couple, all landlords interviewed in Oregon in the early 1970s answered positively, but they estimated that only 50% of other landlords would accept an unmarried couple as tenants (Dawes 1972). Such cases are rather common; what is puzzling is that people may expect a given norm to be upheld in the absence of information about other people's conforming behavior and in the face of personal evidence to the contrary. Thus, simply focusing on people's expectations may tell us very little about collective behavior.

If a purely behavioral definition of norms is deficient, and one solely based on expectations is questionable, what are we left with? Norms refer to behavior, to actions over which people have control, and are supported by shared expectations about what should/should not be done in different types of social situations. Norms, however, cannot just be identified with observable behavior, nor can they be equated with normative beliefs, as normative beliefs may or may not result in appropriate actions. In what follows I introduce a definition of social norms that will be helpful in shedding light on the conceptual differences between different types of social rules. My definition coincides with ordinary usage in some respects but departs from that usage in others. Given the fact that the term has been put to multiple uses, it would be unrealistic to expect a single definition to agree with what each person using the term means. The goal of giving a specific definition is to single out what is fundamental to social norms, what differentiates them from other types of social constructs.

Besides helping in drawing a taxonomy of social rules, a successful definition should provide conditions under which normative beliefs can be expected to be consistent with behavior. This means that those conditions that are part of the definition of social norm would be used as premises in a practical argument whose conclusion is the decision to conform to a norm. This does not entail that we normally engage in such practical reasoning and deliberation and are consciously aware of our conforming choices. We should not confuse adopting a belief/desire explanatory framework with assuming awareness of our own mental processes. As I shall discuss in the last section, the fact that we are mostly unaware of our mental processes, and often are not fully conscious of what we are thinking and doing, is no objection to a belief/desire model of choice.

The definition I am proposing should be taken as a *rational reconstruction* of what a social norm is, not a description of the real preferences and beliefs people have or the way in which they in fact deliberate (if at all). The advantage of a rational reconstruction is that it substitutes a precise concept for an imprecise one, thus removing the conceptual difficulties and vagueness related to everyday usage. A rational reconstruction of the concept of norm specifies in which sense one may say that norms are rational, or compliance with a norm is rational.[4] Not every rational reconstruction will do, though. For example, a rational reconstruction that is built on a belief/desire structure is constrained by the requirement that, were beliefs to be different (in a specified sense), we would expect behavior to change in predictable ways. In other words, a successful rational reconstruction must allow meaningful, interesting predictions to be made.

Conditions for a Social Norm to Exist

Let R be a *behavioral rule* for situations of type S, where S can be represented as a mixed-motive game. We say that R is a social norm in a population P if there exists a sufficiently large subset $P_{cf} \subseteq P$ such that, for each individual $i \in P_{cf}$:

> *Contingency*: i knows that a rule R exists and applies to situations of type S;
> *Conditional preference*: i prefers to conform to R in situations of type S on the condition that:
> (a) *Empirical expectations*: i believes that a sufficiently large subset of P conforms to R in situations of type S;
> and either
> (b) *Normative expectations*: i believes that a sufficiently large subset of P expects i to conform to R in situations of type S;
> or
> (b′) *Normative expectations with sanctions*: i believes that a sufficiently large subset of P expects i to conform to R in situations of type S, prefers i to conform, and may sanction behavior.

A social norm R is *followed* by population P if there exists a sufficiently large subset $P_f \subseteq P_{cf}$ such that, for each individual $i \in P_f$, conditions 2(a) and either 2(b) or 2(b′) are met for i and, as a result, i prefers to conform to R in situations of type S.

There are several features of the above definition that need explanation. First, note that a rule R can be a social norm for a population P even if it is not currently being followed by P. I defined P_{cf} as the set of 'conditional followers' of R, those individuals who know about R and have a conditional preference for conforming to R. I defined P_f as the set of 'followers' of R, those individuals who know about R and have a preference

---

[4] E. Ullmann-Margalit (1977) made one of the first attempts at explaining norms and norm compliance in a rational choice framework.

for conforming to R (because they believe that the conditions for their conditional preference are fulfilled). A behavioral rule R is a social norm if the set of its conditional followers is sufficiently large; a social norm is followed if the set of its followers is sufficiently large. Second, note that a social norm is defined relative to a population: A behavioral rule R can be a social norm for one population P and not for another population P'. Finally, the 'sufficiently large subset P_{cf} of P'' clause reflects the fact that social norms need not be universally conditionally preferred or even universally known about in order to exist. A certain amount of opportunistic transgression is to be expected whenever a norm conflicts with individuals' self-interest. The 'sufficiently large subset P_f of P_{cf}' clause reflects the fact that, even among conditional followers of a norm, some individuals may not follow the norm because their empirical and normative expectations have not been fulfilled. Moreover, even among the members of P_f, occasional deviance due to mistakes is to be expected. How much deviance is tolerable is an empirical matter and may vary with different norms. For example, we would expect P_{cf} (the proportion of conditional followers) to be equal to P in the case of group norms, especially when the group is fairly small, whereas P_{cf} will be close to P in the case of well-entrenched social norms. For new norms, or norms that are not deemed to be socially important, the subset P_{cf} could be significantly smaller than P. I will discuss deviance and its effects in later chapters, when I address the issue of norm dynamics. It should also be noted that I do not assume P_f (the proportion of actual followers) to be common knowledge. Different individuals will have different beliefs about the size of P_f and thus have different empirical expectations. If so, they will have different thresholds for what 'sufficiently large' means. What matters to actual conformity is that each individual in P_{cf} believes that her threshold has been reached or surpassed.

Condition 1, the *contingency condition*, says that actors are aware that a certain behavioral rule exists and applies to situations of type S. This collective awareness is constitutive of its very existence as a norm. Note that norms are understood to apply to classes or families of situations, not to every possible situation or context. A norm of revenge, for example, usually applies to members of a kinship group and is suspended in case of proven accidental death. A norm of reciprocity may not be expected to apply if the gift was a bribe, and the rules that govern fair allocation of bodily organs differ from those that regulate the fair allocation of university Ph.D. slots. Situational contingency explains why people sometimes try to manipulate norms by avoiding those situations to which the norm applies (as the Ik did with food sharing and gift reciprocation) or by negotiating the meaning of a particular situation.

Condition 2(a), the *empirical expectations condition*, says that expectations of conformity matter. I take them to be *empirical expectations*, in the sense that one expects people to follow *R* in situations of type *S* because one has observed them to do just that over a long period of time. If the present situation is of type *S*, one can reasonably infer that, *ceteris paribus*, people will conform to *R* as they always did in the past. Notice that the fulfillment of Condition 2(a) entails that a social norm is *practiced* (or is *believed to be practiced*) in a given population (which may be as small as a group comprising a few members or as large as a nation); otherwise there would not be empirical expectations. Sometimes expectations are formed not by directly observing conforming behavior, but rather its consequences. This would happen, for example, with norms regulating private behavior. In this case, public support might be voiced for a norm that is seldom adhered to in private. If conformity to such a norm is believed to produce observable consequences, then observing such consequences will validate the norm. But if these consequences are the effect of other causes, people will draw the wrong inference and continue to believe that the norm is widely followed even when support is dwindling. Consider a norm of private behavior such as avoiding premarital sex; what we observe are the consequences of such behavior (teen pregnancy, etc.) or the lack thereof. If people take adequate precautions, there might be greater deviance than expected, but people might still believe that the norm is widely practiced in the population.[5] Norms regulating private behavior may thus present us with cases in which Conditions 2(a) and 2(b) are satisfied. However, as I shall make clear in discussing Conditions 2(b) and 2(b′), there are many individuals for whom 2(b′), the possibility of sanctions, is a *necessary* condition for compliance. Such individuals will believe they are expected to follow the norm but will not expect to be sanctioned for transgressing it [Condition 2(b′)], because deviance can be concealed. In this case, public endorsement of the norm may coexist with considerable private deviance.

The expectations mentioned in Condition 2(a) could, besides being empirical, also be *normative*, in the sense that people might think that

---

[5] I would venture the hypothesis that norms regulating private behavior may survive longer than other norms precisely because of the lack of direct observation of compliance. On the other hand, they may decay very quickly once the magnitude of deviance becomes public knowledge, as I discuss in Chapter 5.

everyone 'ought to' conform to *R* in situations of type *S*. The 'ought' implicit in a normative belief does not necessarily state an obligation. Take, for instance, a well-known convention such as the rule of driving on the right side of the road. We believe that people ought to follow that rule simply because, if they do not, they risk killing or being killed. If a person does not want to jeopardize her life, nor does she have an interest in causing harm to others, then we believe she 'ought to' follow the driving rule. The 'ought' in this case expresses prudential reasons and is akin to saying that, if you have goal *x* and the best available means to attain *x* is a course of action *y*, then you ought to adopt *y*. Consider, on the other hand, a rule of equal division. In this case, we may believe that others ought to 'divide the cake in equal parts' because this is the fair thing to do. We think they have an obligation to follow the rule, a duty to be fair. I do not ask for the moment what grounds this obligation, though I shall come back to this question later. At this point it is only important to make a distinction between a prudential 'ought' and the statement of an obligation. From now on, when I mention 'normative expectations' I will always refer to the latter meaning.

Normative expectations do not necessarily trump empirical ones, and very often they coexist. Many well-entrenched social norms are thought to be good or reasonable, and people often refer to these qualities in justifying their own compliance, as well as in expecting other people to comply. Yet there are also cases in which most people do not think that others ought to conform to a norm, even when they observe widespread conformity (i.e., the number of those prepared to sanction others is very small). This happens with norms that many, maybe most, people dislike and yet are followed by everyone. Wearing a veil may be an unpleasant requirement for many Muslim women, and they may not believe that one 'ought to' wear it (apart from prudential reasons). But if each woman holds the belief that she is expected to wear a veil, in the sense of believing that a sufficiently large number of people think she ought to wear a veil and prefer that she wears a veil (because it is her religious duty to do so), then she will feel great social pressure in that direction, and the result will be overall collective compliance. In this case the norm regulates public, observable behavior; hence a transgression is easily detected and likely to be punished. If it is not public knowledge that most women dislike the veil, a woman may even take widespread adherence to this norm as evidence that other women follow this practice out of a deep religious conviction, and infer that she is expected by everyone else to fulfill her religious duty as well. Everyone may secretly feel she is a deviant, but they will never openly question the norm. I will discuss in Chapter 5 how such 'pluralistic ignorance' may be responsible for the survival of norms that most people dislike.[6] For now it is enough to emphasize that a normative interpretation of Condition 2(a) is not necessary for my argument.

Conditions 2(b) and 2(b′) tell us that people may have different reasons for conditionally preferring to follow a norm. Condition 2(b), the *normative expectations condition*, says that expectations are *believed to be reciprocal*. That is, not only do I expect others to conform, but I also believe they expect me to conform. What sort of belief is this? On the one hand, it might just be an empirical belief. If I have consistently followed *R* in situations of type *S* in the past, people may reasonably infer that, *ceteris paribus*, I will do the same in the future, and that is what I believe. On the other hand, it might be a normative belief: I believe a sufficiently large number of people think that I have an obligation to conform to *R* in the appropriate circumstances. For some individuals, the fulfillment of Conditions 2(a) and 2(b) is sufficient to induce a preference for conformity. That is, such individuals recognize the legitimacy of others' expectations and feel an obligation to fulfill them. For others, the possibility of sanctions is crucial to induce a preference for conformity. Condition 2(b′) says that I believe that those who expect me to conform also *prefer* me to conform, and might be prepared to sanction my behavior when they can observe it. Sanctions may be positive or negative. The possibility of sanctions may motivate some individuals to follow a norm, either out of fear of punishment or because of a desire to please and thus be rewarded. For others, sanctions are irrelevant, and a normative expectation is all they need. Condition 2(b′) does not say that transgressions *will* be punished and compliance rewarded. It only states that a sufficiently large subset of *P may* be capable and willing to sanction others. As we shall see in a moment, normative expectations are essential for the enforcement of social norms.

Now suppose Conditions 1, 2(a), and either 2(b) or 2(b′) hold. Each of them is a necessary condition for conformity to *R*, but *contingency*, *empirical*, and *normative expectations* are not jointly sufficient to produce conformity to rule *R* in situations of type *S*. I might expect others to follow a rule of equal division, and believe that I am expected to follow that rule

---

[6] What social psychologists call *pluralistic ignorance* is a psychological state characterized by the belief that one's private thoughts, attitudes, and feelings are different from those of others, when in fact they are not, in a situation where public behavior contradicting these private thoughts and attitudes is identical (Allport 1924; Miller and McFarland 1991).

too, but when it is my turn to 'cut the cake,' I may be tempted to get a larger share, especially if nobody is observing my action. If I do not, it must be that I *prefer* to conform to the rule. However, this is no simple, unconditional preference for conformity. Condition 2, the *conditional preference condition*, says this preference is *conditional* on expecting others to conform to R and either believing that one is expected to conform to R or believing that those who expect one to conform also have a preference for collective conformity and are prepared to punish or reward. If so, the counterfactual "If I were to believe that others do not follow R or do not expect me to follow R, then I would not want to conform to R" must be true. What I am saying suggests that following a social norm may be contrary to self-interest, especially if we define it in purely material terms. Thus it may be the case that, in the presence of monetary or otherwise 'material' rewards, I have a tendency to prefer more to less but will prefer to 'share' if I believe that I am in a situation in which some form of generosity is the norm, if I expect others to be generous, and if I believe them to think I 'ought to' be generous in the circumstances. In this case, I might prefer to behave generously. Note that the generous behavior induced by adherence to a norm should not be confused with other motives, such as altruism or benevolence.

Before we continue our discussion of Condition 2, let us look at an example that will hopefully clarify what I mean by saying that the motive to follow a norm should be distinguished from other motives. Consider playing a one-shot prisoner's dilemma, where C stands for Cooperate and D stands for Defect.

If the payoffs in Figure 1.1 represent sums of money, just by looking at them it is not obvious what a player will choose. Suppose Self, the row player, only cares about his 'material' self-interest and thus prefers DC to CC, CC to DD, and DD to CD. If B stands for best, S for second best,

FIGURE 1.1. One-shot Prisoner's Dilemma

Others

		C	D
Self	C	S	W
	D	B	T

FIGURE 1.2. One-shot Prisoner's Dilemma from the perspective of narrowly self-interested Self

T for third best, and W for worst, the preference ranking of a narrowly self-interested Self would look like that shown in Figure 1.2.

The narrowly self-interested person will always choose D, her dominant strategy. Self-interest, however, should not be confused with the desire for material incentives. A self-interested person is one whose ultimate desires are self-regarding, but these desires can involve 'immaterial' goods such as power and recognition, or the experience of 'benevolent' emotions. A self-interested person may want to 'feel good' (or reap social rewards like status and love) by reciprocating expected cooperation and in this case her preferences would look like those in Figure 1.3.[7]

Others

		C	D
Self	C	B	T
	D	W	S

FIGURE 1.3. One-shot Prisoner's Dilemma from the perspective of benevolent Self

---

[7] I am assuming for simplicity that the benevolent individual is concerned with the material well-being of another. The same assumption holds for the pure altruist. However, their utility functions look very different. If x_i and x_j are the payoffs, respectively, of player i and player j, the pure altruist's utility will be $U_i f(x_j)$, and $\delta U_i/\delta x_j > 0$. The benevolent player's utility instead will be $U_i f(x_i, x_j)$, and the first partial derivatives of U_i with respect to x_i, x_j, will be strictly positive.

Others

		C	D
	C	S	B
Self	D	W	T

FIGURE 1.4. One-shot Prisoner's Dilemma from the perspective of altruistic Self

Note that a benevolent person would prefer CD to DC; that is, she would prefer, *ceteris paribus*, to be the righteous sucker rather than the spiteful cheat. This preference would probably be cost-sensitive, but if the costs are not too high, it makes sense to prefer to 'feel good about oneself' and be the loser rather than penalizing another to get some small benefit.

Benevolent motives are different from those of a pure altruist, whom I take to be a person whose ultimate desires are completely other-regarding. A pure altruist wants, first and foremost, the satisfaction of another's desires, at whatever cost to the self.[8] If the altruist believes his partner to be a narrowly self-interested type, the altruist's preference ranking would look like the one in Figure 1.4.

The person who instead follows a norm of generosity or cooperation need not have a desire to 'feel good': If the established norm is a coop-erative one, provided Conditions 2(a) and either 2(b) or 2(b′) are met, the preference ranking of the norm follower will look like the one in Figure 1.5.

The norm follower's preferences are similar to those of the self-interested, benevolent person, with a crucial difference: For the benev-olent person, it is better to be the 'sucker' than the 'crook' (CD is pre-ferred to DC); but for the norm follower, the reverse may be true.[9] This distinction should not be interpreted as denying that individuals can be both benevolent and norm followers. Benevolence, however, is usually

---

[8] The choice to donate part of one's liver to an anonymous recipient is an example of altruism, because the risk of complications and even death from the procedure is sizable.

[9] Again, I am assuming for simplicity that the norm follower is not also benevolent. If this were the case, Figures 1.3 and 1.5 would coincide, at least in all those situations to which benevolence applies. In large, anonymous groups, where the effects of one's actions are insignificant, we may expect less cooperation (or not at all) from the benevolent person, whereas the norm follower would not be affected.

Others

C   D

	C	D
Self C	B	W
Self D	T	S

FIGURE 1.5. One-shot Prisoner's Dilemma from the perspective of norm-following Self

directed to people with whom we habitually interact and know well. As social distance increases, benevolence tends to decrease. If most people were benevolent toward strangers, we would need no pro-social norms of fairness, reciprocity, or cooperation. In particular, we would have no need for those norms that 'internalize' externalities created by behavior that imposes costs on other people. Thus it is plausible that one is guided by benevolence (or even altruism) in interacting with family and friends, but when interacting with strangers, be guided by social norms. Moreover, whereas benevolence toward those who are close to us should be a relatively stable disposition, generosity or cooperativeness with strangers will vary according to our expectations, as defined in Conditions 2(a) and 2(b) or 2(b′).

It may be objected that motivational distinctions are futile, because often observation cannot discriminate among them. If in a one-shot social dilemma experiment we observe consistent cooperative behavior, what can we say about the underlying preferences? If, as economists do, we take preferences to describe behavior and not motivation, what we observe is a 'revealed preference' for taking into account other people's welfare. *Why* we do that does not matter. Still, I believe motivations carry some weight. Up to now, most experiments have been geared to show that human behavior consistently deviates from the narrow, self-interested paradigm postulated by traditional economic models. Experiments have been very successful in this respect, yet they do not tell us why actors have other-regarding preferences. Is it altruism, benevolence, or are we priming norms of fairness and reciprocity? The answer is clearly important, and not just for the policymaker. What we now need is to test more sophisticated hypotheses about what goes on in the black box. To do so it is important to pay attention to the meanings of the concepts we use (and test). To tell altruism and benevolence apart is not very difficult: If an altruist is informed that the other defected, the altruist should keep cooperating. Never mind there are very few such people around: If they exist, that is the way altruists will behave. The benevolent individual and the norm follower are more difficult to set apart. For one, a norm follower may also be motivated by benevolence. If, however, some norm followers are not benevolent, the distinction would be most clear in all those situations in which people are forced to choose between CD and DC. Suppose we identify a subset of people who 'conditionally cooperate' in one-shot Prisoner's Dilemmas. That is, controlling for their expectations, they cooperate whenever they expect others to cooperate, too. It should be possible to perform another experiment on the same individuals in which the only choice is one between being the sucker or the crook: The subject might be told that the other player will choose next, and will have to choose the opposite of what she does. Provided the personal cost is not too high, the benevolent person should prefer being the sucker. A person who instead followed a cooperative norm for reasons other than benevolence would see no reason to be the sucker (possibly provided the cost to the other person is not too great).

Condition 2 (the *conditional preference condition*) marks an important distinction between social and personal norms, whether they are habits or have moral force. Take the habit of brushing my teeth every morning. I find it sanitary, and I like the taste of mint toothpaste. Even if I came to realize that most people stopped brushing their teeth, I would continue to do so, because I have independent reasons for doing it. It is likewise with moral norms: I have good, independent reasons to avoid killing people I deeply dislike. Even if I were to find myself in a Hobbesian state of nature, without rules or rights, I would still feel repugnance and anguish at the idea of taking a life. With this I do not mean to suggest that moral norms are a world apart from other rules. Instead, by their very nature, moral norms demand (at least in principle) an unconditional commitment.[10]

---

[10] It might be argued that even what we usually understand as moral norms are conditional. One may be thoroughly committed to respect the sanctity of human life, but there are circumstances in which one's commitment would waver. Imagine finding oneself in a community where violence and murder are daily occurrences, expected and condoned by most. One would probably at first resist violence, then react to it, and finally act it out oneself. Guilt and remorse would in time be replaced by complacency, as one might come to feel the act of murder to be entirely necessary and justified. The testimonies of survivors of concentration camps, as well as the personal recollections of SS officers, are frightening examples of how fragile our most valued principles can be.

Commitments of course may falter, and we may run afoul of even the most cherished obligations. The point is that, under normal conditions, expectations of other people's conformity to a moral rule are not a good *reason* to obey it. Nor is it a good reason that others expect me to follow a moral rule. If I find their expectation reasonable, it is because I find the moral norm reasonable; so the reason to obey it must reside in the norm itself. What I am saying goes against the well-known Humean interpretation of our moral obligation to follow the requirements of justice (Hume 1751). This moral obligation is, according to Hume, *conditional* on the expectation that others are following the norms of justice too. In my interpretation, Hume's requirements of justice are social norms, because they fulfill my conditions for a social norm to exist. What distinguishes norms of justice from other social norms is that many of us would have a conditional preference for abiding by such norms because we acknowledge that the normative expectations expressed by Condition 2(b) are *legitimate* and should therefore be satisfied. Their legitimacy may stem from recognizing how important it is for the good functioning of our society to have such norms, but of course their ongoing value depends on widespread conformity. There is nothing inherently good in our fairness norms, above and beyond their role in regulating our ways of allocating and distributing goods and privileges according to the basic structure of our society.[11] However, many of us would feel there is something inherently bad in taking a life, especially when the victim is a close kin. All known societies have developed similar rules against killing one's kin or mating with one's parents. The *unconditional* preference most of us have for not committing such acts may have an evolutionary origin, and typically contemplating killing or incest elicits a strong, negative emotional response of repugnance. What needs to be stressed here is that what makes something a social or a moral norm is our attitude toward it.[12] How we *justify* our conditional or unconditional allegiance has no bearing on the reality of the distinction, and the latter is all that matters to my definition of social norms.

Condition 2 also helps in distinguishing a social norm from a collective habit. People in Pittsburgh wear coats in winter. I expect them to keep

[11] The fact that 'fair' allocations reflect the structure of society is well known to anthropologists. In traditional, authoritarian societies, for example, the allocation of goods is based on rank. Such allocations are accepted by all the involved parties as just (Fiske 1992).

[12] Our attitudes are also shaped in part by the norms that we internalize, which results in a positive feedback loop between attitudes and adherence to norms.

wearing coats in winter and, were anyone interested in my attire, I would
say they expect me to wear a coat in winter. But these expectations have no
bearing on my decision to wear a coat. There is no connection between
my preference for wearing a coat and my expectations about the rest
of the population. My not wearing a coat in winter may violate their
expectations, and it may cause surprise and puzzlement, but does it matter
to my choice? It does not, because I have independent reasons to wear a
coat in winter. Condition 2 instead tells that my preference for conformity
depends on the expectation that others conform, and either the belief that
they expect me to conform or the belief that they also prefer me to
conform (and may sanction my behavior). Using the language of game
theory, we may say that compliance with R is not a strictly dominant
strategy.[13] If it were, one would want to follow R irrespective of one's
expectation about others' behavior.

Taken together, the conditions I have stated tell us that social norms
motivate action, but they do so only indirectly. The direct, underlying
motives are the beliefs and desires that support the norm. Thus the presence of a norm of reciprocity, and its salience in a particular situation,
motivate me to act in a congruent manner, but my behavior is ultimately
explainable only by reference to my preferences and expectations. This
statement should not be surprising to those who adopt a methodological
individualist perspective. In this perspective, a norm is a social construct
reducible to the beliefs and desires of those involved in its practice; if
individuals for some reason stopped having those beliefs and desires, the
norm would cease to exist.

The conditions for a norm to exist entail, when they are fulfilled, that
a social norm is an equilibrium. First, let me briefly define the notion of
equilibrium as it is widely used in the social sciences. An *equilibrium* is a
situation that involves several individuals or groups, in which each one's
action is a best reply to everyone else's action. It is a situation of stable
mutual adjustment: Everyone anticipates everyone else's behavior, and all
these anticipations turn out to be correct. In other words, an equilibrium
is a set of self-fulfilling prophecies that individuals formulate about each
other's actions. Social norms, as I stated before, have no reality other
than our beliefs that others behave according to them and expect us to

---

[13] A (strictly) dominant strategy is a strategy that gives the individual who chooses it a
better payoff (usually expressed in utility) than any other available strategy. In a game-
theoretic context, a (strictly) dominant strategy gives a better payoff than any other
available strategy independently of what the other players do.

behave according to them. In equilibrium, such beliefs are confirmed by experience and thus they become more and more ingrained as time goes on. A norm of reciprocity is supported by our beliefs that people will comply with it, and that they expect us to comply with it too. Each time we reciprocate we strengthen the norm and confirm those expectations. In equilibrium everyone reciprocates and is right to do so. But there could also be another equilibrium in which nobody reciprocates. If people expected no reciprocity, there would be no trust in the first place, and again expectations would be self-fulfilling: Everyone would distrust and would be right to do so, because nobody would reciprocate. A situation in which some reciprocate and some do not would not be stable, for the second group might learn that they would do better by reciprocating, and thus switch their strategy (or the first group might learn not to recipro-cate, and change their strategy). In some recent work on norm emergence (Bicchieri et al. 2004), I looked at how a norm of trust/reciprocity can emerge in a situation in which different groups display different behav-iors, and how they may solidify into an equilibrium. For now, let us agree that social norms, those bundles of self-fulfilling expectations we live by, are equilibria.

If a social norm is followed, then by definition individuals' expecta-tions are self-fulfilling, in the sense that the combination of empirical and normative expectations [Conditions 2(a) and 2(b) or 2(b')] give one a reason to obey the norm. What sort of reason is this? As I already mentioned, I believe different people may have different reasons for com-pliance that extend beyond the standard reasons given by many social scientists, namely, that we fear punishment when we disobey a norm. It is certainly possible that some may *fear* the consequences of violating oth-ers' normative expectations, because violation may trigger resentment and unpleasant consequences for the transgressor.[14] Such individuals would be motivated to follow a norm to avoid negative sanctions. Yet I would argue that another reason for compliance is the *desire to please* others by doing something others expect and prefer one to do. In this case, the expectation of a positive sanction would be a reason for com-pliance. A third reason for compliance with a norm is that one accepts others' normative expectations as well founded. In this case, sanctions

---

[14] This is often the case when members of group A *impose* certain norms on members of group B (the target group). In this case most members of B would conform out of fear of punishment or because of the desire to be rewarded for good behavior. Conditions 2(a) and 2(b') would in this case refer to expectations about the targeted members of P only.

have no weight. If I recognize your expectations as reasonable, I have a reason to fulfill them. I may still be tempted to do something else contrary to your expectations, but then I would have to justify (if only to myself) my choice by offering alternative good reasons and show how they trump your reasons. This need to offer a justification (to myself as well as others) signals that I recognize others' expectations as cogent. The acceptance of others' expectations as legitimate is usually accompanied by the recognition that negative sanctions against transgressors are also legitimate. If your expectation is reasonable, I must also acknowledge that it is reasonable for you to punish my transgression, even if the reprimand is nothing more than an expression of disapproval of my behavior. The common observation that norm transgression is often accompanied by punishment (or the expectation of punishment) does not entail that norms are only *supported* by sanctions, in the sense that if sanctions were not there, conformity would be entirely absent. Recognizing punishment as legitimate is different from acknowledging that, de facto, violations are punished. The latter does not involve understanding conformity expectations as valid, whereas the former presupposes the acceptance of a norm. It is important to acknowledge that different individuals may need different normative expectations in order to be prepared to obey a norm, and that an individual may follow some norms, but not others, in the absence of any expected sanction.[15]

Fear and the desire to please are powerful motives, but they imply that a norm would only be followed in circumstances in which either there is monitoring of one's actions and sanctioning is possible (as in repeated interaction) or there is some way to ensure that one's action is acknowledged by the people one wants to please or else has a noticeable effect on their well-being.[16] Under anonymity conditions, and when one's action effects are insignificant (as when contributing to some public goods), the motivation to obey a norm would falter. A possible objection to this conclusion is that we may feel *guilt* at violating a norm, and the emotion of guilt supports conformity even in the absence of external monitoring and sanctioning (Elster 1989). According to this view, emotions directly *cause* conformity. But why and when do we feel guilt? Imagine a situation in which someone does not expect others to conform to a practice of truth-telling. He has observed people openly lying and has been lied

---

[15] In Chapter 3, I discuss the differences we observe in the behavior of Proposers in Ultimatum versus Dictator games.

[16] Individuals differ as to the scope of people they want to please. Most of us stop at family and friends, but some may include acquaintances and even strangers.

to often enough to expect further dishonesty. Yet he is made to believe that he is expected to conform to a norm of truth-telling. It is likely that this individual would consider the expectation illegitimate, and he would feel no guilt at violating it. Guilt, as well as resentment, presuppose the violation of expectations we consider *legitimate*. It is irrational to resent a malfunctioning computer, but it is reasonable to resent the seller if we think he should have known (and told us) the computer was defective. We trusted him, and he flouted our legitimate expectations of honesty and good faith. Guilt and resentment *signal* that a social norm is in place and that mutual conformity expectations are legitimate. It is reasonable to feel guilt or resentment precisely because there is a norm, a set of mutual expectations that we recognize should be met. The existence of an accepted norm that one contemplates violating is the source of guilt, but it is the recognized legitimacy of mutual normative expectations, not the emotion of guilt, that motivates conformity.

Notice that I am not postulating a generic desire to meet, whenever possible, other people's expectations. In his analysis of conventions, Sugden (2000) assumed we possess a 'natural aversion' toward acting contrary to the preferences (and expectations) of others. This propensity may be true for the preferences and expectations of family and friends, but it is hardly at work with strangers. As social distance increases, we tend to care less and less for others' preferences and expectations, especially when these preferences and expectations run counter to other interests we have. Sugden's assumption would restrict norm-abiding behavior to a circle of family and friends, but these are precisely the circumstances where norms are not needed. In large, anonymous groups, if we do not want to act contrary to others' normative expectations, it must be because we find such expectations reasonable. The acceptance of others' normative expectations as reasonable is the third kind of motive to conform to a social norm I mentioned before. This need not be a motive for everyone, but in all cases in which anonymity and the absence of sanctions tempt us to defect, for a norm to survive there must be a critical number of people for which such reasons have power.

Since social norms often go against our self-interest, especially if we narrowly interpret it as a desire for material possessions, a social norm need not be an equilibrium of an ordinary game in which payoffs represent self-interested preferences. Thus, for example, a cooperative norm cannot be a Nash equilibrium of the PD game represented in Figure 1.1.[17] If

---

[17] A Nash equilibrium is a combination of strategies, one for each player, such that each player's strategy is a best reply to the strategies played by the other players.

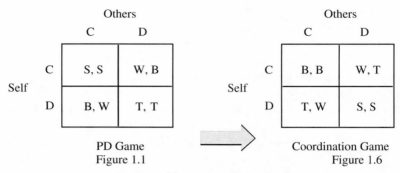

FIGURE 1.6. Norms transform games

such a norm exists and is followed, however, the original PD game would be transformed (at least for the norm followers) into the subsequent, very different game shown in Figure 1.6.

In the traditional Prisoner's Dilemma game, each player's preference ranking is DC > CC > DD > CD. As before, B stands for 'best,' S for 'second best,' and so on. In the symmetric game of Figure 1.6 instead, each norm follower's preference ranking is CC > DD > DC > CD. That is, the players who follow a cooperative norm will do it because their empirical and normative expectations have been met and hence they *prefer* to obey the norm. The new game in Figure 1.6 is a coordination game with two *strict* Nash equilibria, one of which is Pareto superior to the other.[18,19] When a norm of cooperation is obeyed, a game like the PD of Figure 1.1 is *transformed into a coordination game*: Players' payoffs in the new game will differ from the payoffs of the original game, because their preferences and beliefs will be as in Conditions 2, 2(a), and 2(b) or 2(b′) previously outlined. Indeed, if a player knows that a cooperative norm exists and expects a sizeable part of the population to follow it, then, provided she also believes she is expected (and maybe also preferred) to follow such norm, she will have a preference to conform to the norm in a situation in which she has the choice to cooperate or to defect. Note that what I am saying implies that a social norm, unlike a convention, is never a solution

---

[18] In a strict Nash equilibrium each player's strategy is a unique best reply to the other players' strategies. This means that a strict Nash equilibrium cannot include weakly dominated strategies.

[19] A coordination game is a game in which there are at least two Nash equilibria in pure strategies, and players have a mutual interest in reaching one of these equilibria (CC or DD in Figure 1.6), even if different players may prefer different equilibria (which is not the case in Figure 1.6).

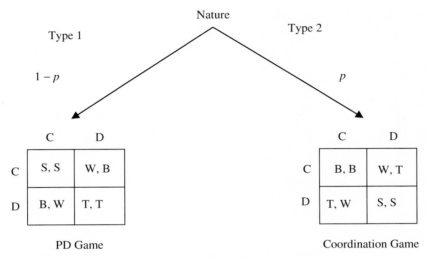

FIGURE 1.7. A Bayesian game

of an original coordination game, though it is an equilibrium of the new, transformed game it *creates*.

It is important to recall that my definition of social norm does not entail that *everybody* conforms. In fact, the definition says that a social norm may exist and not be followed. For some, the PD game of Figure 1.1 is never transformed into any other game. And even a person who starts playing a coordination game like the one in Figure 1.6 may revert to playing the regular PD game if she realizes that Condition 2(a) (*empirical expectations*) is violated. Let me clarify this point with a simple example. Suppose an actor is faced with a finitely repeated PD, and suppose the situation is such that a 'cooperative' norm is primed.[20] The player knows there exists a cooperative norm that applies to this kind of situation. The player also knows that there are several types of players, some of which would not see the game as he does. To make matters easy, suppose there are two types of players, those who simply see the game as a PD and those who follow a cooperative norm.[21] In this case we may model the choice situation as a Bayesian game (Figure 1.7) in which Nature picks a player type with a given probability, so that with prior probability p the opponent one faces

---

[20] In Chapter 4 I discuss in detail how such 'cooperative' norms might be primed.

[21] In a finitely repeated game, even a 'selfish' player may want to cooperate for a while, if it is not common knowledge that all players are rational and selfish (Kreps et al. 1982). This consideration, however, has no bearing on my argument because, until a defection is observed, a player cannot distinguish between a forward-thinking selfish type and a true cooperator.

is playing a coordination game, and with probability $(1 - p)$ he is playing a PD game.[22] If a norm-follower assesses a sufficiently high probability to being matched with a similar type, he will cooperate.[23]

When faced with a defection, however, the player will reassess his probabilities and possibly revert to playing the equilibrium strategy (defect) for the traditional PD game. One might thus say that the *existence* of a norm always presents a conditional follower with a Bayesian game: If the normative and empirical expectations conditions are fulfilled, she will assess a higher probability to being matched with a similar player type (a norm follower) and act accordingly. But she must also be prepared to revise her probabilistic assessment in case experience contravenes her previous expectations.[24] Note that the existence of a social norm facilitates equilibrium selection in the Bayesian game faced by the conditional norm followers. If the probability of being matched with a similar type is high enough, C,C is the selected equilibrium; otherwise D,D will be selected. (Appendix 1 presents a formal treatment of a norm-based utility function and the conditions under which a PD game becomes a coordination game.)

This simple and elegant game-theoretic model offers a language, built on the notions of belief and preference, in which to cast what we commonly observe: In an experimental setting in which repetitions of a PD-like game are allowed, we witness high initial levels of cooperation. Yet cooperation precipitously declines as soon as some players defect (Fehr and Gachter 2000a). Whether a game-theoretic model provides an acceptable explanation for what we observe depends in part on our willingness to take 'as if' models seriously, which in turn relates to the possibility of drawing interesting predictions from them. In the case at hand, people may not be aware of their preferences and never have made a probabilistic assessment of the situation; yet, if we take their behavior to reveal certain dispositions, we may predict that, *ceteris paribus*, factors that we expect will change their expectations will have a measurable effect on future choices.

---

[22] When players are uncertain as to the type of player they are facing, they will assess some probability that the other player is of a certain type. Typically the list of all possible types and their prior probability of occurring in the population are taken to be common knowledge among the players (Harsanyi 1967, 1968).

[23] If players use an availability heuristic to come to this probability assessment, the probability of playing a coordination game might initially be much higher. That is, if a player is the type who follows a cooperative norm, he tends to believe there is a high probability that others are like him.

[24] This revision is governed by a "learning rule." I discuss one such rule in Chapter 6.

Descriptive Norms

Let us now look at how the definition of social norms given above differentiates several types of social constructs and behaviors that are often lumped together. Sometimes 'norm' means what people commonly do in certain situations, what constitutes 'normal' or 'regular' behavior. This notion of regular behavior differs in important respects both from a shared habit and from what people believe ought to be done, what is socially approved or disapproved. The regular behaviors I am referring to, and their influence on people's choices, have been extensively studied by social psychologists, most notably Cialdini et al. (1990), who dubbed them *descriptive* norms. Examples of descriptive norms are all sorts of fashions and fads, in addition to the many collective behaviors that people (rightly or wrongly) deem to convey important information about the surrounding world. Conventions, as we shall see, are a kind of descriptive norm, but not all descriptive norms become stable conventions. Note that there is no intrinsic property of a behavioral pattern that makes it a descriptive norm: What is a descriptive norm for one group may be an entrenched social norm for another. Dress codes are a case in point. For the office workers at a particular firm, a 'dress-down Friday' informal rule is nothing more than a fashion code that, though widely adopted, remains entirely discretionary. For teenage members of a Los Angeles gang, on the contrary, a dress code may signal group loyalty, so much so that every member is expected to rigidly adhere to the code and transgressions are punished. What makes a collective behavior a descriptive or a social norm are the expectations and motives of the people involved. This point is worth emphasizing: It is the way we relate to behavioral rules by way of preferences and expectations that gives them their identity as habits, norms, or mere conventions.

We conform to social norms because we have *reasons* to fulfill others' normative expectations. These reasons often conflict with our self-interest, at least narrowly defined. Conformity to descriptive norms is, on the contrary, *always* dictated by self-interest: We conform because such norms make life easier for us, because we want to 'fit in' or do the right thing – as when we adopt a new fashion – or simply because they provide evidence of what is likely to be effective, adaptive behavior, as when we bought Internet stocks because many people we know were buying them and were doing well. Often there are good prudential or informational reasons to "do as the Romans do." Conformity to a descriptive norm may be motivated by a desire to imitate others' behavior in uncertain or ambiguous situations. In such circumstances, others' behavior provides us with information about the appropriate course of action, as when a young employee imitates older, more experienced colleagues' way of handling complaints. Imitation may be a reasonable, cost-effective choice, provided we believe that the majority's behavior or opinion conveys the information we lack. There are many occasions in which we have to make a quick decision without much information about the environment: Gathering information may be unfeasible or have too high an opportunity cost in terms of resources (such as time and money) that one would more effectively employ elsewhere. Or we may be in a condition in which the wrong decision could have serious consequences, and we lack the expertise to properly evaluate the situation. Conversely, there are circumstances in which the consequences of a decision are not too important, and here again gathering information seems a waste of resources. In all these cases, we look at the choices other people make as a guide to our own choices. While this may seem like a good deal for the actors at the time, it can ultimately mean all actors depend on the choices of one (or a few) first mover(s), and those choices may or may not be good ones. This type of 'informational cascade' (Banerjee 1992) may be the reason why some inefficient descriptive norms emerge and persist, as I will discuss in Chapter 5.

For now let me stress that conformity to a descriptive norm need not involve an obligation or normative expectations: We do not feel any group pressure to conform, nor do we believe that others expect us to comply with what appears to be a collective behavior. Deviation from the 'norm' is not punished, nor is compliance overtly approved. For example, if I decide – alone among my friends and co-workers – not to invest my retirement money in stocks, I do not expect to be blamed or ostracized. At worst, they will think I am overly cautious. A crucial feature of *descriptive norms* is thus that they entail *unilateral* expectations. Though we may have come to expect others to follow a regular behavioral pattern, we do not feel any social pressure to conform. That is, Conditions 1, 2, and 2(a) apply but Conditions 2(b) and 2(b') do not. In most cases of descriptive norms, there simply are no reciprocal expectations: We do not believe others care about our choices or expect us to follow any particular behavior. When I choose to adopt a new fashion, I usually do not think I am *expected* to follow it. But even in those cases in which we are aware that we might be expected to follow the majority's decision or opinion, we do not count on being blamed if we follow a different path. Others may think it would be prudent or reasonable for us to behave as they do (for example, to pick a certain stock portfolio), but the 'ought' involved in stating prudential reasons is very different from a normative ought. I might recognize the reasonableness of others' expectations, but not their legitimacy.

Fulfilling others' expectations in this case is not a reason for compliance, whereas expecting a majority of people to behave in a given way is a *necessary reason* to adopt that behavior. It is only a necessary reason, however, because one must also have a *conditional preference* for conforming. Expectations alone cannot motivate a choice: My choice to conform depends on expecting a majority of people to conform, but it must be that I prefer to follow such 'normal' behavior on condition that it is the majority's behavior. This latter condition differentiates a descriptive norm from a collective habit: In the example of wearing a coat in the Pittsburgh winter, I have an independent reason (and thus a preference) to wear a coat, irrespective of what other people do. But in the case of a new fashion, following it depends on one's perception of what other people do. After Mary Quant introduced the miniskirt in the 1960s, it probably took a small number of trendsetters to reach a critical mass and start what became a major change in women's fashion. That critical mass of women, however, was crucial in determining the success of the new attire: Most women would not have started wearing a miniskirt if not for the sense that it was now 'in' and many celebrities were wearing it. It should be noted that often it is the *perception* of a critical mass, rather than a real critical mass, that tips the balance in favor of the new behavior. A small but vocal minority, or an endorsement by some celebrity, may thus be enough to induce a change in mass behavior.

The conditional preference for conformity may be dictated, among other things, by a desire to 'fit in' or be fashionable, or just by prudential reasons; it does not, however, spring from a desire to fulfill other people's expectations or from fear of being punished if one does not meet them. For a descriptive norm to exist, the following conditions must be met.

Conditions for a Descriptive Norm to Exist
Let R be a *behavioral rule* for situations of type S, where S is a coordination game. We say that R is a descriptive norm in a population P if there exists a sufficiently large subset $P_{cf} \subseteq P$ such that, for each individual $i \in P_{cf}$,

1. *Contingency*: i knows that a rule R exists and applies to situations of type S;
2. *Conditional preference*: i prefers to conform to R in situations of type S on the condition that:

(a) *Empirical expectations*: i believes that a sufficiently large subset of
P conforms to R in situations of type S.

A descriptive norm is followed by population P if there exists a sufficiently large subset $P_f \subseteq P_{cf}$ such that, for all $i \in P_f$, Condition 2(a) is met
for i and as a result i prefers to conform to R in situations of type S.

A descriptive norm thus tells what a person would do if he had certain
expectations. For instance, "walk on the left side of the sidewalk" and
"walk on the right side of the sidewalk" are both descriptive norms. Some
people may follow the first rule (because they expect others to do the
same), some people may follow the second rule (again, because they
expect others to do the same), and some people may follow neither rule
(because they do not expect a sufficient number of other people to walk
on a specific side of the sidewalk). Even in a society where one of the
rules has been conventionalized, it is clear that the other rule still exists
as a possibility: I drive on the right side of the road, but if I observed
large numbers of people driving on the left side of a particular road, my
expectations would change and I would consider driving on the left side
of that road.

As in the case of social norms, the preference for conformity is conditional, but this time it is only conditional on expecting others to follow
the behavioral rule in a given class of situations. Note that a descriptive
norm that is followed is an equilibrium, in the sense that followers' beliefs
will be self-fulfilling: If one believes R to be widely followed, then it is in
one's interest to follow R, too. Thus, if enough people come to believe R
is the 'norm,' they will behave in ways that further validate those beliefs.
The conditional preference for conformity may be driven by the desire
to imitate those we believe are more informed or by the hope of 'fitting
in' a group we value. Or it may simply be the wish of doing what we think
most people do. Be it as it may, a preference for conformity depends on
expecting others to conform to R.

If a descriptive norm is an equilibrium, what sort of game is it an equilibrium of? Consider again the miniskirt fashion: In this case, a woman
has several choices of attire, of which the miniskirt is one. Assume for
simplicity that there are only three possible types of clothes women can
choose from: M (miniskirt), L (long skirt), and P (pants). Assume also
that a woman already has L and P in her wardrobe, and has to decide
whether to buy and wear M. The choice of M is thus more costly than L
or P, but she prefers above all to be fashionable. Her choice matrix would
look like the one in Figure 1.8.

Others

	M	L	P
M	1, 2	0, 1	0, 1
Self L	0, 2	2, 1	0, 1
P	0, 2	0, 1	2, 1

FIGURE 1.8. An Imitation game

Notice that the payoffs of 'Others' need not be the same as the payoffs of 'Self.' Indeed, suppose 'Others' are the trendsetters that start a new fashion. I assume the trendsetters will not care whether 'Self' follows the new fashion; what the trendsetters care about is self-expression, and starting a new fashion is not their goal [M may have a higher payoff (2) for trendsetters because they always prefer to do the 'new' thing]. 'Self' instead wants to imitate the trendsetters; hence she cares about whether she coordinates with 'Others.' Because 'Others' may not care at all about being imitated, the three Nash equilibria of the game are not strict. Imitation is a one-sided coordination game.[25] Even if the choice of M is more costly than P or L for 'Self' (it has a lower payoff), if it is believed that now "it is *in* wearing miniskirts," the imitators' choices will converge to M. The example shows that a descriptive norm may be a suboptimal equilibrium and still be the one chosen by the players. It also shows that the class of games of which descriptive norms are equilibria is much larger than the class of coordination games of which conventions are equilibria. As I shall discuss shortly, the latter are always coordination games without nonstrict Nash equilibria and for that reason, in such games, all players prefer that everybody conforms. Such preferences are absent in a descriptive norm.

Earlier I represented social norms as coordination games, too. There is a crucial difference, though. The existence of a social norm *transforms* a game like the Prisoner's Dilemma (or any other mixed-motive game) into

---

[25] Note that 'most other women' need not refer to an entire population or even a large group. Some descriptive norms are *exclusive*, in that they signal belonging to a special, selected group. Fashion may play that role on occasion.

a coordination game (or a Bayesian game, in which we may be playing a coordination game with a given probability), by providing actors with an alternative set of expectations and preferences. But the problem that a social norm is solving in the first place is *never* a coordination problem. If I expect everybody to cooperate, to be fair, or to reciprocate favors, I may be tempted not to, and only a desire to fulfill others' expectations may induce me not to stray. This desire may spring from fear, benevolence, or the acknowledgment of the legitimacy of others' reasons and expectations. Social norms by and large apply to situations in which there is a conflict between selfish and pro-social incentives. In contrast, descriptive norms *solve* a preexisting coordination problem (even if it is a unilateral one, as in imitation). If so, following a descriptive norm is not in opposition to self-interest. Indeed, it is usually in one's self-interest (however narrowly defined) to follow a descriptive norm. In sum, we may say that a descriptive norm is always an equilibrium strategy of an original coordination game. In a given situation S, a descriptive norm is followed if and only if the players of the coordination game expect (with sufficiently high probability) a particular equilibrium strategy to be played, and thus they play that strategy as well.[26]

Note that the game-theoretic representation is silent about the dynamics leading to one particular equilibrium. We still need a plausible story about the dynamics that led women to adopt *en masse* the miniskirt. For the moment, however, this should not be a matter of concern; for now all we want to answer are questions about conformity and norm elicitation.

Conventions

Descriptive norms, such as fashions and fads, can wane rather quickly, but some of them may crystallize into stable *conventions*, such as signaling systems or dressing codes. Such conventions are useful because they coordinate our expectations and often act as signals that facilitate interaction and communication. Usually no intrinsic value is attributed to a convention, although violating it can be costly, as the cost is directly related to the consequences of breaching a coordination mechanism. For example, the trader on the stock exchange floor signals with her fingers how many shares she wants to buy or sell. The failure to do so is not socially

---

[26] A definition of descriptive norms that *requires* them to be followed would limit descriptive norms to a time-varying and imprecisely defined subset of the equilibria and would also make it hard to talk about equilibrium strategies that are not currently being played.

condemned, sanctioned, or accompanied by guilt. Not following the convention simply means the trader will not be able to communicate what she wants and lose an opportunity to gain. When a convention is in place, expectations of compliance are *mutual.* An actor expects others to follow the convention, and she also believes she is expected to follow it by the other participants in the conventional practice. The traders expect each other to follow the signaling convention, as much as we normally expect a competent speaker to stick to the rules of English usage. Yet such mutual expectations are never a sufficient reason to adhere to a convention. It must be that one has a conditional preference for coordinating and communicating with others, as failure to coordinate and communicate comes with a personal cost.

David Lewis first defined conventions as equilibria of coordination games (Lewis 1969). According to Lewis, a convention is a regular pattern of behavior that is a strict Nash equilibrium in a coordination game with $n \geq 2$ strict Nash equilibria.[27] This requirement is meant to capture the *arbitrariness* of conventions, in particular the awareness on the part of those participating in a convention that there are possible alternative arrangements. In a coordination game, the interests of the participants may or may not perfectly coincide. In the miniskirt example, all the followers had the same (ordinal) preferences. In the game in Figure 1.9, instead, the players' interests do not exactly coincide. What matters though is that everyone does better by coordinating with the choices of other players than by 'going solo.'

The game in Figure 1.9 can be interpreted as a situation in which two people want to coordinate or 'be together,' but one would prefer to go to the Opera whereas the other prefers playing Golf. The game has two strict Nash equilibria in pure strategies, (Golf, Golf) and (Opera, Opera), and a mixed-strategy equilibrium in which 'Other' chooses Golf with probability 1/3 and Opera with probability 2/3, and 'Self' chooses

---

[27] Lewis's account of convention is quite different from mine, and it runs as follows (p. 78):

> A regularity R in the behavior of members of a population P when they are agents in a recurrent situation S is a *convention* if and only if it is true that, and it is common knowledge in P that, in almost any instance of S among members of P, (1) almost everyone conforms to R; (2) almost everyone expects almost everyone else to conform to R; (3) almost everyone has approximately the same preferences regarding all possible combinations of actions; (4) almost everyone prefers that any one more conform to R, on condition that almost everyone conforms to R; (5) almost everyone would prefer that any one more conform to R', on condition that almost everyone conform to R', where R' is some possible regularity in the behavior of members of P in S, such that almost no one in almost any instance of S among members of P could conform both to R' and to R.

Other

Golf   Opera

		Golf	Opera
Self	Golf	1, 2	0, 0
	Opera	0, 0	2, 1

FIGURE 1.9. A Coordination game

Golf with probability 2/3 and Opera with probability 1/3. Clearly the preferences of the players are not identical. They do, however, prefer to be together rather than be separate. The players may settle on one of the equilibria for whatever reason, but once they are in equilibrium, they have no incentive to deviate from it.[28] When I say that a convention is 'self-sustaining,' I just mean that each actor has a self-interested motivation to conform to the convention.

The matrix in Figure 1.9 does not tell us *which* equilibrium is played, because it all depends on the expectations players bring to the game. Thus 'Self' may have to settle for Golf, if he expects 'Other' to make that choice, and vice versa. But how are these expectations justified? This is a well-known problem in game theory: Even if players have common knowledge of the structure of the game and of their mutual rationality, usually this information is not sufficient to select a particular equilibrium strategy (Bicchieri 1993). In this case, we must introduce some salience criterion of choice, and common knowledge thereof, to solve the equilibrium selection problem. Salience may be provided by precedent or by an explicit agreement. Lewis (1969) unambiguously referred to precedent as a mechanism by which players succeed in coordinating on one particular equilibrium. Schelling (1960), on the other hand, referred to focal points. However, salience and focal points are not satisfactory solutions, because for them to do their coordination job it must be common knowledge among the players that they describe the game in the same way; but unless it is explicitly assumed, there is no reason to believe that common knowledge exists. This interpretation of the coordination

[28] An account of how a convention emerges would look at repetitions of the stage game depicted in Figure 1.9. The convention in this case might be that people alternate between Golf and Opera, or that they do one or the other with fixed probabilities.

game in Figure 1.9 is a static, stylized description of the conditions under which a convention is likely to *emerge*, not an analysis of how players attain common knowledge of the shared criteria that will help them solve their coordination problem.

Another possible interpretation of the game in Figure 1.9 is that one of the two equilibria has already been selected and consequently a convention is in place. 'Self' will know, for example, that in situations of type *S* almost everyone chooses to play golf. She thus has an empirical expectation about what 'Other' will do and a conditional preference for conformity given her expectation. In this case 'Self' will conform and, if 'Other' has a similar expectation and preference, he will follow the established convention, too. In this case no common knowledge is necessary for players to play the 'play golf' equilibrium: First-order expectations are all that is needed. This interpretation of the game refers to the *survival* of a convention: A convention persists if agents have the right kind of empirical expectations. The question now becomes how agents come to form such expectations, or reason inductively from past cases. For example, when 'Self' is faced with situation **s**, she will look for analogies with past situations she has experienced and eventually decide there are enough relevant similarities to categorize **s** as a member of *S*, the class of situations to which a given behavioral regularity applies. The next step for 'Self' is to decide that that particular behavioral regularity can be projected as a genuine regularity; otherwise she would have no reason to expect it to persist. Sugden and Cubitt (2003) point out how Lewis explicitly recognized that inductive inferences are crucial in maintaining a convention and offer a formal model of Lewis's informal description of how common knowledge that a behavioral regularity will persist is attained. Without entering into the details of Sugden and Cubitt's formal reconstruction of Lewis's argument, let me point out that Lewis's argument is crucially dependent on assuming shared inductive standards, and one of these standards is the common recognition that only certain behavioral patterns can be projected. In the next chapter I address the problem of what grounds inductive inferences (especially inferences about social behavior); for now let me point out that a game-theoretic account of norms and conventions, insofar as it describes them as equilibria of particular types of games, is both inescapably static and epistemically inadequate. Not only do we need dynamic accounts of how norms and conventions emerge, but also a better understanding of the kinds of cognitive capabilities that allow us to recognize and project behavioral patterns as such. I will address both issues in later chapters.

All we need to emphasize for the moment is that a convention is a realized equilibrium of an *original* coordination game without nonstrict Nash equilibria, and that it is in a player's self-interest to stick to it. We are now ready to give a more precise definition of convention that hopefully captures its characteristic features.

Conditions for Conventions to Exist

A descriptive norm is a convention if there exists a sufficiently large subset $P_f \subseteq P$ such that, for each individual $i \in P_f$, the following conditions hold:

1. *Empirical expectations:* i believes that a sufficiently large subset of P conforms to R in situations of type S and
2. S is a coordination game without nonstrict Nash equilibria.

Recall that, for a descriptive norm to be followed, empirical expectations [Condition 2(a)] had to be met. Hence, a convention is always a *followed* descriptive norm, because empirical expectations are met. That is, the follower of a convention always expects a sufficiently large subset of P to conform. Note that a descriptive norm could be a nonstrict Nash equilibrium; a follower could imitate a trendsetter, but the latter would not be interested in coordinating with the 'followers.' In the case of a convention, instead, there is no such indifference.

There are several important differences between conventions and social norms. One is that conventions, in order to exist, have to be followed. Social norms (and descriptive norms) instead can exist without being followed. Second, one conforms to a convention because of the belief that others behave in the expected way, because it makes sense to follow a convention only if there is reasonable certainty that it is still in place. Conforming to a social norm, on the contrary, requires that *both* normative and empirical expectations are met. Because conventions do not run counter to selfish motives, but social norms often do, if only empirical expectations were fulfilled, one would have a reason to follow a convention, but he would be seriously tempted *not* to conform to a social norm. In both cases, the players are playing a coordination game without nonstrict Nash equilibria, but whereas a convention solves an original coordination game, a norm transforms (with a certain probability) an original mixed-motive game into a coordination game and at the same time helps players to select one equilibrium.

The neat boundaries I drew between descriptive norms, conventions, and social norms are quite blurred in real life: Often what is a convention to some is a social norm to others, and what starts as a descriptive norm may in time become a stable social norm. Sometimes (but by no means always) the passage is marked by the presence of a new preference for universal conformity. In the trading example, the trader does not prefer that every other trader follow that specific signaling convention. Of course, she prefers that there is a signaling system, but she does not care if some traders do not follow it (provided the system is still in place). If another trader suddenly decides to make different signals, he is the only one to bear the cost of deviating from the conventional sign language. The case of traffic rules, the quintessential example of a convention, is quite different. Driving according to 'personal' rules may cause severe damage. The reckless driver is prone to cause accidents involving other people, who thus have to bear the costs of his infraction. When breaking a convention creates negative externalities, people prefer not just that the convention is in place, but also that everyone follows it. Such violations are usually legally sanctioned, but, even more importantly, they are also informally sanctioned by society. A reckless driver is blamed as irresponsible: We think he should have observed traffic rules. When breaking a coordination mechanism produces negative externalities, we may expect conventions to become full social norms.

A good example of such a transformation would be the stag-hunt game (Hume 1739). In this game, the hunters could coordinate their efforts and get a stag, which is a much bigger and valuable prey than a hare, which they could hunt alone and get with certainty. The game can be represented as shown in Figure 1.10.

If the players agree to hunt the stag together, they may get a better payoff (2) than hunting alone (1). However, even if a stag-hunting convention is in place, the larger the number of hunters, the higher the

	Others	
	Stag	Hare
Self Stag	2, 2	0, 1
Hare	1, 0	1, 1

FIGURE 1.10. The stag-hunt game

probability that someone might deviate from it. The (Stag, Stag) equilibrium, though Pareto dominant, is risky because, if someone deviates from it, Self risks remaining empty-handed. The (Hare, Hare) equilibrium is risk-dominant, because by hunting hares alone success is guaranteed.[29] Thus, if p (Others play S) is greater or equal to 1/2, Self will choose Stag; otherwise she will choose Hare. In this case the players might agree to impose sanctions on the lone hunters, especially when the hunting group is small and even a single deviation risks preventing the stag from being successfully hunted. What started as a convention may thus in time become a full social norm.

This does not mean that a social norm is in place *because* it prevents negative externalities from occurring. Many social norms are not the outcome of a plan or a conscious decision to enact them; they emerge by human action but not by human design. Some conventions may not involve externalities, at least initially, but they may become so well entrenched that people start attaching value to them. For example, a group of people may routinely avoid smoking before there arises a consensus disapproving this behavior. Once a public consensus is reached, smoking incurs new costs. Not only would one be expected not to smoke, but the occasional smoker would incur the blame of the entire group. At this point, a social norm is born. It may also happen that some conventions lend themselves to purposes they did not have when they were established. Norbert Elias (1978) illustrated how rules of etiquette, such as proper ways to eat and drink, developed to become a sign of aristocratic upbringing and refinement, and were effectively used to exclude those who did not belong to the ruling class. Thus a thirteenth-century peasant, and even a city burgher, would be excused if he slurped with his spoon when in company, drank from the dish, or gnawed a bone and then put it back on the communal dish. It would have come as no surprise if the ill-bred blew his nose in the tablecloth, poked his teeth with the knife, and slobbered while he drank, but no nobleman was allowed such lack of manners. Definitions of socially unacceptable behavior, or 'coarse manners,' were uniformly shared by thirteenth-century writings on table manners – simultaneously appearing in Italy, Germany, and England – that recorded for the first time a long-standing oral tradition reflecting what was customary in society. The standard of good behavior promoted in these works is the behavior of the aristocracy, the courtly circles gathering around the great feudal lords. Social differences were much more important than they are today, and

---

[29] For a definition of risk-dominance, see Harsanyi and Selten (1988).

they were given unambiguous expression in social conduct. Because at that time eating together was a significant moment of socialization, table manners came to play an essential role in shaping the identity of the aristocracy. A member of the ruling class was *identified* as such through his 'courtesy' or good manners. Had he not respected the rules of etiquette, he would have been met with contempt and perceived as threatening the established class boundaries.

Another example of a convention that evolved to become an important social signaling device is footbinding in China (Mackie 1996). The practice of footbinding might have been invented by a dancer in the palace of the Southern T'ang emperor, or it may have originated among slave traders as a restraint on female slaves, but it soon spread to all but the lowest classes in the population, becoming a sign of gentility and modesty and an essential condition for marriage. A family that did not impose such painful mutilation on its female children would have come to signal, among other things, a dangerous disregard for tradition and custom. As a consequence, it would have been ostracized and its young females regarded as unsuitable mates. Given enough time, what starts as a descriptive norm may become a stable convention. And conventions that prevent negative externalities, or those that come to fulfill an important signaling function, especially when the signal is related to social status or power, are easily amenable to being transformed into social norms.

There are many rules of social interaction we usually think of as mere conventions but, on closer inspection, show all the characteristics of social norms. These rules have become so entrenched in the texture of our lives, so imbued with social meanings, that we cannot ignore them with impunity. Everyday life is rife with implicit conventions directing the way we speak, walk, make eye contact, and keep a distance from other people. We are seldom aware of them until they are broken; however, when they are breached we may experience anger, outrage, and confusion. A person who speaks too loudly, stands too close, or touches us in unexpected ways is usually perceived as disturbing and offensive, if not outright frightening. Cultures differ in setting the boundaries of personal space, but once these boundaries are in place, they define 'normal' interactions, help in predicting others' behavior, and assign meaning to it. The rules that shape the perimeter of our personal sphere thus have an important signaling function: We resent those who trespass these boundaries precisely because we perceive those individuals as being hostile and threatening. Conventions of public decorum, such as manners and etiquette, are more explicit but not less important because, among other things, they signal respect for others and for social relationships. Breaching them can offend and bring forth retaliation. Simmel's example of the dangers of failing to greet an acquaintance on the street underscores this point: "Greeting someone on the street proves no esteem whatever, but failure to do so conclusively proves the opposite. The forms of courtesy fail as symbols of positive, inner attitudes, but they are most useful in documenting negative ones, since even the slightest omission can radically and definitely alter our relation to a person."[30] When a conventional manner of interaction has acquired such an important social meaning, we would rather refer to it as a social norm. Such norms, as opposed to conventions, are accompanied by what are perceived as legitimate expectations of compliance: We feel almost entitled to a courteous greeting, and the annoyance and resentment we direct against those who willingly ignore us indicate we are in the realm of normative expectations.

Following Social Norms

Social norms prescribe or proscribe behavior; they entail obligations and are supported by normative expectations. Not only do we expect others to conform to a social norm; we are also aware that we are expected to conform, and *both* these expectations are necessary reasons to comply with the norm. Contrary to what happens with descriptive norms and conventions, being expected (and preferred) to conform to a social norm may also give us a sufficient reason to conform. I have mentioned fear, benevolence, and the desire to fulfill others' legitimate expectations as three different reasons why normative expectations (and preferences) matter to conformity. Fear should never be discounted, because there are many cases in which one obeys a norm only because neglecting others' expectations and preferences will bring about some form of punishment. We may conform without attributing any intrinsic value to the norm and without finding others' expectations legitimate. Some Arab women may observe Muslim sexual mores, and Corsican men embrace norms of revenge, for fear of being punished if they break the rules. In both cases, they may find their community norms oppressive and ill-suited to modern life, but whoever speaks or rebels first runs the risk of bearing huge costs. Breaking the rules looks like the risky cooperative choice in a social dilemma. Freedom from a bad norm is a public good that is often very difficult to bring about.

[30] Cf. G. Simmel (1950, p. 400).

At the opposite end of the spectrum are those who conform because they attribute some value to what the norm stands for. People vary in the degree to which they are prepared to stand for a given norm. Some of us value a rule of reciprocity, because we see how it helps society function smoothly, but we would be prepared to shed the rule in an environment where it is consistently violated. Others might find deep moral reasons for upholding it even in the face of betrayals. A thirteenth-century member of the ruling class would have refrained from blowing his nose in the tablecloth because that behavior was not 'courtly' or appropriate for a nobleman. Nowadays most of us would be ashamed at displaying such bad manners in front of a table companion. Even if alone, we tend to avoid this kind of behavior, finding it not just unsanitary but also a little demeaning. The negative social sanctions that may follow a transgression are usually reasons for compliance when a social norm is not well established. But later, when the norm has become a well-entrenched practice and we have come to attribute a certain virtue to what it prescribes, external sanctions seldom play a role in inducing conformity. Thus a smoker who avoids smoking in public places for fear of being reprimanded may in time come to see the merit of this policy and refrain from smoking in public places even when alone. Philosophers have pointed out that it is a fallacy to infer *ought* from *is*, but personal as well as historical evidence tells us that we are readily victims of this 'naturalistic fallacy': When a practice is well entrenched, we often come to attribute to it some intrinsic value. In such cases we recognize the legitimacy of others' expectations and feel an obligation to fulfill them.

Neither the person who obeys a norm because a reward or a punishment is in place, nor the person who always obeys out of a deep conviction of the norm's merits presents us with a particular problem. Sometimes, however, we follow social norms even in the absence of external sanctions: Our choices are anonymous, and we are reasonably sure nobody is going to monitor us and detect behavior that runs counter to the norm. Even if a choice is not strictly anonymous, there are many cases in which we can easily turn our backs to the situation and leave without risking any penalty. When we leave a tip at the diner sitting along the motorway we happen to be passing, we are behaving like regular customers even if this is the first and probably the last time we will see that waiter, so there is no obvious punishment or reward in place. It might be argued that in this case we are in the grip of personal norms and would experience guilt or shame were we to transgress our self-imposed rules. If this were the case, we should observe consistent compliance with a tipping norm in a variety of circumstances, but often the same individual who is ready to leave a tip at the diner may not do so when in a foreign country, even in those cases in which the 'service included' clause is not present. The same inconstancy we encounter with tipping may occur with respect to much more important social norms, such as those regulating fair division or reciprocation. People who reciprocate on one occasion may avoid reciprocating on others without apparent reason. I am not referring here to cases in which it is acceptable to transgress a norm.[31] For almost every norm one can think of, there are socially acceptable exceptions to it. Thus I am normally expected to return favors, but an intervening hardship may excuse me; similarly, many would deem it inappropriate to return a favor that was not requested and looks like a veiled bribe. The cases of interest are rather those in which one is expected to adhere to a norm and does not, but we have evidence that on other, similar occasions, the same person complied with the norm even in the absence of any obvious sanction. I am interested in explaining such apparent inconsistencies across and within individuals.

The brief taxonomy of norms I have proposed is of some help here, because what is baffling is not inconsistency in following a descriptive norm or a convention, but the inconsistency we experience with regard to social norms. For example, when a coordinating convention is in place, it is in everybody's interest to follow it, and when we observe inconsistent behavior we are likely to attribute it either to a misunderstanding of the situation or to poor learning about how and when to follow the convention. Whenever I go back to England, I have to pay special attention the first few days I drive a car, because driving on the left side of the road feels unnatural. If I were tired or absentminded, I would be prone to make a dangerous mistake. Since expectations play such an important role in supporting conventions – as well as descriptive norms – a change in expectations (of others' conformity) may be another reason why we stop following a convention we observed until now. We may subsequently realize it was a mistake, because the convention is still followed, and revert to the old behavior. Alternatively, when a new convention is in place we are more likely to fluctuate in compliance. Dress codes are a good example. It is now customary in many American companies to have a day (usually Friday) of "business casual" dressing. Many friends reported embarrassing situations in which they were the only ones in jeans and sneakers, only

---

[31] Even criminal law recognizes mitigating circumstances such as duress, coercion, insanity, and accident.

to realize that the following Friday, when they reverted to dressier suits, more coworkers had adopted the "dress down" code. It usually takes some time to stabilize on a common dress code, and in the meantime behavior can be quite hectic.

The case of social norms is more complex. Norms are sometimes stated in vague and general terms and operate in the presence of areas of indeterminacy and ambiguity. Several norms may apply to the same situation, or it may not be clear which norms have a bearing in a given case. Whenever it is unclear which norm applies to a given situation, we may of course expect irregular behavior, as the former example of tipping in a foreign country illustrates. Variance is also to be expected (or at least it is explainable) when sanctions have been introduced or removed or, for some reason, there has been a change in expectations. With fairness and reciprocity norms, it is often in one's interest to break the norm, to yield to temptation. Why should I accept a fair division if I have the upper hand and, moreover, I will not interact with my partner in the future? Why should I reciprocate my neighbor's favors if I am moving to a different town soon? My sudden transformation can be altogether explained by self-interest, boosted by a change in sanctions and expectations. Another possible reason for inconsistent behavior is weakness of the will. Whenever the temptation is too great, the bait too alluring, I may break a norm that I otherwise approve of and regularly obey.

Yet, if no such reason is apparent and we know that a person (a) approves of a given norm and (b) has conformed to it on other, similar occasions, we could either conclude that norms' influence on behavior has been overstated or that we need a better understanding of the role of situational cues in inducing conformity. Indeed, factors having nothing to do with the norm in question – including other norms, attitudes, or environmental factors – may attenuate or emphasize its impact on actions. Environmental stimuli in particular have been reported by psychologists to cause major changes in the kinds of behaviors, such as the propensity to help other people, that we usually expect to manifest a certain consistency and that are taken to signal a character disposition. Several studies of helping behavior indicate that people are more likely to help others if they are in a familiar environment, or if the request comes from a female. When facing emergencies, people are much more likely to intervene if they are alone. The presence of other bystanders to an accident seems to consistently dampen altruistic ardor (Latane and Darley 1968). Similarly, we have no indication of a general disposition to take normative considerations as overriding, or of an unfailing inclination to obey a norm whenever a norm is in place. Quite to the contrary, all the evidence we have points to situational factors as having a significant influence on behavior. However, as much as situational factors may attenuate the impact of norms on behavior, the opposite is also true: Situational factors may increase the effect of norms on behavior by making a norm salient. Unfortunately, there are no experiments tracking personal (as opposed to interpersonal) variations in behavior in similar situations, where the experimenter slightly varies the environment or the description of the situation. In the following chapters, I will present some indirect evidence that supports the hypothesis that situational variables are extremely important in focusing actors on social norms, thus inducing or preventing conformity.

Awareness and Choice

In the next chapters, the idea that norms influence behavior only when they are salient or focal for the individual at the time of behavior will be expanded on and put to the test. If people are not strongly focused on a norm, I shall argue, even strong personal norms are not predictive of relevant behavior. Normative focus, in turn, is enhanced or mitigated by situational cues that draw attention to (or distract attention from) a relevant norm. There is by now a large database of experimental results from Trust, Ultimatum, and Social Dilemma games, in which small alterations in the environment or the way in which the game is presented produce major behavioral changes. Individuals may be cooperative on some occasions and selfish in others, give generously or reciprocate at times and be 'mean' at other times. If a fairness norm is activated in condition x, when the game is one-shot and the players anonymous, why is it not activated in the slightly different condition y, in a similar one-shot, anonymous encounter? Because the apparently inconsistent behaviors are not correlated with the presence or absence of sanctions, this variability has led several authors to discount the importance of norms as explanatory variables in such experiments (Dawes et al. 1977). The reasoning leading to this conclusion is that – if a person were to uphold a norm – then that person would conform to it in all circumstances to which the norm applies. This belief presupposes that (a) we are always aware of our personal standards and ready to act on them, and (b) situational factors have no influence on our behavioral dispositions. Because I will focus next on situational factors and their influence, I will now restrict my attention to the issue of normativity and choice. For example, when situational factors are paramount, in the sense that their presence is crucial in priming a norm, does it make sense to say that a person *chooses* to follow a norm? If one is unaware of the stimuli and the cognitive process whose outcome is norm-congruent behavior, can we still claim that it is *rational* to follow that norm?

When mentioning the expectations and preferences that support conformity to a social norm, I referred to *reasons* for following a norm, and having reasons can be interpreted as mentally referring to a norm before acting, having intentions, and making a reasoned (and rational) choice. For example, we may say that the trader who uses the conventional signaling system is making a rational choice, because we assume she wants to communicate and, through communication, reach her goal of buying and selling shares. There is a difference, though, between choosing rationally and choosing a course of action *because* it is the rational thing to do. In light of the coordinating role played by the trading-signaling system, and assuming the trader's goal is to make trades, we judge the trader's choice to be rational, but the trader herself may have been totally unaware of having a choice. In this case, what has been activated is not the deliberational route to behavior but rather the heuristic one. The trader may have never thought about the signaling convention being a coordinating device, nor might she be aware of any goal or plan that following the convention helps her to achieve. This, I must add, is a common experience; frequently we do not think much before acting, in the sense that our behavior does not consciously follow from intentions or plans and is carried out without awareness or attention. To engage in thoughtful processes, we must be sufficiently motivated: The situation must have high personal relevance, our action must have important consequences, we are held responsible for our choice, or there is some challenge present. As opposed to this thoughtful evaluation of pros and cons, we usually engage in a more rapid, heuristic form of processing. The trader uses the signaling convention as a default, without a thought to the benefits her behavior yields.

Even obeying a social norm can be, though by no means has to be, an entirely automatic affair. We are, so to speak, in the grip of the situation that primed the norm and are following it through the heuristic route. Those individuals who cooperate in the initial stages of an experimental, finitely repeated public good game do not seem to have gone through a mental process in which they calculated the costs and benefits of being nice. Indeed, a simple calculation of costs and benefits might have induced them to defect immediately, as game theory predicts they will do. On the other hand, these people are not dupes: Cooperation precipitously decays whenever people realize they have been cheated by others (Dawes and Thaler 1988; Fehr and Gachter 2000b). My hypothesis is that subjects in experiments act like any of us would in a new situation and use social norms as defaults, at least initially. If not challenged, a cooperative norm is adopted in all those situations in which it is made focal. If, however, the norm is violated often enough to be noticed, people will stop following it, at least in that situation. Recall that my definition of social norms entails that an individual needs to have conditional preferences and the right kind of expectations in order to follow a norm. The potential norm follower was represented as facing a Bayesian game. If he initially assesses a higher probability to being matched with another norm follower, he will behave cooperatively. But he will revert to defecting if he realizes his expectations are not met. I am not claiming here that mine is a realistic model of how we reason, but, as will be made plain in the following chapters, I maintain it is a fairly good explanatory and predictive model, because my definitions are operational and their consequences are testable. Furthermore, the fact that we are not aware of our mental processes does not mean that the beliefs and preferences that underlie the choice to conform have no existence. On many occasions our conscious awareness of a norm, and of the expectations and preferences that trigger conformity, is only brought about by the realization that the norm has been violated.

Suppose you are one of the nice guys who choose to cooperate in a finitely repeated public good game. When asked to explain your behavior, you may offer a rational justification and refer to the choice to obey a norm: You may say that you would really feel guilty not to give it a chance and signal your good intentions. Or you may say that being cooperative is a good rule, and that it is better, in the long run, than being a defector, and therefore you are committed to it even on those occasions in which you may cheat with impunity. Your rational justification is part of a narrative, an acceptable account of why we act as we do. Cognitive psychologists tell us that we often have little direct introspective awareness or access to our higher level cognitive processes (Nisbett and Wilson 1977).[32] We may be unaware that certain stimuli influence our responses, or we may even be unaware of the existence of stimuli that have a causal effect on our responses. Yet when questioned about our choices, judgments, and

---

[32] A high-order cognitive process mediates the effects of a stimulus on a complex response such as judgment, inference, problem solving, and choice.

evaluations, we are usually quite articulate in offering credible reasons. A plausible explanation is that our reports are based on implicit theories about the causal connection between stimulus and response. The causal theory we put forth may happen to be an accurate account of what stimulus was influential in producing our response, but accuracy, according to Nisbett and Wilson, is not synonymous with awareness. We may accurately report that a particular stimulus was influential in producing a behavioral response because the stimulus is available and salient, and it appears to be a plausible cause, not because we have a privileged access to our higher cognitive processes. If the actual stimulus is not available, salient, or not deemed to be a plausible cause of the response, it will regularly be discounted as uninfluential.[33]

Latane and Darley's (1968) experiments on helping behavior offer a disturbing example of how choices may be influenced by factors that are outside our immediate awareness. Their subjects were progressively more unlikely to help somebody in distress as the number of bystanders increased, but they were entirely unaware of the effect that the presence of other people had on their behavior. Moreover, when the experiments were described in detail to different, nonparticipating subjects, who were then asked to predict how others (and perhaps themselves) would behave in similar circumstances, they concurred that the presence of other people would have no effect on helping behavior. In this as well as other similar experiments, the congruence between the participants' reports and the predictions made by nonparticipants suggests that both are drawn from a similar source. Nisbett and Wilson explain the congruence by referring to common, shared causal theories that make both actor and observer 'perceive' covariations between particular stimuli and responses.[34]

Some of our reports may instead be highly accurate, as when we apply the sequential steps of a decision process we have learned. A business school graduate who is making the decision whether to buy a particular stock, for example, will apply learned rules for evaluating the stock and weighing all the factors that have a bearing on its price. Her report on

---

[33] We are usually blind to contextual factors, as well as to position, serial order, and anchoring effects. Most people would think it is outrageous that the choices they make might be influenced by such irrelevant factors as the position (say, from left to right) of the object chosen.

[34] The criterion for awareness proposed is a "verbal report which exceeds in accuracy that obtained from observers provided with a general description of the stimulus and response in question" (Nisbett and Wilson 1977, p. 251).

her final choice will accurately list the weighted factors as reasons for her choice. Similarly, we might be fairly accurate about the weights we assign to various factors in deciding what a fair division of a particular good should be. But this may happen because our culture (or subculture) specifies rather clearly which factors should count in such a decision. Still, being able to describe the evaluative criteria one has applied is not evidence of direct access to one's mental evaluation process.

The existence of a norm and of reasons for conformity might thus be correctly reported as an explanation for our behavior, even if we are unaware of the complex mental process that resulted in that behavior. Situational dependency can in turn be understood in two different ways. One is that the environment or situation we are in provides perceptual stimuli to which we respond in an 'automatic,' unreflective way. *Ex post*, we may or may not accurately report on the importance of the stimuli, depending on whether they are available and how plausible they are as causal factors. Alternatively, we may see the situation as influencing the way in which we consciously interpret and understand our surroundings. A norm in this case can be made salient by particular situational cues, but we still *choose* to follow it, that is, consider alternatives and make mental reference to the norm before we act. I believe both accounts of situational dependency to be valid, depending on the level of awareness we experience at any given time. There are occasions in which we are unaware of the reasons why we do what we do, and occasions in which we are consciously thinking of a norm, and the reasons for following it, before acting.[35] Also in this second case, though, we should not confuse access to our private store of knowledge, emotions, or plans with access to our cognitive processes, which are opaque to introspection.[36]

Lack of awareness should not be equated with lack of rationality. It is possible to maintain that it is rational to follow a norm, even if for the most part our subjective experience of conformity to a norm is beyond

[35] A mental state is *conscious* when it is accompanied by a roughly simultaneous, higher order thought about that very mental state. For example, a conscious experience of pain involves more than the simple registering of a painful sensation in the mind. It also includes a realization that one is having this sensation, a thought that "I am feeling pain."

[36] Jones and Nisbett (1972) distinguish between *content* and *process*. Content includes all sorts of private knowledge we possess: We know personal historical facts, our focus of attention at any given time, what we feel and sense, our evaluations, and our plans. They convincingly maintain that we have introspective access to content but not to mental processes.

rational calculation. Compliance may look like a habit, thoughtless and automatic, or it may be guided by feelings of anxiety at the thought of what might happen if one violates the norm. Yet conformity to a norm may be rational, and may be explained by the agents' beliefs and desires, even though one does not conform out of a conscious rational calculation. As David Lewis himself pointed out in his analysis of habits, a habit may be under an agent's rational control in the following sense: If that habit ever ceased to serve the agent's desires according to his beliefs, it would at once be overridden and abandoned.[37] Similarly, an explanation in terms of norms does not compete with one in terms of expectations and preferences, because a norm persists precisely because of certain expectations and preferences: If I ever wanted to be different, or if I expected others to do something different, I would probably overcome the force of the norm.

We may conclude that awareness is not a necessary condition for being rational, in the sense that, even if unaware, we may still act according to our beliefs and desires. To maintain that following a norm can be described, at least in principle, in terms of beliefs and desires and hence as a (practically) rational choice allows us to think of norms as a special kind of unintended collective outcome of individual choices.[38] Such outcomes have desirable properties, for example, they are equilibria of coordination games. Note that being an equilibrium does not make a social norm good or efficient; there are lots of bad equilibria around. It simply means that the expectations and actions of all the parties concerned are consistent, or that their expectations are self-fulfilling. This raises the important question of how such consistency comes about, but we will discuss this later. Another important advantage of defining norms in terms of beliefs and preferences is that we are providing an operational definition of what a norm is. This is important in experimental studies, where we want to assess whether the behavior we observe is due to the presence of norms or to something else. If we know that norms are only followed if certain expectations exist, then it is possible to verify if indeed people have those expectations, or to manipulate them in order to see whether their behavior changes in predictable ways.

---

[37] D. Lewis, 1975, p. 25.

[38] It is important to distinguish between *practical* and *epistemic* rationality (Bicchieri 1993). Practical rationality is the rationality of an action, given the agent's goal and beliefs. Thus goals may be unrealistic and beliefs false, and an action still may be practically rational. Conversely, epistemic rationality is the rationality of the beliefs we hold.

Appendix to Chapter 1

In this short appendix I introduce a general utility function based on norms. Consider a typical n-person (normal-form) game. For ease of formal treatment, think of a norm as a function that maps one's expectations concerning the behavior of others into what one "ought to do." In other words, a norm regulates behavior conditional on other people's behavior.

Denote the strategy set of player i by S_i, and let $\boldsymbol{S}_{-i} = \Pi_{j \neq i} S_j$ be the set of strategy profiles of players other than i. Then a norm for player i is formally represented by a function $N_i: L_{-i} \to S_i$, where $L_{-i} \subseteq \boldsymbol{S}_{-i}$.[39] In an n-person Prisoner's Dilemma game, for example, a shared norm may be to cooperate. In that case, L_{-i} includes all the strategies of all players (excluding player i) that prescribe cooperation.

Two features of this definition are worth noting. First, given the other players' strategies, there may or may not be a norm that prescribes how player i ought to behave. So L_{-i} need not be, and usually is not, equal to $\boldsymbol{S}_{-i}$. In particular, L_{-i} could be empty in the situation where there is no norm whatsoever to regulate player i's behavior. Second, there could be norms that regulate joint behaviors. A norm, for example, that regulates the joint behaviors of players i and j may be represented by $N_{i,j}: L_{-i,-j} \to S_i \times S_j$, where $L_{-i,-j}$ is the set of strategies adopted by all players other than i and j. Because I am primarily concerned with two-person games, I will not further complicate the model in that direction.

A strategy profile $s = (s_1, \dots, s_n)$ *instantiates* a norm for j if $s_{-j} \in L_{-j}$, that is, if N_j is defined at s_{-j}. It *violates* a norm if, for some j, it instantiates a norm for j but $s_j \neq N_j(s_{-j})$. Let π_i be the payoff function of player i. The norm-based utility function of player i depends on the strategy profile s and is given by

$$U_i(s) = \pi_i(s) - k_i \max_{s_{-j} \in L_{-j}} \max_{m \neq j} \{\pi_m(s_{-j}, N_j(s_{-j})) - \pi_m(s), 0\},$$

where $k_i \geq 0$ is a constant representing a player's sensitivity to the relevant norm.[40] The first maximum operator takes care of the possibility that the norm instantiation (and violation) might be ambiguous, in the sense that a strategy profile instantiates a norm for several players simultaneously. However, this situation never occurs in my examples, so the first maximum

---

[39] Note that N need not be deterministic. As we shall see in Chapter 3, when we look at Ultimatum games, N can also be a random variable.

[40] k_i is only unique up to some positive factor that varies according to the players' payoff functions.

operator degenerates. The second maximum operator ranges over all the players other than the norm violator. In plain words, the discounting term (multiplied by k_i) is the maximum payoff deduction resulting from all norm violations.

As an example to illustrate the above norm-based utility function, consider the Prisoner's Dilemma, where each player has two possible strategies: C (Cooperate) and D (Defect). The norm-based function for either player is defined at C and undefined at D. The utility function for player 1 is then the following:

$$\begin{aligned}
U_1(C, C) &= \pi_1(C, C) - k_1(\pi_1(C, C) - \pi_1(C, C)) = \pi_1(C, C) \\
U_1(D, D) &= \pi_1(D, D) - k_1(\pi_1(D, D) - \pi_1(D, D)) = \pi_1(D, D) \\
U_1(C, D) &= \pi_1(C, D) - k_1(\pi_1(C, C) - \pi_1(C, D)) \\
U_1(D, C) &= \pi_1(D, C) - k_1(\pi_2(C, C) - \pi_2(D, C)).
\end{aligned}$$

Player 2's utility function is similar. The game turns out to be a coordination game with two equilibria when $U_1(D, C) < U_1(C, C)$ and $U_2(C, D) < U_2(C, C)$, that is, when[41]

$$k_1 > \frac{\pi_1(D, C) - \pi_1(C, C)}{\pi_2(C, C) - \pi_2(D, C)}$$
$$k_2 > \frac{\pi_2(C, D) - \pi_2(C, C)}{\pi_1(C, C) - \pi_1(C, D)}.$$

Otherwise it remains a PD game.

As an example, take the PD game in Figure 1.1 and assume the players' payoffs are as follows:

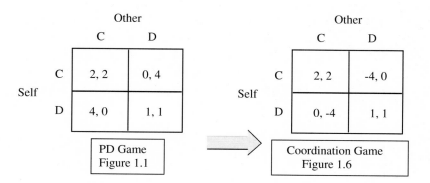

		Other: C	Other: D
Self	C	2, 2	0, 4
	D	4, 0	1, 1

PD Game
Figure 1.1

→

		Other: C	Other: D
Self	C	2, 2	-4, 0
	D	0, -4	1, 1

Coordination Game
Figure 1.6

[41] Note that $U_1(D,C)$ stands for the utility of player 1 when 1 plays D and 2 plays C. Analogously, $U_2(D,C)$ stands for the utility of player 2 when 1 plays D and 2 plays C.

In this case, $\pi(C, C) = 2$ and $\pi(D, D) = 1$.
However,

$$U_1(C, D) = 0 - k_1 \max \left\{ \begin{array}{l} \pi_1(C, C) - \pi_1(C, D) \\ \pi_2(C, C) - \pi_2(C, D) \\ 0 \end{array} \right\} = 0 - k_1(2)$$

and

$$U_1(D, C) = 4 - k_1 \max \left\{ \begin{array}{l} \pi_1(C, C) - \pi_1(D, C) \\ \pi_2(C, C) - \pi_2(D, C) \\ 0 \end{array} \right\} = 4 - k_1(2);$$

similar calculations hold for player 2.

For both players to prefer to cooperate with each other, it must be that both k_1 and k_2 are greater than 1. For example, if we assume that, say, both k_1 and k_2 are equal to 2, we obtain the above coordination game (Figure 1.6). Note that it is not necessary to assume that k_1 and k_2 are the same. In fact, players may have different degrees of 'sensitivity' to a norm. Being 'sensitive' to a norm simply means that one dislikes being the victim of a norm violation as well as being the transgressor. We may thus say that k defines different types of players. In our simple example, there can be only two types of players: Either a player's k is greater than 1, or it is equal to or less than 1.

In this case, player i (with $k_i > 1$) is rational iff she chooses a strategy s_i such that the expected utility $EU(s_i) \geq EU(s_i')$ for all $s_i' \neq s_i \in S_i$, calculated with respect to the probability that $(k_j > 1)$. It is important to remember that when a player is faced with a PD game and has no information about the identity or past actions of the other player, she will rationally choose to 'follow the cooperative norm' if *two* conditions are satisfied. She must be a potential norm-follower (i.e., her k must be greater than 1) and she must believe that the other player's k-value is such that it makes him sensitive to the norm (in our example, it must also be greater than 1). In other words, a norm-follower faced with a PD game will have to assess the probability that the other player is the norm-following type. In our case, if $p(k_2 > 1) > 1/2$, player 1 will choose to cooperate.

2

Habits of the Mind

Introduction

In the previous chapter, I presented some 'internal' existence conditions for social norms. Without normative beliefs, empirical expectations, and conditional preferences for conformity by a sufficient percentage of individuals in a population, no norm would survive. My definitions were meant to highlight the interdependence of beliefs and actions that create and support this kind of collective phenomena. I left open the question of how expectations and beliefs exert their influence on social behavior, and under which conditions the norms they support become prescriptively or proscriptively operative. These questions arise from the fact that norms are not continuously activated; rather, they become salient and active only under certain situational conditions. Even when active, norms operate along with other dynamics, sometimes competitively. Thus, under any given set of circumstances, observed behavior may be due to factors other than the operation of norms, but this fact per se does not deprive the concept of scientific validity. What needs to be demonstrated is that norms have predictable effects on social behavior and that we can make interesting and accurate predictions about the influence of norms in specific social situations.

To fully accomplish this goal a good *operational* definition of social norms is in order. By 'operational' I mean that such a definition must have an empirical, testable content. The definition provided in Chapter 1 lends itself to empirical testing, because we can establish whether individuals have certain beliefs and expectations and whether their behavior is consistent with their expectations. It must be noted that it is important to have an assessment of individuals' expectations that is independent of their observed behavior. This is because expectations help to tell apart different motives. Observing what looks like 'fair' behavior, for example, leaves us in the dark about the motives behind the choice. Yet knowing motives is important in making predictions about individual behavior and collective outcomes. Social scientists have traditionally only been interested in collective predictions such as determining aggregate demand and supply of goods and labor, voting patterns, or the dynamics of social movements. However, because collective phenomena are ultimately the outcome of a myriad of individual decisions, knowing what motivates people to act one way or another is a stepping stone in any satisfactory explanation. Economists have come to recognize that people are not just motivated by narrow monetary incentives, but often act in ways that suggest they have a 'preference' for fairness, reciprocity, retaliation, and so on (Camerer 2003). To say that a person's behavior has revealed a preference for fairness, however, does not tell us much about the circumstances under which such a preference will be manifested, or about the reason why a specific interpretation of fairness (equity, equality, etc.) has been chosen. We have plenty of anecdotal evidence and personal experience suggesting that, though people are usually capable of being fair and cooperative, they are by no means uniform in their propensities. Our preferences, in other words, are *conditional* on the decision context. But *what* exactly in a context elicits a preference for fairness is difficult to establish, unless we have a theory about how people 'map' contexts into specific interpretations that involve, among other things, expectations and inferences about other people's motives and future behaviors. Such interpretations, I argue, often imply shared rules about what is to be done in specific situations.

Figure 2.1 briefly outlines what the remainder of this chapter will address. To say that preferences (and beliefs) are context-dependent is to say that they are sensitive to situational cues, and the subject's

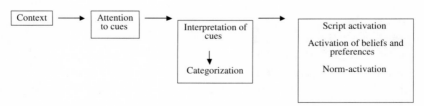

FIGURE 2.1. Mapping from context to beliefs/preferences

interpretation of these cues. It follows that particular preferences and beliefs may not always be activated; rather, they are the result of an interpretation of specific cues, a categorization of the situation based on those cues, and the consequent activation of appropriate scripts. Social norms, as I shall argue later on, are embedded into scripts.[1] Once a script has been activated, the corresponding beliefs, preferences, and behavioral rules (norms) are prompted. I have argued that activating a norm informs the subject about what to expect others will do and what he himself is expected to do. Given these expectations, an agent will have a conditional preference for conforming to the norm.

The reader may at this point note that the operational definition of social norms provided in Chapter 1 opens the black box that economists have hitherto left untouched. It does so by explaining how it is that we move from context to preference. Research by economists, decision scientists, psychologists, and other social scientists seems to agree that context matters. However, a model of just how context matters is absent. In my view, it is precisely the mapping from context to interpretation, and thus to beliefs and expectations, that elicits a preference for conformity to, say, a fairness norm. In other words, people usually do not prefer to be fair, *tout court*, but instead conditionally prefer to follow a norm of fairness if they interpret the decision context as one calling for such a norm.[2,3]

It must be added that another important difference between a simple preference for fairness and a conditional preference for conforming to a norm of fairness involves a distinction between consequentialist and process-oriented modes of appraising outcomes. A model that assumes a preference for fairness presupposes that people value the distributive consequences of outcomes. How such consequences are obtained does not matter (Fehr et al. 2003). It is well established, however, that identical outcomes are evaluated very differently, depending on the perceived

---

[1] I shall discuss scripts in detail later in the chapter.

[2] Note that the definition of social norms I have provided helps in designing experiments that can potentially distinguish between different kinds of motives. For example, if people are aware of fairness norms, Proposers in Ultimatum games should be able to anticipate rejection rates in different situations (Fehr and Schmidt 1999). Then observing a 'preference' for fairness in the absence of the relevant normative expectations (independently assessed) would suggest that in this case obeying a norm is not the main motive, and we would have to search for a different explanation. A norm-based approach predicts congruence between expectations and actions, and lack of consistency would suggest other factors are at work.

[3] The interpretation of the decision context as one that calls for a fairness norm is not necessarily a conscious process, as I outlined in the previous chapter.

'intentions' of the parties. Recognizing the role played by intentions and beliefs about intentions means recognizing that people care about how an outcome is obtained. Models that include judgments about other players' intentions (Rabin 1993), however, do not explain how we are able to detect intentions. People are not transparent, and usually all we can observe are their actions and the circumstances of choice. I argue that it is precisely the specific interpretation of a context that lends meaning to an action, and judging an act as fair or unfair, cooperative or mean makes sense only against the background of shared norms defining and prescribing fair or cooperative behavior. If people are indeed process-oriented, if they care about the way an outcome is obtained, they need social norms to guide them in judging whether the process was fair or the intention kind.

I have also stated that norms are activated only under certain stimulus conditions, that we must be 'focused' on a norm to obey it. This statement risks being hopelessly vague (and untestable) unless we have a plausible theory of what makes norms salient – a theory that is grounded in what we know about cognitive processes and the place of rule recognition and following in such processes. If a social norm exists, it must be recognized to apply and be expected to apply to an identifiable class of situations (this is Condition 1 in my definition of social norms). Again, as Figure 2.1 shows, attention to cues is critical. If two subjects are presented with the same context, but are focused on different cues, then they will probably interpret the situation very differently.[4] In such cases we would expect different behaviors. It also follows that for two culturally homogeneous subjects to express the same preference (say splitting something evenly) in a given context, they must pay attention to the same cues and interpret them the same way. Consequently, the same script will be activated in each of them and elicit the same normative behavior. We thus want to learn as precisely as possible about the conditions under which a given norm becomes operative, that is, when the mapping from a context to a specific interpretation involving a norm will occur.

Controlled experiments are essential tools for learning what makes a norm focal. Yet such experiments must be guided by a theoretical understanding about the individual cognitive mechanisms underlying the activation of expectations and preferences that result in norm-congruent behavior. Otherwise, even if we were to become reasonably certain that

---

[4] As I will discuss in Chapter 3, people have a tendency to interpret ambiguous situational cues in a way that elicits a norm-following response that is most beneficial to them.

particular stimuli reliably activate normative expectations, and that activating such expectations produces measurable and significant behavioral effects, we may still be far from understanding through which cognitive mechanisms norms produce measurable changes in behavior. To 'activate' a norm means that the subjects involved *recognize* that the norm applies: They infer from some situational cues what the appropriate behavior is, what they should expect others to do, and what they are expected to do themselves, and act upon those cues. It is the cues one focuses on that govern the mapping from context to interpretation and, ultimately, the activation of social norms.

In this chapter I shall undertake the task of examining some results of field experiments that unambiguously demonstrate how dependent norm abidance is on the cues made salient in a given context. The results of these experiments lend support to the view that norms have a demonstrable impact on action, but they also show that impact to vary depending on the kind of norm the actor is focused on, as well as on the simultaneous presence of conflicting norms. I also examine the possible cognitive mechanisms that mediate the effects of social norms on behavior, paying particular attention to spreading activation theory and social categorization.

Experiments

A good starting point to explore which norms become salient in particular settings, and whether they affect subsequent behavior, is the experimental literature in social psychology and economics. Experiments can be roughly divided into two large categories: laboratory experiments and field experiments. The latter are deemed to be more realistic, as one unobtrusively observes subjects' behavior in a host of real-world situations. The problem with such observations is that we lack control over the situation, and this may make us less confident about the validity of the results. Take, for example, the hypothesis that social norms (the independent variable) have a demonstrable effect on behavior (the dependent variable). In an unobtrusive field experiment it is possible to make a norm cognitively accessible and then observe behavior that goes in the direction predicted by the normative influence hypothesis. But how can one be sure that the observed behavior is actually caused by the presence of a norm that has been made readily available? Can there be any other cause for the observed behavior? Laboratory experiments are explicitly designed to provide an answer to these kinds of questions: There is much more control over an environment that has been artificially created, and one can test whether some other factor may cause the observed behavior with well-designed control groups. The drawback is that too much control in a laboratory setting may mean an artificial situation has been created that is far apart from any real-life experience, and this may affect the generality of the results. As such we need both nonintrusive (field) experiments and a series of laboratory experiments to cross-verify results.

An example may clarify why both kinds of experiments are needed in a study of normative influence. Suppose we conjecture that priming a norm of beneficence will induce a significant increase in generous behavior in situations in which there might otherwise be little giving. A field experiment might proceed as follows. As is often done in psychology, subjects may be exposed to stimuli (visual, verbal, etc.) aimed at making a norm of beneficence highly available. Exposure to the relevant stimuli typically takes place in a lab, where subjects may be told that they are participating in an experiment on perception. Subsequently the subjects leave the 'experiment' and are unobtrusively observed while they walk back home. On their way home, they find a highly visible envelope that the experimenter has positioned in the middle of the street. The envelope has no name on it, and it contains $20 in various note sizes. After the subject takes it, she will come across a beggar (a confederate of the experimenter). The original conjecture was that priming a beneficence norm would significantly increase people's disposition to be charitable and generous to strangers, and so let us assume that a high percentage of subjects (say, 70%) offer some money to the beggar. Now one might wonder whether priming the beneficence norm was the real cause of such generosity. One would want to know, for example, what subjects would do with the money they found if they had not been previously exposed to the norm (box B, Figure 2.2). But it is also important to compare behavior in two

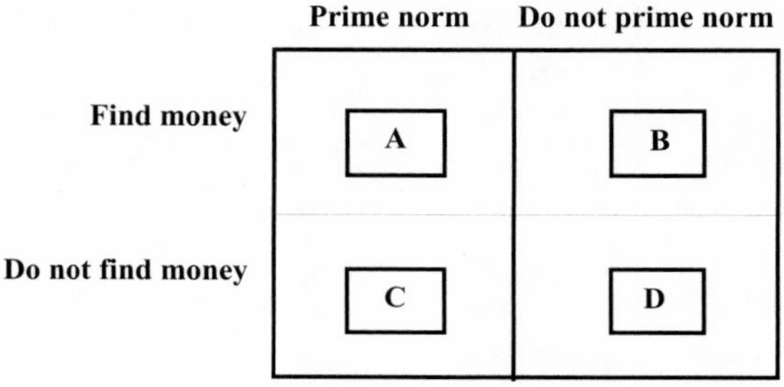

FIGURE 2.2. Money × norm priming possible combinations

other situations: priming the norm and not finding any money (box C), and not priming the norm and not finding any money (box D).[5]

Examining behavior under conditions B and C is important because we need to be able to tease apart the effect of priming a norm (column 1) and the possible effect of finding money in the street (row 1). If a group of subjects were to be exposed to 'neutral' stimuli and then find the money and meet the beggar (condition B), and one were then to observe an increase in charitable giving over the known base rate, one might conjecture that the very fact of finding money on the street had put subjects in a good mood and made them more disposed to act generously. Observing such behavior would make us doubt a researcher's claim that only explicit norm priming was at work here. Further, we might be concerned that there are other, unobservable confounding elements that are influencing the subjects' behavior. Despite their value, field experiments, such as the one detailed above, only allow for a limited number of environmental manipulations, and the presence of confounding elements is difficult to quantify and control.

A lab experiment instead is much more amenable to a variety of treatments that help to exclude alternative causes for the behavior one observes. It is possible, for example, that *seeing* the beggar has an effect on giving, quite independently from norm-activation. In the lab, it would be feasible to design an experiment that could ascertain whether a face-to-face encounter has an independent effect on giving, and measure the magnitude of this effect if indeed there is one. As an example of a lab experiment, think of one in which each subject is given $20 and then plays a double-blind Dictator game[6] in which they must decide whether to give any part of it (or nothing at all) to some other player they can see (but who cannot see them).[7] The other player, in turn, is forced to accept whatever the subject offers, and thus has no means to penalize an ungenerous giver such as rejecting the offer and thus causing both to lose the money (as would occur in the Ultimatum game, which I will discuss in the next chapter). If it were to be discovered in our lab experiment that seeing the recipient has a positive effect on giving (beyond control conditions), then we might want to return to our original field experiment

---

[5] In all these cases, the subjects would still meet a beggar.

[6] In a double-blind experiment, the subject knows that her choice will be anonymous (she will not be identified by the recipient) and that not even the experimenter will know what she chose.

[7] If no effect is apparent, one may want to check whether seeing and being seen has any effect, and so on.

with the beggar and compare the lab results to the condition in which the subject finds the money but where no norm has been explicitly primed (box B). Suppose the effect on giving is bigger in that variant of the Dictator game experiment than in the field experiment under the condition find money–do not prime norm and the difference is statistically significant. In the Dictator game, no beneficence norm has been explicitly primed by the experimenter. It is, however, possible that in the field experiment the *combination* of being forced to make a choice *and* seeing the potential recipient has in fact activated a norm of beneficence. In other words, norms can be primed by simply making some aspect of the situation salient. To address *why* the combination of receiving some money from the experimenter and seeing the potential recipient prime a beneficence norm, we need a model about how people interpret and categorize social situations such as the one I outline in the rest of the chapter.

An oft-cited problem with lab experiments such as the Dictator game is that they force subjects to make a *choice*, thus invoking the deliberational route. Subjects have to decide what to do, and it could be argued that this very fact may distort the results by producing behavior quite different from the behavior we would observe in a field experiment, where observations are unobtrusive and subjects are put in situations in which they are not asked to deliberate. Nonetheless, it is not obvious that being faced with a choice means that we are conscious of each step of the mental processes that are involved in making the choice. Even when deliberating, we are still subject to many stimuli we are unaware of, some of which may be causally involved in activating a norm. Several studies in social psychology have shown that social judgments and stereotyping processes, for example, operate without conscious attention, even though in all these studies participants were explicitly instructed to engage in social perception or judgment tasks (Bargh 1994). It thus seems that automatic processes can be prompted by a control process, such as being asked to give a judgment or make a choice. The value of well-designed lab experiments lies in the possibility of systematically varying the subjects' environment to detect if indeed the presence of some environmental stimuli is (automatically) triggering social norms, even when the subjects are explicitly asked to make a choice.

Cialdini et al. (1990) conducted a series of experiments that subtly and systematically varied the environmental cues to detect whether norms can be primed and which norms (descriptive or social) can be primed. The main contribution of their experiments lies in highlighting the role that situational cues play in focusing people's attention on different kinds of norms. Thus, an analysis of their experiments and their shortcomings may serve as a benchmark for future field experiments on the elicitation of relevant pro-social norms such as fairness, trust, reciprocity, and beneficence.

I believe the greatest help in understanding the effects of social norms on behavior will come from a combination of field and lab experiments that is yet to come. Knowing what makes people focus on particular norms, what may happen if they face conflicting norms, and how sensitive norms are to the framing of a situation is of great practical importance. To promote socially beneficial behavior, it may be unwise to rely on such scarce personal qualities as benevolence or altruism. A better course of action may consist in altering the environment in such a way that individuals will find certain desirable norms salient and act on them. Norms of beneficence, fairness, promise-keeping, and reciprocity, to name but a few, are critical in maintaining social order and stability, and many of them are prominent in all sorts of negotiations and public policies. Knowing how to make them focal may render obsolete more costly and dubiously effective policies of social control.

Trigger Cues

Though there is some consensus among social psychologists about the importance of situational factors in activating a norm, there has been very little empirical research on what makes particular norms salient, a notable exception being the Cialdini et al. (1990) field experiments on littering. Their work on littering aims to distinguish the influence of descriptive versus social norms on behavior, as well as assessing the relative power of social and personal norms as motivating factors.[8] Cialdini et al. did not offer a precise definition of social versus descriptive norms, but what they say is consistent with the more precise definitions I provided in Chapter 1. In their words, a descriptive norm tells what is 'commonly done' and a social norm tells what others 'commonly approve or disapprove of.' Their understanding of social norms, in particular, is consistent with the presence of normative beliefs that is the hallmark of a social norm in my own definition.

Cialdini et al.'s goal was to separate two sets of motives, informational and normative influence, prime them independently, and assess their

---

[8] Cialdini et al. (1990) call 'injunctive norms' what I call social norms (see my definition in Chapter 1), so I shall keep using the latter term.

relative strength. In so doing they were drawing on a distinction first
made by Deutsch and Gerard (1955) between informational and normative influence. *Informational influence* means that we take the behavior
or opinions of other people to convey important information about the
environment, and thus imitate or adopt them. This kind of conformity
would typically occur in new or ambiguous situations, when we face particularly difficult tasks, or when the cost of gathering information is too
high. In all these cases, we take 'what most people do' to clarify reality.
Normative influence instead means we seek social approval, want to 'fit in' a
valued group, or simply avoid negative social sanctions. In this case we pay
attention to what people approve or disapprove of, and 'what most people do' is taken to clarify what is expected of us. Because frequently what
we approve of is also what we normally do, it is difficult to disentangle the
influence of normative reasons from that of a desire to imitate others'
behavior. Similarly, when we observe norm compliance, it is impossible
to determine if it is due to a personal norm or to the desire to conform
to what is perceived as a shared norm.

Though Cialdini et al.'s experiments are only focused on littering, they
highlight a general difference between descriptive and social norms. To
have a clear view of what the determining factors might be in different decision-making contexts is of practical consequence. We are constantly exposed to descriptive norms that are socially harmful. Not only
littered environments, but also drinking, smoking, or binge eating among
teenagers; speeding on certain highways; extensive bribing practices in
several countries; or precincts with low voter turnout, to list but a few
examples, convey the message that what is observed is normal behavior,
that 'everyone does it,' and thus focus our attention on a detrimental
descriptive norm to the exclusion of other considerations. There are
many possible means to curb such negative practices. Some of them
would be very costly, such as putting in place an effective monitoring-
plus-sanctioning system. It is thus important to know whether we can
find ways of 'refocusing' individuals on less harmful behaviors, possibly
by making salient some social norms that proscribe the damaging practices. Cialdini's work is narrowly focused on littering, but, as I will show
in later chapters, being able to distinguish between descriptive and prescriptive (social) norms, and being able to focus people's attention on
ether of them, can become a powerful public policy tool.

In a series of nine studies of littering in public places, Cialdini and
his colleagues observed littering decisions in real-life settings, such as a
hospital garage, the lobby of a college dormitory, an amusement park,

and a stairwell. In all instances, the environment was manipulated in several ways. The environment was either clean or littered (whereby littered meant the presence of numerous pieces of trash). Cialdini et al. put subjects in the condition of having to dispose of a piece of trash and established base-rate behavior in the clean and littered settings.[9] Then they modified the experiment in two ways. First, they put one prominent piece of trash in an otherwise pristine environment and compared littering behavior in this new situation to littering in the clean (no trash present) environment. In a second set of experiments, they introduced a confederate who, walking before the subject, either littered if the environment was clean or threw his own trash (which he was carrying) in a garbage dump in a dirty environment, or picked up a piece of trash in the dirty environment and threw it in the trash can. When a confederate was present, he quickly exited out of view, so that there were no witnesses to the subject's action. Further, the same subjects did not participate in more than one experiment. The results show that subjects littered more in a dirty rather than in a clean environment (32–40% versus 11–18%), and they littered even more in an already dirty environment if they observed a confederate littering (54%). In the latter case, the experimenters verified that they could influence behavior by focusing subjects on the descriptive norm: The confederate's littering in an already dirty environment presumably had the effect of further drawing subjects' attention to the dirty environment, and to a descriptive norm suggesting that littering was common and 'normal.' If the environment was clean, only 11–18% (depending on the experiment) of the subjects littered, but a smaller number (6%) littered whenever they were exposed to a confederate throwing a flyer on an otherwise clean floor.[10]

What emerges from the data is that there are three types of subjects: a minority who always litter no matter what, another small fraction who never litter, and a large majority of subjects who are sensitive to the state

---

[9] For example, in one treatment the subjects, leaving for the hospital garage one by one, found a handbill on their car windshield. In another treatment they were left to walk down a stairwell with a messy paper towel they had used to wipe off some jelly left on their hands by a previous experiment measuring physiological reactions. In both cases, their behavior was unobtrusively observed by the experimenter.

[10] At a college dormitory, the experimenters placed fliers in mailboxes situated in a mailroom. As usual, they varied the cleanliness of the environment. They found that the littering rates in a clean environment, one with a piece of trash, and a dirty environment were 10.7%, 3.6%, and 26.7%, respectively ($p < .001$).

of the environment and imitate whatever they perceive "most people" do. Note that the choices of the majority of subjects are *conditional*: They will not litter in a clean environment but will litter in a dirty one. The 'preference' for littering thus appears to be conditional on what other people have done, and presumably will continue doing, and the state of the environment is taken to be a good indicator of that. Notice that even a person who would otherwise prefer not to litter might think that, in a dirty environment, the relative impact of her not littering would be nil. As I discussed in Chapter 1, conformity to a descriptive norm involves 1) realizing there is such a norm and thus 'focusing' on it, and 2) preferring to conform to the norm on condition that one expects a sufficiently large number of people to conform. Being exposed to a clean (dirty) environment in a situation in which one has to dispose of a piece of trash seems to induce people to draw inferences about what is commonly done and litter less (more) than they otherwise would.

The subjects may have been only vaguely aware of how dirty or clean their environment was, but such a vague awareness was enough to induce different behaviors in different environments. Interestingly, in a clean environment, the subjects were *even less* inclined to litter after observing a confederate throwing a handbill on the floor or, alternatively, after seeing a single noisome piece of garbage on the floor. However, there appears to be no statistically significant difference between the amount of littering by subjects when there was one piece of trash as opposed to a pristine environment. Cialdini does not highlight this result, but its implications have great import. It seems that only a very small percentage of individuals need *further* inducement, such as a clear-cut stimulus that points unequivocally to the state of the environment (and the underlying descriptive norm). The great majority of subjects are conditional choosers who do not need extra stimuli (the confederate or the extra pieces of trash) to act in accordance with what appears to be the descriptive norm. We may conclude that further manipulations of salience (beyond presenting a clean versus dirty environment) have only a *small* effect with regard to descriptive norms.

The problem with descriptive norms is that they are susceptible to *threshold effects*. Even the most socially beneficial descriptive norm can quickly degrade when people are exposed to a small number of 'transgressions.' For example, whenever trash is introduced in a pristine environment, a threshold effect seems to take hold. Once trash begins to accumulate and it becomes less clear what the descriptive norm is, the restraining effect is lost and more people litter.[11] The results hold across experiments and are statistically significant.[12] Threshold effects are important, as in many social situations a small signal is known to generate a 'snowball' effect.[13] Rudolph Giuliani's success in curbing criminality in New York may be due to his 'zero tolerance policy': catch the smallest criminal offense in order to discourage more serious violence. The underlying idea is that condoning small offenses, such as graffiti on the subway, signals that such behavior is acceptable and normal, thus opening the door to more serious transgressions. Focusing people on beneficial descriptive norms is a double-edged sword, though. As Cialdini successfully argued, whenever the state of the environment points to an identifiable descriptive norm, people will *focus* on it and norm-congruent behavior will follow. This is fine if the descriptive norm is in line with behavior we want to encourage. Thus we might conclude that, if we want to discourage harmful behavior, we should expose individuals to an environment in which there is little evidence of it. But, as parents of teenagers know too well, this is not a foolproof strategy. In a 'clean' environment, even a small number of transgressions can have a dramatic snowball effect.

Socially harmful descriptive norms abound, and they seem to persist even when they are in open conflict with existing legal rules. As an example of a conflict between legal behavior and a descriptive norm, consider driving in Naples. Running a red traffic light in Naples is illegal, yet running a red light if no other car is in sight is a rule most people will follow. After making a small inquiry among several acquaintances, the most common answers I collected were, in this order: "Why wait at an empty intersection?," "It's silly to wait if everyone else goes," and "If I stop and wait, I will be honked at and insulted by the drivers behind me." In fact, driving only when the light turns green is no longer a safe bet: The coordination mechanism provided by traffic lights has broken down and now everybody relies on his own sight and reflexes. This is an example of how a new convention might emerge: The way people act depends on

[11] For example, in one experiment (in an amusement park) 18% of the subjects littered in a clean environment, 10% did so in the presence of one piece of trash, 20% littered with two pieces of trash, and 40% littered if there were four pieces of trash in an otherwise clean environment.

[12] It would be interesting to check how subjects react to being exposed, in a clean environment, to a confederate that throws several pieces of trash at once on the floor. The descriptive norm is still made salient, but now the environment may be dirty enough to elicit a "what the heck!" response.

[13] This is very similar to familiar collective action or public good problems in economics literature.

how many are behaving one way or another, and once enough people run red lights, it becomes a self-sustaining practice.

If beneficial descriptive norms are fragile, and a change in the dominant, harmful descriptive norm is difficult or impractical, focusing people on social norms can become an alternative, successful strategy.[14] Social norms, as I defined them in Chapter 1, involve normative expectations, that is, people believe that they are under some sort of obligation to conform and that they may be sanctioned if they do not conform. The obligation may or may not be felt as binding, and indeed the motives behind conformity could vary from fear of a negative sanction, the desire for positive sanctions, to the acceptance of others' expectations as legitimate. Because social norms usually prescribe behavior that may be in conflict with other, narrowly self-interested motives, it is not *prima facie* clear which motives will dominate. As an example, if everybody litters and refraining from littering has a cost, why should one feel obliged to conform to a social norm that condemns littering?

This question is only germane if we think of conformity in terms of conscious deliberation and intentional choice, in other words, if we accept the deliberational route to behavior. In the deliberational mode, one may weigh the costs and benefits of actions and choose in a way that maximizes the difference or net benefit. However, costs and benefits need not be narrowly selfish. A benevolent or even altruistic individual may choose in favor of pro-social actions and deliberation can also take a less consequentialist direction, in that it may lead to recognizing the legitimacy of others' normative expectations and thus provide the subject with good reasons to meet them, since it is very difficult to recognize something as a legitimate claim and not find oneself under some sort of obligation to grant it. What needs emphasizing is that taking the deliberational route does not guarantee compliance with a norm, and may frequently have the opposite effect, especially in situations in which there is anonymity and thus little chance of being monitored and sanctioned.

But, as I stated in Chapter 1, the deliberational route to behavior is hardly the most common *modus operandi*, and social norms are habitually

---

[14] I believe there is an asymmetry between socially beneficial and socially harmful descriptive norms. Small threshold effects will be much more effective in reversing beneficial norms, whereas large threshold effects will be necessary to displace harmful descriptive norms, as socially harmful descriptive norms typically promote individual interests at the expense of societal benefits. The opposite is generally true of beneficial descriptive norms. Note that this is not going to be the case with other classes of norms, such as social norms.

followed in an automatic way. We leave a tip in a foreign country although we know service is included, trust strangers, exact revenge, donate to charities, reprimand transgressors even when we are not directly harmed, and show favoritism toward groups to which we belong without much thought to the reasons for, or the consequences of, what we are doing. More often than not, we behave in the 'right' way, in that we follow the established rules of our group, subculture, or society. In so doing we coordinate with others, fulfill their normative expectations, and collectively behave in ways that validate our mutual expectations. Coordinating behavior requires skilled performance, but this performance is usually below the level of conscious awareness. If we consider the alternative, heuristic route to behavior, social coordination seems less mysterious, since it results less from conscious intention than from priming shared behavioral rules that are then automatically followed. In this second scenario, priming a social norm that prescribes action x in the presence of a descriptive norm that condones $\sim x$ would induce conformity to x, *provided people are focused strongly enough on the social norm.* Focusing people on a social norm means that they know the situation is one to which the norm applies, expect a sufficiently large number of people to obey the norm, and also believe that a sizable number of other people expect and prefer them to obey the norm, and may even be prepared to sanction violations. Under these conditions most people would prefer to conform to the norm. Recall that a rational reconstruction of norms in terms of preferences and expectations does not require conscious deliberation. As I discussed in Chapter 1, rational choice does not entail awareness. Thus, one may follow a rule in an automatic way even if following the rule is ultimately explainable in terms of preferences and beliefs.

Turning again to the experiments of Cialdini et al., they provide some evidence that when subjects' attention was strictly focused on a *social norm* against littering, they refrained from littering even in the presence of strong evidence that a conflicting descriptive norm existed. In one condition, subjects observed a confederate picking up a piece of litter from the ground. Regardless of the state of the environment, almost all refrained from littering. However, the amount of littering was not diminished beyond control conditions if the confederate was seen throwing his own handbill in a trash can.[15] Presumably the two actions convey quite different messages. In the second case, the confederate throwing

---

[15] In this case the control condition was one in which no focusing on social norms was induced.

his own handbill in the trash can conveys the message that the (confederate) passerby personally disapproves or dislikes littering and thus avoids it. However, picking up other people's trash unambiguously expresses strong disapproval. It is other people's behavior that one finds objectionable, and this evokes the sanctions connected to norm violation, as well as focusing attention on the social norm itself. In other experiments, subjects did not encounter a confederate but were instead made to focus on social norms by means of messages written on handbills. The messages referred to norms with more or less conceptual similarity to the no-littering norm. These handbills were designed to "cognitively prime" subjects and focus their attention on the relevant social norm. The experimenters predicted that there would be less littering as the norm on the handbill increased in similarity to the anti-littering norm. Indeed, a request to refrain from littering had a behavioral effect close to that of an appeal to recycle, whereas a plea to vote had little effect. This monotonic trend was significant. Focusing subjects on social norms always produced the expected effect, irrespective of the prevailing descriptive norm. The effect was particularly strong when anti-littering behavior was elicited against a descriptive norm that condoned littering. It should be noted that priming effects are possible only when a norm is *recognized* as such within a given culture.[16] A stimulus, in other words, has to be interpreted within a context of background (collective) knowledge to be effective in activating norm-abiding behavior. If no anti-littering norm existed, or if there were no shared recognition that the situation is one to which the norm applies, neither the confederate's actions nor the appeals to recycling would have had any consequence on behavior.

Spreading Activation

There are a few interesting conclusions one may draw from the littering experiments. One is that subjects behave differently depending on whether their focus is on what people do versus what society approves of. Another is that to promote socially beneficial behavior social norms should be made *salient*. Social norms are usually more general than descriptive norms, in the sense that they prescribe or proscribe an entire class of actions in a variety of different situations, and have the added property that they can be elicited *indirectly* by focusing on other, conceptually similar norms. The latter claim is not just based on the

---

[16] This is Condition 1 of my definition of social (as well as descriptive) norms in Chapter 1.

experimental results illustrated here; rather, it is an example of how the design of an experiment involves auxiliary hypotheses drawn from other theories, in this case, cognitive psychology. It seems almost trite to say that any experiment is built on a set of accepted or at least plausible theories that inform the way the experiment is designed, the data collected and analyzed, and the findings interpreted. The point is an important one to make, however, because more often than not the role of auxiliary hypotheses is not made explicit, and this is a serious weakness in experiments whose design and results can only be properly understood in the light of such hypotheses.

Cialdini's idea of providing subjects with different but related normative messages, for example, builds on Collins and Loftus's (1975) theory of semantic memory. A central feature of Collins and Loftus's theory is the *spreading activation process*, which refers to the way in which a memory search proceeds. Simply stated, spreading activation works as follows: When the memory representation of a concept is activated, the activation spreads to neighboring stored representations. The greater the semantic similarity (relatedness) of two concepts, the higher the probability of activation of one of them if the other is activated. For example, if one is presented with the stimulus word *table*, what is activated is not just the representation of the concept table, but also representations of related concepts such as chair, furniture, and so on. If a person is subsequently presented with an ambiguous stimulus that could be interpreted as a chair or as a cube, it is more likely that it will be reported as a chair because of greater prior activation of the concept *chair*. The spreading activation model has gained widespread acceptance, especially because it explains (and predicts) an important phenomenon called *semantic priming*. Priming is an increase in the speed or accuracy of a decision that occurs as a consequence of prior exposure to some of the information in the decision context, without any intention or task-related motivation. A typical demonstration of priming is the lexical-decision task (Meyer and Schvaneveldt 1971), in which a series of decisions is made about whether letter strings are words. Priming is predicted to occur in cases where two successive letter strings are semantically related words. For example, the decision that 'doctor' is a word is faster if the preceding letter string was 'nurse' as compared to 'horse' or a meaningless string of letters.[17] The

---

[17] Note that priming occurs in lexical-decision tasks in which neither instruction nor any task-related incentive is provided that induces participants to base their responses on memory for prior experimental tasks. Hence it is believed that priming occurs automatically and without awareness. Further studies of priming have shown that priming

spreading activation model thus also explains why, when a neighbor concept is presented as the next letter string in a lexical decision task, it is identified sooner than less close concepts, since it was partially activated by the prime word even before being presented.

The spreading activation process presupposes that concepts are organized in a network structure: A node is a concept representation linked to other nodes, and the links correspond to associations between related concepts. Links between concepts may vary in length, and the length of each link is a function of the relatedness (similarity) of concepts, so activation is more likely to spread to a nearby concept rather than to a farther one (Collins and Quillian 1969). Priming is therefore proportional to semantic relatedness. The way concepts are linked to each other is related to category membership, and I will come back to this topic in the next section, when I explicitly introduce categories and schemata. For now, it is important to stress that the assumption that knowledge is represented in networks is well accepted in cognitive psychology and has been further developed in neural network models (Rumelhart 1997), in which the activation of a single node causes pathways to other, connected nodes to become active simultaneously. Such models have the added advantage of mapping well into our present knowledge of the structure of the cerebral cortex, in which an action potential in one neuron may activate other neurons along what is known as a 'neural pathway.'

Social norms might be similarly represented in memory within an organized cognitive structure, so that whenever a specific norm is made salient, we access the representation of that norm *and* of other norms that are closely related. Harvey and Enzle (1981) studied helping behavior in this light and demonstrated that observing a helping norm transgression, when followed by an opportunity to help, increases the probability of helping. Their results fit with previous observations that when individuals were exposed to a 'model' that donated/refused to help in a Christmas charity setting, there was greater donating when the model either donated or explicitly refused to donate (Macauley 1970). Note, however, that if the situation is ambiguous, in the sense of not being clear what the appropriate behavior is, observing a refusal to help consistently induces less helping, probably because it is taken to be the 'right' or 'normal'

---

is related to a basic perceptual processing that permits us to translate sensory inputs into perceptions of objects, words, etc. (Jacoby 1983), and that priming tasks tap into brain systems different from those involved in intentional recall. Many amnesic patients, for example, retain priming capabilities but have deficits in intentional retrieval of information (Graf and Schacter 1985).

response. Here, I propose that the transgression/helping effect might be explained by the following sequence: (a) Observing transgressions activates a relevant transgression-proscriptive norm and other, closely related norms; (b) subsequently subjects are exposed to an opportunity to help; and (c) the help-prescriptive norm relevant to the new situation will become more easily accessible to the degree to which it is closely related to the previously activated norm.[18] This effect of transgressions increasing the probability of activating a proscriptive norm almost certainly is subject to *threshold effects*: If all norm transgressions were to encourage norm adherence, Guliani's zero-tolerance policies would not have been needed. Once several transgressions occur, people's expectations about others' behavior change. In this case, a new descriptive norm that *condones* transgressions may emerge.

An obvious problem facing network theorists is the construction of these hypothesized structures in an objective way. By objective I do not mean that any two concept representations must be necessarily close because of some 'essential' semantic similarity; rather, it is the case that, in a given culture, we tend to collectively conceive of certain concepts as closely related. Our conceptual networks are for the most part intersubjective and shared, and successful social interaction rests on such collective representations and common forms of thinking: People are able to coordinate actions and expectations despite limited access to the operation and contents of their and others' minds and despite limited ability to communicate these contents to other people. Such coordination is possible because people share collective perspectives that have led them to develop similar inferences and interpretations of common situations, objects, and events.

Recent anthropological literature (Henrich et al. 2004) has examined how members of different small societies play experimental games. Such studies are particularly interesting because they show a strong intracultural consistency in interpreting and responding to various experimental games and an equally strong cross-cultural variance in such interpretations. However, as I shall discuss shortly, despite the heroic efforts to maintain the integrity of the experimental design across settings, this body of literature fails to explicitly account for cultural differences in the way in which subjects categorize these games. That is to say, Mapuche

---

[18] Note that the particular norm seen by the subject as most salient might, under certain conditions, be the most "self-serving" norm that could be activated. Chapter 3 discusses this *self-serving bias* in detail.

Indians may interpret the same game played by Los Angeles students as a sharing game, whereas students in Los Angeles interpret the game as a power game.[19] Cross-cultural studies are valuable, but, when studying the normative system of a particular human group, it is also important to be able to trace a map of the connections that exist between different norms and measure how central a norm is to a particular domain. For example, scaling procedures might be developed that derive network representations from judgments of word relatedness or similarity ratings (Cooke et al. 1986). Such procedures would be very valuable in assessing the closeness or similarity of different norms in a given culture.

There are important consequences to assuming that our knowledge of norms is represented by a network of concepts that are more or less semantically related to each other. A norm of reciprocity, for example, may be semantically closer to a norm of revenge (negative reciprocity) than to a norm of beneficence. According to the spreading activation hypothesis, a norm of reciprocity will be highly accessible once a norm of revenge has been primed, even if the emotions involved are very different (gratitude versus anger). Unfortunately there are no systematic studies of how representations of social norms are organized, though such studies would be of enormous practical value.

For example, suppose we were to discover that a norm of reciprocity is in fact closely connected to a norm of revenge. We would then predict that: (a) any event that primes a norm of revenge is sufficient, *ceteris paribus*, to activate a norm of reciprocity.[20] Note that such events would include instances of norm compliance as well as instances of norm transgression: It only matters that the first norm is primed, not whether it is obeyed;[21] (b) when faced with a subsequent choice in which positive reciprocation is a salient option, and provided activation of the first norm has been maintained until that moment, activation of a positive reciprocity norm will produce behavior consistent with it. That is, we would expect reciprocation levels to be significantly higher than in a

---

[19] As an example, some of Henrich's subjects seemed to interpret the Ultimatum game as a gift-giving game. The result was that their monetary offers were greater than 50% of the allotted sum, and such offers were systematically rejected because the gift recipients did not want to be obliged to repay the proposer's generosity.

[20] Subjects could read a story, watch a movie, or observe a confederate that takes (or does not take) revenge after a slight.

[21] This might explain the puzzling result of many helping experiments: Observing a confederate that refuses to help someone in need *also* increases subsequent helping behavior (Macaulay 1970). Similarly, it has been noticed that priming nonconformist behavior may simultaneously prime conformity (Epley and Gilovich 1999).

control group where no prior norms were made accessible. This hypothesis lends itself to empirical testing and is clearly falsifiable. I am inclined to interpret Cialdini's norm-activation experiments as providing evidence for a spreading activation mechanisms: The target norm (anti-littering) was activated when the subjects received an explicit message referring to another, closely related norm.

Yet, we cannot be sure that the observed effect is not due to the fact that we are priming those people who already embrace the norm. If this were the case, then we would be just *reminding* them that the norm applies to a given situation, but people who did not internalize the norm would not be induced to change their ways. If so, the social benefit of making a norm focal in order to induce behavior consistent with another, closely related norm would be moot, because we would be 'preaching to the converted.' It might be that making people focus on social norms elicits appropriate behavior simply because it evokes some internalized norm or standard of conduct (a *personal* norm, in the language of Chapter 1). In a similar vein, Elster's (1989) emphasis on emotions as mediators of norm observance suggests that, when individuals are made aware of some relevant social norm, they will obey it because feelings of guilt, shame, or self-enhancement have been activated. In Elster's case, too, the activated norm, to produce such emotions, must be internalized. To test the hypothesis that focusing people on social norms has an effect on behavior because it triggers internalized norms, it should be possible to design experiments in which one would first measure to what extent an individual has a personal norm that prescribes/proscribes a given behavior[22] and then observe whether those who have either a weak personal norm or no norm for/against the target behavior (and hence would 'transgress' under control conditions) conform when induced to focus on a norm that prescribes/proscribes that behavior. Cialdini et al. (1990), for example, discovered that 50% of those individuals who had a weak personal norm or no norm against littering did litter under control conditions, but only 22% of them littered if the relevant social norm was activated.[23] Though we need much more data to be sure of the generalizability of the priming effects, the littering experiments unequivocally indicate that

---

[22] To measure personal norms, subjects may be asked to answer a questionnaire that contains questions like the following: Do you feel a personal obligation to not litter when you are holding an empty soft-drink can and there are no trash cans available? The answer takes the form of deciding where – along a line that goes from 'No personal obligation' to 'Very strong obligation' – one's position would be (Cialdini et al. 1990).

[23] Cialdini et al. 1990.

making social norms focal induces conforming behavior even in those individuals who would otherwise break the rules without qualms.

I shall explore in the following sections the likely mechanisms by which a focus on social norms elicits compliance. What seems clear, however, is that norms, to be efficacious, have to be made salient, and that it is situational, contingent cues that lead people to interpret the situation as one to which a given norm applies, focus on the norm, and act on it. *The predictive power of a theory of norms therefore depends on knowing which situational cues trigger which norms.* Experiments are crucial in obtaining such knowledge, because only under controlled experimental conditions can we manipulate various features of the environment and find out which ones focus individuals on different normative considerations. This task was fairly simple in the case of the littering experiments, because the meaning of an anti-littering norm is unambiguous, as much as it is apparent when a descriptive norm pro or against littering is in place. Even in a controlled environment, focusing individuals on more complex social norms, such as norms of fairness and reciprocity, may present a greater challenge. As I shall discuss in the next chapter, fairness has several different interpretations, and the context within which a fairness norm is elicited determines the meaning individuals attribute to fairness.

Local Norms

Even within the same culture, fairness and reciprocity usually mean different things in different circumstances (Bicchieri 1999). Fairness, reciprocity, trust, and so on, are *local* concepts, in the sense that their interpretation and the expectations and prescriptions that surround them vary with the objects, people, and situations to which they apply. Some norms are more 'local' than others, though. Fairness norms, for instance, are conceived (at least in our society) as impartial, in the sense that they are meant to apply to everyone who is in a given position. For example, a norm of fairness in college admissions may dictate that merit be the only ranking criterion. Merit is supposed to be judged according to impersonal criteria (like standardized tests). It would be thought unfair to admit a candidate just because she is the niece of an admission committee member. Indeed, institutions go to great lengths to avoid 'personalizing' fairness (rules against nepotism are an example). Trust is very different in this respect. In most societies, there are implicit rules and expectations about who should be trusted. We ought to be fair in all of our interactions, but we ought not to trust everybody. Trust is thus partial and local in a stronger sense than fairness. Note that it is precisely the existence of such 'personalizing' rules that modulates emotional responses to a failure to trust. A spouse will be very upset and offended if he is not trusted (without good, explicit reasons) by his partner. Likewise, trust is expected in any long-term, close relationship, such as labor or commercial relations. For example, Macaulay's (1963) extensive study about Wisconsin manufacturing companies and their purchasing practices showed that most transactions were based on personal knowledge and trust, and in the context of long-standing relations the reference to contracts or legal sanctions was taken to signal a breakdown of trust (and of the relationship).[24] Similarly, Yamagishi (1998) pointed out that, though it may be inefficient to only deal or trade with members of the same network, we do not look elsewhere mainly because by so doing we would ruin our present relationship.[25] Looking elsewhere would send a clear signal that we do not care about the relationship and value money or profit more. In contrast to trust, fairness is expected to be insensitive to the identities of the parties. Fairness, however, is not insensitive to the personal attributes of the parties that are relevant to the allocation being considered. As an example, an allocation based on need, such as one in which an organ for transplantation has to be allocated, will be determined considering the potential recipients' health, life expectancy, age, and so on. On the other hand, an allocation based on merit, such as college slots, should take attributes such as standard aptitude test (SAT) scores and high school grades into account.

If norms are local in the above sense, interpreting experimental results will be complicated in several ways. A given situational cue may not just elicit a norm of fairness, but also a very *specific interpretation* of fairness. However, even when shared, fairness criteria such as 'give according to merit,' or 'give according to contribution,' or 'distribute according to need' leave the door open for comparison among the claimants as to who is needier, how important a contribution is, and so on. The more similar the claimants, the greater the scope for comparison and disappointment.

---

[24] Macauley (1963, p. 61) quotes what is a common business attitude expressed by a purchasing agent: "If something comes up, you get the other man on the telephone and deal with the problem. You don't read legalistic contract clauses at each other if you ever want to do business again. One doesn't run to lawyers if he wants to stay in business because one must behave decently." Similar attitudes were expressed by the traders in the diamond industry studied by Lisa Bernstein (1992).

[25] Note that inefficiency is determined only by comparison with a perfect information benchmark.

Experimental research on social justice consistently finds that the judgments people make about whether they are being treated fairly derive not
from the actual value of their outcomes, but from comparisons between
what they have and what they expected to have. If I get a 10% salary
rise, but I expected 20%, I will feel unjustly treated; if I expected less, I
will feel favored. Expected outcomes, in turn, are often determined by
interpersonal comparison between oneself and similarly situated others.
If others get more than I do, I feel deprived. If everyone else is equally
deprived, I do not feel so bad. This phenomenon occurs at a collective
level, too. In a well-known study done in the 1960s, Runciman (1966)
found that English manual workers felt more resentment if other manual workers' incomes exceeded their own, but they were less concerned
about the incomes of nonmanual workers. Similarly, philosophy profes-
sors are not usually affected by the higher salaries of the business school
faculty: Because the latter have alternative opportunities for nonacademic
employment, whereas philosophers usually do not, the salary differential
is perceived as market-driven and thus (at least in the United States) not
unfair. Changing the comparison class will therefore radically alter the
perception of what counts as fair and produce unexpected results. This
fact suggests that experimenters should pay particular attention to the
different ways in which an experiment could be perceived. As we shall
see in the following chapter, in Ultimatum games the slightest suggestion
that one of the parties is 'more deserving,' or the explicit introduction
of alternative monetary divisions one might choose (Fehr et al. 2003),
alters the perception of what a fair share is.

Further difficulties in interpretation arise because, although there is
usually substantial agreement within a culture's boundaries about what
counts as a fair allocation or distribution of particular goods (kidneys,
school slots, auction goods, etc), conflicts may still arise. In fact, the more
ambiguous a situation appears to be, the greater the potential for conflicting interpretations, where each interpretation invokes a different norm.
It is rather common for groups with conflicting interests to try to impose
a reading of the situation that allows them to benefit from the application
of a particular norm. For example, we know from experience that sacrifices are easier to bear if they are shared, or at least appear unavoidable.
This knowledge is often exploited to the advantage of one of the parties
in bargaining. A common tactic in wage bargaining between unions and
management when cuts are needed is for the management to impute
losses to market conditions, because sacrifices to make up for losses due
to managerial ineptitude are not likely to be accepted. Manipulation of

norms may thus be a conscious, intentional process, but there is also evidence that where we come from and our previous experiences and frames of reference influence our perceptions in an unconscious way. In a situation of conflict, uncertainty over appropriate behavior leads us to anchor the current situation to what we perceive are similar, previously experienced situations (Bettenhausen and Murnighan 1985). Different groups may just adopt different reference points, without any conscious attempt to manipulate norms, by reinterpreting the situation in their favor.

The foregoing complications depend on the fact that the most important prosocial norms, like fairness, reciprocity, or beneficence, are *local*, insofar as their content and recommendations are context-dependent. Different contexts will activate different interpretations of what it means to be fair, to reciprocate, or to be generous, and will therefore generate different beliefs, expectations, emotions, and behaviors. I mention these difficulties because I want to dispel the impression that priming a norm is a simple process. Individuals must be able to *focus* on a norm, that is, there must be enough cues in the environment to make a norm salient, and not too many conflicting cues pointing to different, sometimes opposing norms, or even different interpretations of the same norm.[26] As I discuss in the next chapter, the more ambiguous the situation, the greater the likelihood that different interpretations of the same norm will crop up, opening the door to self-serving biases.

It is worth repeating that there exists a common misconception about norms: If we take norms to have motivational power, then the mere existence of a shared norm is expected to induce compliance *in all sorts of situations* to which the norm might apply. The erroneous assumption that if a norm motivates, then it will always produce the same observable behavior, has prevented many social scientists from considering social norms as explanatory variables in their models and consequently in their experiments. For example, if we know that a group shares a norm of reciprocity, we would be mistaken in expecting to observe reciprocating behavior in a variety of circumstances that call for it. *Social norms are not internalized generic imperatives such as 'reciprocate,' 'commit,' or 'cooperate.'* One does not feel a generic obligation to cooperate with strangers in regard to unspecified issues, as much as an art lover is unlikely to buy any piece of art she comes across and likes, however vast her means may be. Rather, norm activation is context-specific and relies on past experiences and

---

[26] Note that, as I discussed in Chapter 1, 'enough' may be different for different norms.

present perceptions that shape our expectations of other people's behavior. If a specific situation does not activate the relevant expectations and beliefs, then there is no reason to expect a norm to be active. Thus, even if a norm applies to situation s, if there are not enough cues in s to activate it, conforming behavior will not be observed. Cognitive heuristics play a crucial role in interpreting the situation. Consequently, heuristics are fundamentally responsible for some norms rather than others (or none at all) being activated in different situations. I shall discuss these heuristics and their consequences presently.

A second misconception I discussed in Chapter 1 is the belief that people consciously deliberate about norms, that they mentally refer to them before acting. Obeying a norm, in this view, is always a conscious, intentional action. The propensity to explain behavior as resulting from an intentional choice is an instance of a common tendency to overattribute behavior to dispositional factors (abilities, preferences, or character traits) and underestimate the influence of situational factors (cues). Ross (1977) called it the *fundamental attribution error*, and social scientists are not immune to it. Hence a person whom we observe helping the victim of an accident may be deemed to be generous, and we expect her future behavior to be consistent with the alleged character trait. Similarly, someone who, facing a choice between stocks and bonds, is observed to choose stocks is thought to be displaying a preference for risky assets. There is much evidence, however, that the most important determinant of behavior is the situation in which one is. As Latane and Darley (1968) demonstrated, my disposition to help in an emergency may depend on the number of bystanders, and my choice of stocks may be driven by imitating what people around me do. I may choose to buy stocks even if I still prefer a less risky portfolio, and indeed would have chosen otherwise if I had no information about other people's choices. The overriding motive, in this case, is the desire to imitate the choices of what one takes to be more informed actors (Bicchieri and Fukui 1999).

Having established that norms may or may not be activated in a given situation, and that norm activation is usually an automatic, unintentional process, it remains to be explored what sort of cognitive mechanism is at work. If we rely on a 'stored,' shared set of behavioral rules, it is important to describe how such rules are connected with the circumstances we find ourselves in. We want to know what drives our attention to specific situational cues, how those cues are interpreted, and how these interpretations lead us to act in predictable ways. Psychological research suggests that categories, scripts, and schemata are the answer.

Categories, Schemata, and Role-Playing

Every single day of our lives we have to understand, interpret, and make a host of more or less significant decisions about people and social situations. Is that person trustworthy? Is she happy or aggressive? Is he smart? Is he romantically interested? Is this a friendly occasion, or should I worry about being judged and evaluated? Should allocating time slots for discussion among students be a matter of equality or equity? In any social situation we face, we go through a complex set of mental operations of interpreting, understanding, encoding, and inferring, the output of which is meaningful, appropriate behavior. These operations include (but are not limited to) the perception of a stimulus, be it a person or an event, focusing attention on particular cues or dimensions of it, activating a comparison process to assess similarities and differences with past episodes stored in memory, grouping the stimulus with others in a specific category, and finally invoking a cognitive schema that will specify beliefs, expectations, and behavioral rules. This simple serial, step-by-step account is an idealization, because it is likely that some information flows in both directions, or even that several cognitive operations overlap (McClelland 1979). For our purposes, however, it is useful to separate the cognitive operations, to distinguish the general process of categorization (e.g., defining something as a 'market interaction') from the more specific activation of a schema or script (e.g., understanding a problem as involving a 'fair division of the sale proceeds').

Categorization is a crucial step in the process of interpreting the social world, as it activates schemata (or scripts) that may be likened to personal theories of the way social situations and people work. Such 'theories' allow us to function in society: As they ground our inductive inferences and predictions about others' future behavior, they make the world intelligible and predictable. For example, once I cast the person I am facing into the category 'waiter,' a script about what happens in restaurants is primed, followed by the prediction that this person will come to my table with a menu, take orders, bring food, and so on. A script may also contain rules and expectations about the restaurant client's behavior, including ways of addressing waiters and tipping policies. Thus my tipping at a foreign restaurant could be the result of script activation, not generosity. Scripts and schemata help fill gaps when information is lacking, but they also bias our perceptions in the direction of schema-confirming information; for instance, people labeled 'attractive' are generally perceived as possessing the finest qualities. More negatively, minorities are often seen by members of a majority group as possessing the worst personality traits, such as being lazy or untrustworthy. Though the perceptual biases they induce may lead to negative stereotyping that is difficult to eradicate, the other, positive side of the coin is that scripts and schemata perform the invaluable task of channeling attention to specific, relevant stimuli (e.g., looking at a person's face when engaged in a conversation), as far too much information is available for processing at any given time.

Scripts and schemata are important in understanding how norms work, because norms are embedded into such cognitive structures. Schemata, for example, contain social roles and expected sequences of behaviors that help us to behave appropriately (and know what to expect) in specific settings. For example, suppose you observe individual A giving B $100, and B subsequently giving C $20 and keeping $80 to herself. What is B doing? Is she behaving fairly, generously, dishonestly, or spitefully? There are many ways to describe the same action sequence, depending on our goals and information. If the situation is ambiguous, in that we do not have much detailed information about A, B, and C, we will try to 'fill in' the missing data with cues derived from the context, including the reactions of the parties. Suppose all we know is that A, B, and C work together; A is the boss, and B and C often do joint work. If we are further told that today was B's birthday, she may have received the money as a birthday gift, in which case she is being very generous in donating part of it to C. In this context, we think C has no right to any of it and that he should feel grateful for the unexpected boon.

If C looks irritated, is he being unreasonable or is something else going on? Because we tend to attribute 'reasons' to emotions, we would probably look for further cues that explain C's anger. If we know that B often does joint work with C, it may be the case that B received the money from her boss for a shared job, but then, depending on other situational and cultural cues as well as on C's reaction, we may judge the division to be fair or unfair and C's anger unreasonable or justified. If we live in a culture where authority and seniority matter, the unequal division would be fair if B is more senior or has greater authority than C. Is this the case? Are there outward signs of B's greater authority? What if we suspect C put much more effort than B in the task? This suspicion would only have a bearing in a culture that applies equity rules such as 'give to each according to effort or contribution.' In this case, B's action would be perceived as unfair, prompt legitimate feelings of anger in C, and we would understand and possibly sympathize with C's anger.

On the other hand, if we believe a rule of equality applies, B's and C's unequal contributions would not matter, and in this case C would rightly expect half of the sum. He would still be angry at receiving $20, but for different reasons, and we would still sympathize with him. How B's and C's behaviors are interpreted depends on how the interaction is categorized and what kind of schema is applied. In all cultures, norms of fairness are *local*, in the sense that different situations, objects, and people will produce different interpretations of what counts as fair: In present-day America, for example, it is generally agreed that a kidney to be transplanted should not be allocated by auction, merit, or by a 'first come, first serve' principle, whereas merit or 'first come, first serve' are acceptable grounds for allocating college slots. Whether we perceive a new situation as more similar to allocating a kidney or a college slot will make all the difference regarding subsequent beliefs, emotions, and behavior. My discussion of categories, scripts, and schemata is meant to offer a description of the way in which contexts can trigger particular beliefs and preferences, and thus particular actions.

Categories

Cognitive psychologists regard categories as collections of instances that have a family resemblance (Rosch 1978). Like the Wittgensteinian definitions of "game," we can almost never identify a set of attributes as necessary and sufficient criteria for category membership. Instead, instances are more or less typical in terms of a range of attributes, with maybe a most typical, or prototypical, instance representing the category. A prototypical car has four wheels, a roof, seats, and so forth. When faced with a new object, we compare it with category prototypes, paying particular attention to attributes that are perceived as diagnostic of category membership. The more similar the object is to the prototype of a category, the more likely we are to assign it to the category. A prototypical car has a roof, but we assign a Cabriolet to the car category because it shares many other important features with the prototypical car.[27]

---

[27] This view of categories is presupposed by Collins and Loftus's (1975) theory of spreading activation discussed earlier. Recall that if concept representations are organized in a network structure, then the activation of a concept is likely to spread to nearby concepts. Distance, in turn, is a function of the similarity of two concepts, defined in terms of category membership. Thus, when making decisions about category membership, the probability that a stimulus s_i is classified in category J depends on its similarity to the

Categories may also be represented by sets of exemplars, that is, specific instances one has encountered (Estes 1986). Thus, deciding that an event, person, or situation belongs to a certain category involves comparing it to several exemplars stored in memory. This latter view does not imply that people are able to recall every single instance in memory. It just states that instances leave traces in memory, and these traces are accessed in categorizations. Access may not be a conscious process at all. Indeed, psychologists treat knowledge of exemplars as nondeclarative because subjects are not usually aware that they have acquired such knowledge. As I am exposed to a series of examples of a category, I learn about each individual example, but I also learn about the items as a group. I might be aware that I have learned about a specific example, but I might not be aware that I have acquired category-level knowledge. The latter kind of knowledge only emerges when I am confronted with new examples of the category and have to classify them. For example, I may be aware that I have heard several pieces by Mozart, but I may not be aware that I also learned something about the pieces as a group, or what is common to all of them. When I hear a new Mozart piece, however, I will be able to recognize it, even if I am unable to describe the features that make it a Mozart piece. The exemplars view has the advantage of representing information about variability, but perhaps its greatest advantage is flexibility: Some categories do change as we acquire more information, and adding new instances as exemplars seems easier than changing the prototype.[28]

Among cognitive psychologists the jury is still out, though some have conjectured that people use both prototypes and exemplars, depending on how well they know a particular category (Elio and Anderson 1981). Prototypes are preferentially used when we know less, whereas

---

prototypical category member and to the prototypes of all other categories **k** that may be relevant, i.e.,

$$\text{Probability } (s_i \in J) = \frac{\text{similarity } (s_i, \text{ prototype}_j)}{\sum_k \text{similarity } (s_i, \text{ prototype}_k)}.$$

[28] Exemplar theory does not conceive of memory as containing a separate, prototypical representation of the category itself. It is rather hypothesized that our knowledge of, say, birds is based on the features stored with various examples of birds. The probability that a stimulus s_i is classified in category **J** will thus depend on the summed similarities of s_i and the exemplars from different categories $\mathbf{k_1}, \ldots, \mathbf{k_n}$, i.e.,

$$\text{Probability } (s_i \in \mathbf{J}) = \frac{\sum_{j \in J} \text{similarity } (s_i, \text{ exemplar}_j)}{\sum_{k=1}^{n} \sum_{j \in k_1} \text{similarity } (s_i, \text{ exemplar}_j)}$$

(Note that **J** is part of the set of **k** categories considered in the denominator.)

exemplars represent richer, more detailed knowledge. This latter view, however, still presupposes a basic, elementary memory encoding in terms of prototypes.

From Attention to Interpretation

Any person, object, or event we face possesses a variety of features, and our attention will be typically focused on some of them to the exclusion of others. Without attention to particular cues, the activation of the comparison process that is the hallmark of *categorization*, the mental activity of recognizing something as belonging to a given category, would be impossible. When we compare a person, object, or situation with others stored in memory, we assess the similarity of the present stimulus with members of a given category we know. Any stimulus, however, possesses an infinity of dimensions and can potentially be described in innumerable ways. This is an obvious problem when trying to determine similarity relations. Nelson Goodman (1972) pointed out that any two objects or situations have infinite sets of properties in common, and also infinite sets of properties that are not shared. I can describe the child sitting in front of me according to spatial location, height, weight, physical features, name, dressing, family relations, and so on. This child and his little chair both share the property of weighing less than 20 kilos, 21 kilos, 22 kilos, and so on. He also may share with other individuals the properties of being first born, of having parents in their twenties, and so on. Clearly similarity is a meaningful notion only when we specify some relevant *respect* in which two things may be judged similar. It is realistic to assume that our background knowledge, the decision context, and our purposes will focus our attention on particular features, affect our judgments of relevance, and thus constrain the number of stimulus dimensions on which we base category membership decisions, as empirical studies have repeatedly demonstrated (Barsalou 1982; Roth and Shoben 1983; Lamberts 1994).

Research suggests that our goals tend to automatically influence what grabs our attention. When one has a conscious goal, objects, people, and events relevant to the goal seem to "pop out" from the background. Our goals determine what we pay attention to, and which of its aspects we pay attention to as well (Bruner 1957). A second, entirely 'automatic' attention response exists that is independent of our goals and relies on chronic sources of influence such as self-relevant information, frequently experienced information, negative social behavior, and visible features that indicate membership in a social category. For example, we tend to pay automatic attention to behaviors that are relevant to aspects of our lives we frequently think about, such as values, attitudes, or important dimensions of our self-concept. When considering another person's behavior, we tend to pick up information related to frequently used trait constructs, such as hostile, kind, smart, and so on. Negative, potentially threatening social behavior is also immediately noticed (Fiske 1980; Pratto 1994), as are visible personal features (gender, race, age, speech accent, distinctive clothing, etc.) that pre-consciously activate stereotypical categories associated with them (Gaertner and Dovidio 1996, Bargh et al. 1996). Such automatic attention grabbers should not be discounted, because they may compete with our purposes and the decision context for our attention.

Attention lends relevance to a (usually pretty small) subset of features possessed by a given stimulus. Hence, background knowledge, chronic sources of influence, and goals all help in making specific cues salient. The interesting question is, How do we move *from attention to interpretation* or, in other words, how do we come to see a salient stimulus as part of a given class (category)? Note that the set of candidate categories may not be a singleton, in the sense that, in principle, there may be several competing categories under which the stimulus can be classified. Judgments of relevance, familiarity with certain categories, and framing effects are some, but likely not all, of the determinants of our identification of a single category, out of a small set of possible candidate categories, as the one under which we classify a given person, object, or event. For example, *familiarity* with specific categories (or lack thereof) will ease (or instead hamper) the task of recognizing and interpreting social situations, as when an experiment involving monetary manipulations is performed among members of small societies that only infrequently enter into market relations (Henrich 2000). The great variability of the results of Ultimatum and Dictator games played in various small societies points to a shared interpretation *within* a given society, but very different interpretations *between* different societies. In some groups, the proposer in the Ultimatum game offered more than half of the money to the receiver, but the latter consistently refused the offer. Such behavior can only be justified if the game is interpreted as a case of gift giving, where the donor's generosity is both a sign of status and creates an obligation to reciprocate in the receiver. If the most common situation in which goods are exchanged is one of gift giving, it is not surprising that the experimental situation will be categorized accordingly. Easily accessible categories are those more often or more recently used, and consistent with one's goals and expectations in a particular context. For example, when

Cialdini et al. (1990) exposed some of their subjects to a flyer containing an appeal to recycle, they gave them a cue that presumably primed a whole category of environment-friendly behavioral rules. Among them, the one relevant to the context was the anti-littering norm. Indeed, subjects who received the recycling flyer refrained from littering in greater numbers, regardless of the state of the environment.

Framing effects are also important (Kahneman and Tversky 1973), because how a situation is presented or described alters perceptions by guiding the interpretation of cues in a specific direction, such as when two friends are presented either as having a casual conversation or as planning a robbery. It is well known, for example, that people are more likely to cooperate in commons rather than in public-good dilemmas (Brewer and Kramer 1986). In a commons dilemma, subjects start with no money or points, thus it is easy for them to refrain from taking too much of the common good. In a public-good dilemma, they are initially given a sum of money, so they perceive themselves as owning a certain amount of wealth. Contributing to a public good is experienced as a loss, whereas in a commons dilemma refraining from taking from the common pool is perceived as foregoing a gain. In Ultimatum games, we know that the allocation of "property rights" has a major effect on the amount of money offered as well as on how much the responder is willing to accept (Camerer and Thaler 1995).[29] In sum, alternative descriptions of the same situation will induce different categorizations and thus result in

---

[29] An alternative method of subsuming a situation under one specific category would be to calculate the conditional probability of a category given the observed stimulus. If, for example, there are $C_1, \ldots, C_n$ possible candidate categories, of which C_j is one, then we may apply Bayes' rule, i.e.,

$$\text{Probability}\,(C_j, s_i) = \frac{p(C_j)\,p(s_i, C_j)}{\sum_{i=1}^{n} p(C_i)\,p(s_i, C_i)}.$$

Applying Bayes' rule means, among other things, that one takes into account base rates, because one would have to calculate the prior probability of each candidate category occurring. There is much evidence, however, pointing to the fact that people tend to discount base rates, so that $p(C_j, s_i)$ is equated to $p(s_i, C_j)$, the likelihood of the stimulus, given a certain category. This is an example of *representativeness*, a heuristic studied by Kahneman and Tversky (1972, 1973). The typical justification for relying on cognitive shortcuts (heuristics) refers to our limited memory and information-processing capabilities. Heuristics are supposed to reduce complex problem solving to much simpler judgmental operations. Yet if we take similarity judgments to be an example of representativeness, in that $p(C_j, s_i)$ is calculated as $p(s_i, C_j)$ as above, it is not obvious that the sheer amount of calculation involved is less than what it would take to calculate Bayes' rule. Base rates, however, may be more difficult to assess than similarities, and this could explain the preferred reliance on similarity calculations.

different behavioral responses. We may thus assume, for example, that an experimental subject who is about to play a complex social dilemma game will consider how likely it is that the current experimental situation is an instance of a cooperative or a competitive interaction. To which extent the present situation is similar in essential properties, or *represents*, a typical competitive or cooperative interaction may be determined by the subject's familiarity with a specific category, or by a framing effect. In this case the subject will not consider the overall prior probability of competitive versus cooperative interactions occurring in a given context, but instead will focus on how similar the situation is to one of those interactions.

Natural and Social Kinds

Most of the research done on categorization refers to 'natural kind' categories (such as bird, fish, fruit, coal, and so on) as opposed to 'human artifact' categories (such as pencils, chairs, and roads). A way to distinguish between these two types of categories is to think of natural kinds as independent of human beliefs and behaviors, whereas human artifacts are made by man and are there to fulfill some specific function. What makes two pencils similar is just their function; otherwise they can vary in size, material, color, and shape. In contrast, natural kinds are constrained by their genetic and molecular structure to have a particular size, shape, color, and so on.[30] But even more importantly, natural kinds allow a host of inductive inferences to be made, whereas the inductive potential of artifacts is very limited. Once we recognize that what we see is a bird, we can infer a large set of properties this bird shares with other birds. There is little to infer, however, from recognizing an object as a pencil beyond its function. Inductive potential is, of course, limited or enhanced by the amount of background knowledge and the theoretical capabilities of the individual making the inference. A child will not immediately see a penguin as a bird, whereas a zoologist will, because the latter will have a much deeper knowledge of the biology of birds. Hence the child will have a limited capability of drawing inferences about penguins, but what matters is that, in principle, knowledge about a natural kind allows inferences to be made about further unobservable properties, as well as postulating

---

[30] Of course this is a rough and imprecise distinction. By genetic manipulation, humans can create new kinds of, say, fruits and animals that would not have existed if not for human intervention. Still, the members of the new categories would share many more properties than pencils and cars, which share few properties beyond the ones relevant to the functions they were created to fulfill.

links between deeper and more superficial characteristics. Whether there exists an invariant core of essential properties defining a natural kind, or whether instead such core is subject to change and thus new knowledge about, say, electrons produces a radical modification of their meaning, has been the object of much debate in philosophy (Kripke 1982; Putnam 1988; Quine 1974). What matters to the present discussion, however, is not the true nature of categories, but the way people perceive them.

Research has demonstrated that people, even small children, tend to perceive natural kinds as more homogeneous than artifact categories, and to believe that their members have deep underlying similarities (Gelman 1988). There is a widespread tendency to endow members of natural kinds with 'essences' or underlying stable characteristics, and to believe that unobservable essential properties are related to more superficial perceptual characteristics (Medin and Ortony 1989). For example, people tend to think that the perceptual appearances of, say, birds are causally related to hidden essential properties that constitute criteria for inclusion in the bird category, and thus take appearances as diagnostic traits that tell birds apart from other animals. The main feature of what has been called 'psychological essentialism' is that members of a natural kind are thought to have a unique, true identity that persists over time and justifies the inferences and predictions we make about them.

People also seem to have a preferred level of categorization. When observing a canary, for example, most people do not categorize it as an animal or a canary; rather, they prefer to include it in the category 'bird.' The preference for a basic-level categorization appears to be based on the need to maximize inferential, predictive potential (Rosch et al. 1976). Hence, for someone who is not an ornithologist, the basic-level categorization of a canary will be as a bird, as this way to categorize it maximizes at once distinctiveness and informativeness, allowing meaningful predictions to be made. There is a link between 'psychological essentialism' and basic-level categories, because people tend to attribute essences to objects that are categorized at the basic level.

Cognitive psychologists have done little research on social categories and the way people perceive them. Social categorization has traditionally been the province of social psychology, which has preferentially studied how social behavior is categorized in terms of trait concepts (hostility, kindness, etc.) and the pigeonholing of individuals belonging to a particular group in terms of that group's stereotype (Jews, women, blacks, etc.). Evidence about stereotyping suggests that people tend to perceive social categories as natural kinds having high inductive potential and stability.

Gender and race, for example, are common categories people use, but so are caste, national identity, and social roles (mother, laborer, manager, etc.). Though the capability to categorize is clearly adaptive, because it allows one to make inferences and predictions, and thus reduce uncertainty and the amount of information needed to function, it is not clear whether the ways in which we partition our social universe have a biological basis as well. The point is not whether gender and race are 'natural' ways to categorize people (even infants seem to find race and gender salient), but whether the inferences we make from superficial characteristics to essential underlying features are justified. For example, do differences in social roles (mother, manager) reflect different underlying personality traits (caring, ambitious)? Does physical appearance (attractive) reflect some more basic attributes (intelligent, competent)? How many of the group differences that are a function of gender and age are due to biology, and how many to societal expectations? What needs emphasizing is that, in treating social categories as natural kinds, people pay disproportionate attention to surface characteristics and physical signals, taking them as diagnostic of deeper, essential traits.

Social categories are also perceived to be, like natural kinds, discrete and exclusive (Rothbart and Taylor 1992). This might explain why there is a tendency to exaggerate in-group similarities and out-group differences, and why members of a group are usually perceived to possess similar attitudes and traits even when group assignment is arbitrary, as in Tajfel's (1981) minimal group situation. In every culture, conventions develop that signal unequivocally group membership, like the special clothes that prostitutes in Venice had to wear or the yellow star that Jews were forced to display during the Nazi period. When physical signals fail, there seems to be a need to substitute them with man-made ones that fulfill the same function. Rothbart and Taylor (1992) have pointed out another important consequence of perceiving social categories as natural kinds: Social categories will be perceived as unalterable, and there will be a tendency to construct "biological or quasi-biological concepts to convey that inexorability" (Rothbart and Taylor 1992, p. 24). As an example, they consider the vicissitudes of the category *Jew* through the centuries. Though there have been periods (most notably, the Early Christian era) in which converted Jews have been completely assimilated, there are many examples of attempts to make the category inalterable. So, for example, in the Spain of Ferdinand and Isabel, a converted Jew remained a Jew, and in Hitler's Germany the existence of at least one Jewish grandparent branded one forever as a Jew.

'Psychological essentialism' seems to be a feature of social categorization, especially when what is categorized are ethnically, socially, and
racially homogeneous groups. An important question to ask is whether
'psychological essentialism' is at work in the way we perceive a social situation and form inferences about further aspects of it that we may not
immediately assess. How do we categorize social situations? How do we
decide that something is a market interaction, a reciprocal exchange, a
gift-giving occasion, or a status-based exchange? How do we perceive an
interaction as fair or unfair, a person generous or tightfisted, an intention
malicious or benevolent, and why do we apply, at least within the same culture, shared (and fine-tuned) fairness and reciprocity principles? I believe
we learn, through stories, observations, and repeated interactions, that
certain social situations and patterns of interaction are *similar* and can be
clustered together in that they entail specific ways of relating to other people, of allocating and distributing tangible and intangible goods, and of
feeling and expressing these feelings. A market interaction, for example,
involves specific roles (buyer and seller, worker and employer, debtor and
creditor, etc.), the existence (or the possibility) of an exchange among
the parties that is expected to benefit both, a medium of exchange (usually money), and the absence of any thought or intention of promoting
the other party's ends. A market relation is expected to be an impersonal
one, so much so that in my Italian childhood I was repeatedly taught, by
means of ominous examples, that it is better never to enter into such a
relationship with a good friend, on pain of damaging the friendship. As
children, we may learn that buying and selling using money or bartering
objects are prototypical market interactions, and as we grow we fine tune
our understanding of the category through many examples that teach
us, among other things, rules, roles, and feelings fitting market interactions and not other kinds of social relations. It thus seems to me that, at
least with social situation categories, there is a role for both prototypes
and exemplars, though the data collected about memory retrieval of cat-
egorical knowledge point to the centrality of prototypes. However, it is
possible that, though the immediate categorization of an event makes
use of a prototype, the subsequent retrieval of scripts and schemata relies
more on exemplars-based knowledge. I will come back to this point later.

If 'psychological essentialism' is at work in our categorization of social
situations, then it must be true that we treat those categories, at some
level, as natural kinds. But our modes of social interaction, the ways in
which we evaluate them, and the rules we follow are social artifacts, not
natural kinds. Modes of social interaction may have a biological basis, but

the enormous cultural differences that exist in, for example, family structure and relations or market interactions tell us that they are shaped more
by society than by nature. However, we have a tendency to equate at least
some such 'social kinds' with natural kinds. For example, once we categorize something as a market interaction, we tend to form inferences about
other people's expectations and motives as well as about our intentions,
as if the cues pointing to a market exchange were diagnostic of deep and
stable underlying motives, intentions, and personal dispositions. A fairly
common observation is that when people interpret an ambiguous situation as involving a 'fair division' of some good, they may come to expect
equal shares and tend to interpret in this light the parties' behavior. Thus
if one of the parties deviates from the expected fair division, he or she will
be imputed mean intentions and may be punished accordingly. I am not
claiming that all social categories are perceived as akin to natural kinds,
but there is a tendency to endow the most well-entrenched ones with
permanence and high inductive potential, as if such categories reflected
stable underlying regularities. This psychological bent may explain the
frequency, within our culture, of feelings of resentment and anger at
what is perceived as an 'unfair' allocation, as if there were a unique and
unalterable way of dividing things up, a natural right to a fair share, and
a vicious intention in those who deny us our rights.[31] In the next chapter,

---

[31] It has been argued (A. Fiske 1992) that all social relationships and interactions can be
represented by a small number of categories: Communal Sharing, Authority Ranking,
Equality Matching, and Market Pricing. Fiske maintains that such categories are universal and that every social interaction or relationship can be explained as resulting from
some combination of these models of interaction. People relating according to the Communal Sharing (CS) model have a sense of equivalence and attend to what they have in
common, disregarding differences between them. When people coordinate their interactions along the lines of Authority Ranking (AR), they form a linear status hierarchy.
Higher ranking individuals command respect and take responsibility for subordinates.
When people interact in the framework of Equality Matching (EM), they keep track
of the balances or differences among them and aim to reach an even balance. This is
the way people take turns, divide something into equal parts, or restitute in kind. People using the Market Pricing (MP) model operate with reference to socially significant
ratios or proportions such as prices, wages, rents, or interest rates. We are using MP whenever we think in terms of the ratio of benefits to costs or calculate whether it is "worth
spending the time and energy" on some social effort. There is not much experimental
evidence yet to support the existence and effectiveness of Fiske's basic categories, but
there is ample evidence that people do not think of their social life and interactions in
terms of motives such as egoism, altruism, competition, aggression, or cooperation. We
rather seem to put social action 'in context,' quickly determining the type of situation
we are facing and the roles we and others are expected to play within the specific situation (Goffman 1959). Thus though categorizing social situations might involve much
more than the four basic categories identified by Fiske, his analysis goes in the right
direction.

I shall discuss how different ways of categorizing a situation in which a given good has to be allocated or distributed determine the adoption of different allocation procedures and thus focus people on different fairness norms.

Schemata and Scripts

Schemata are cognitive structures that represent stored knowledge about people, events, and roles (Bartlett, 1932; Fiske and Taylor, 1991).[32] When we apply a schema, our interpretation of the situation is theory-driven, in the sense that prior knowledge heavily influences the way we understand and interpret a salient stimulus. I say "theory" because a schema does not represent particular, detailed knowledge, but rather generic knowledge that holds across many instances. A schema is thus concerned with the general case, not the specifics of any situation we have encountered. So when we face a new situation, we quickly form a rudimentary theory of it, draw inferences and make predictions, and interpret subsequent evidence in the light of this 'theory.' Suppose that I understand a new situation as a case of buying; the buying schema contains variables (buyer, seller, money, merchandise, bargaining, etc.) to which I associate people, objects, and events. If there are unobservable variables (I may not see money being exchanged), the buying schema allows me to infer that money was or will be exchanged, and so on. Once a schema is activated, there is a demonstrable tendency to confirm it, as if it were a theory to which we hold on until it is unequivocally demonstrated to be wrong.[33]

The schemata of interest for understanding how norms affect behavior are event schemata that describe appropriate sequences of events in well-known situations. Examples of such schemata are descriptions of what happens at restaurants, soccer games, theaters, and lectures. Consider a 'lecture schema,' which contains roles (student, professor) and

---

[32] The concept of schema was developed in cognitive psychology in the context of research on memory, to explain people's understanding and memory for complex materials such as text passages. It was later transferred to social psychology to model social cognition (see Markus and Zajonc 1985 for an overview, and also Fiske and Taylor 1991).

[33] This tendency is particularly damaging with respect to so-called role schemata: the sets of behaviors and traits we attribute and expect from people who are in a particular social position. When the role is ascribed (as opposed to achieved), as is the case with age, gender, and race, stereotyping may lead to permanent negative attributions of personality traits ('women are too emotional,' 'Chinese are good at math') that are almost never falsified. Because once a schema is activated it affects our subsequent perceptions, attention, recall, and interpretation, it is easy to see how racial or gender biases are difficult to eradicate. Moreover, since schemata are often emotionally laden, racial stereotyping can lead to emotional reactions such as fear or anxiety that may produce the very behavior that is feared.

sequence rules (the teacher enters the classroom, the students seat and prepare to take notes, the lecture starts, the students take notes and ask questions, the lecture ends, all leave the classroom). Schemata for events such as this are called *scripts* (Schank and Abelson, 1977). A script for a lecture thus describes a stylized, stereotyped sequence of actions that are appropriate in this context, and it defines actors and roles. Note that a script also involves beliefs and expectations related to the actors' roles, and that both the expectations and the stereotyped details are cultur-ally consensual. Scripts are the basis of understanding and making sense of events, as they embed knowledge relevant to the present situation. Thus my understanding of an event as a lecture involves comparison and matching of what I experience to pre-stored groupings of actions and sit-uations that I have already experienced. Both the students' and teacher's actions make sense only insofar as I recognize them as being part of a stored pattern of actions that I have previously experienced. The same can be said of what happens in a host of daily interactions in which we can easily interpret what is said and done precisely because we know what usually happens in such situations.

Social norms are embedded into scripts. Once a situation is categorized as being of a certain type, a script is activated that will involve players' interlocking roles, a shared understanding of what is supposed to happen, and even prescriptions for unexpected occurrences. For example, once a particular fair division script is activated, an individual will have definite beliefs and expectations about other individuals she is interacting with, even if (or especially if) she does not know personally such individuals. In Chapter 1, I said that the existence of a social norm presents an individual with a Bayesian game: She may be interacting with other norm followers or instead with agents that do not abide by the norm. I left open the question of where the prior probabilities came from. I want to argue that scripts provide such priors. Once a fair division script is activated, an agent will know what to expect from other agents, and this can be modeled as if the agent were playing a Bayesian game in which the priors are given and favor following the norm.

On the other hand, we seem to know what kinds of events may cause detours or abrupt endings in scripts. We can recognize obstacles, errors, and distractions, and we modulate our emotional reactions depending on the causal attributions we generate for the unexpected events. Frus-tration, anger, and sadness are very different emotions, each appropriate to a different interpretation of the unexpected occurrence. Because a norm is just a prescription about how to behave in a specific situation, violation of a norm will immediately generate a reaction 'appropriate' to the causal explanation of what motivated the violation.

The script–norm connection is important to understand the difficulties we normally experience in abstractly defining general principles of justice, fairness, and so on. Whereas it is reasonably easy to say why and how a specific fairness norm should apply or has been violated, it is very difficult to generally define what fairness is. One explanation for this difficulty is that we reason in modular ways: Most reasoning does not involve the application of general-purpose reasoning skills. Rather, our reasoning is tied to specific schemata or scripts related to particular bodies of knowledge. A demonstration of the role of schemata in reasoning is found in the seminal work of Wason and Johnson-Laird (1972), who showed how subjects systematically fail to solve a simple logic problem involving material implication, but when presented with a formally equivalent problem cast in familiar terms, they are always able to correctly solve it.[34] Once a problem is understood in terms of a familiar schema, reasoning is correctly applied. Logicians and moral philosophers handle abstract concepts professionally, but the vast majority of people need the familiarity of well-known schemata to seamlessly perform logical operations and successfully employ moral reasoning. Imagine being asked what you mean by 'fair division.' What will probably come to your mind will be examples of typical situations that instantiate the concept. Such situations will involve people in various roles, things to be distributed, ways of distributing them, and so on. A schema (script) has been invoked, and with it a series of subschemata (or subscripts) representing specific actors, roles, and things to be distributed. The meaning of 'fair division' is given by the schema and subschemata (or scripts) that we have stored in memory.[35]

In Chapter 1, I said that we are able to accept others' normative expectations as reasonable and legitimate. What confers them legitimacy? I also stated that norms are supported by empirical expectations: We expect

---

[34] One version of the problem is the following: You are told that "Every envelope that has a stamp in the front also has a seal on the back" and are shown four envelopes: two are face-up and one has a stamp whereas the other has no stamp. Two are face-down and one has a seal whereas the other has no seal. Which of the envelopes must be turned over to assess whether the statement is correct? Only a few people will rightly indicate the one with the stamp and the one without the seal. Yet if the problem is presented as involving familiar settings, it is usually correctly solved.

[35] If, as I have hypothesized, a concept representation is like a node embedded in a complex network, a schema will contain the network of relations that link the constituents of the concept in question.

others to keep to certain behavioral regularities. Such regularities are taken to be projectible, but what grounds their projectibility? These two questions seem very different, but I want to argue that, if our social knowledge is organized by means of scripts, then both legitimacy and projectibility have the same source. When people use scripts, they know what to expect of each other. They need not be acquainted with each other or know of each other's past performance. Their expectations are grounded in the certainty that, *if* indeed script *s* is being enacted, *then* actions $a_1, \ldots, a_n$ will follow. This is not unlike our knowledge of Othello's plot: The theater, settings, and actors may differ, but we know exactly what is going to happen after Iago tells Othello about Desdemona's lost handkerchief. Like Othello's jealousy, there is nothing inherently projectible in our social regularities, beside the fact that they have become parts of scripts that guide us in everyday life. Moreover, we tend to perceive scripted interactions as 'right' and appropriate. The attribution of legitimacy and appropriateness stems from our propensity to treat social interactions as 'natural kinds,' as opposed to 'artificial categories.' Artificial categories are, by their very nature, potentially unstable. The projectibility of their members' attributes is not grounded on some essential, invariant properties. However, when we treat social situations as 'natural kinds,' we tend to assume that they possess stable, invariant essential characteristics that we *can* project.

Note that if a category (such as a mode of interaction) is perceived as a 'natural kind,' the scripted interactions it activates are also perceived as stable, projectible, and 'right.' If leaving a tip is part of the restaurant script, then tipping is the normal, appropriate thing to do. We predict its occurrence, and our expectation is legitimized by the very existence of the script. What often ensues is that this empirical legitimacy tends to become a quasi-moral one. We are, in other words, subject to a naturalistic fallacy in most of our daily dealings. The projectible regularity, when human interactions are involved, comes to be perceived as a right or a duty, depending on the role one is playing. If tipping is part of the script, a waiter will feel it is her right to get a tip, and she will get angry if her expectation is not met. If the patron who is not a (possibly ignorant) foreigner does not leave a tip, the most obvious interpretations are that he is either unhappy with the service or miserly. If nothing suggests dissatisfaction, what is left is the attribution of a mean intention, and a justified emotional reaction ensues. The emotions that so often accompany norm violations seem to be the effect of our relying on scripts and acknowledging that our legitimate expectations have been neglected.

It is important to point out that the mental processes involved in categorization and schemata elicitation, as well as our knowledge of categories and schemata, are often unavailable to consciousness and are thus beyond voluntary control (see Greenwald and Banaji 1995, for a review).[36] What we have instead is implicit, nondeclarative knowledge: We are unable to tell how we learned our categories or articulate our present knowledge clearly and precisely. To understand what I mean by implicit, nondeclarative knowledge, think of activities like bicycling or driving a car. Once we are good at it, we drive or bike without paying attention to what we do, and our obvious knowledge of the complex set of operations necessary to safely drive in a crowded street is difficult if not impossible to express. Likewise I can recognize a Mozart piece when I hear one, and my husband can unfailingly diagnose a defective engine from the noise it makes, yet both of us are unable to verbally describe *what* in the music or the engine's noise is the source of our judgment. Our knowledge is expressed in performance, but it is difficult to verbalize. Norm following is similar in this respect to bicycling, or the ability to recognize a piece of music: Once a schema is activated, we tend to follow the norm by default, without being able to tell what prompted it or which features of the situations acquired particular relevance. The bicycling analogy may seem farfetched, because we tend to think of social skills as being more complicated and subtle than motor skills. Yet the study of the neural substrates of intuition found that social learning uses some of the same circuits in the basal ganglia that motor learning does, causing many social skills to become rapid and automatic, like well-learned motor sequences (Lieberman 2000). Not unlike motor skills, we learn social skills and judgmental processes gradually and often implicitly: Children, for example, learn group norms by observing and imitating the practices of older children and adults, without being able to justify or even conceptualize them. Once learned, such norms and practices subsequently operate unconsciously. As I mentioned in the previous chapter, this does not mean that *all* norm following is automatic: There are occasions in which we are consciously choosing to

---

[36] Categorization processes may also be fully conscious. A zoologist who has to decide how to revise the taxonomy of baboons after discovering a new type, or the physicist discovering a new particle and redrawing the boundaries of, say, quarks, are examples of conscious, intentional categorization.

conform (or not to) and are fully aware of the consequences of what we
choose. Most of the time, however, we are on automatic pilot. Note that
whether our choices are made consciously or instead automatically, this
does not preclude explaining them in terms of preferences and beliefs.
That is to say that it is still possible to explain an individual's choice,
when apparently made without conscious deliberation, as determined
by her beliefs and conditional preferences. As I discussed in Chapter 1,
the beliefs that guide our actions may become apparent when they are
called into question or when we are asked to justify our choices. In cases
in which our beliefs about a situation change, we would expect (conditional) preferences to be different. In turn, preferences and beliefs
will be activated by the specific context within which an individual finds
himself.

To summarize: Interpreting and understanding a social situation
involves comparing it to similar ones we have encountered in the past.
What we view as similar will determine which category will be retrieved
and which script or schema will be applied. Social norms, being embedded into scripts, are activated as part of a process that also triggers the
beliefs and expectations that support and justify conformity. The cognitive process of organizing and structuring new stimuli through retrieving
from memory similar situations is thus responsible for framing an interaction as one in which fairness or reciprocity norms are activated. Because
social interactions engage more than one person, the more ambiguous a
situation is, the more likely it will be that several schemata will be retrieved.
If we think of a person's schemata as a kind of private, informal theory
about the nature of the situations, objects, or events she faces, it becomes
apparent that, when several people interact, the potential for misunderstandings and conflicting interpretations of the same situation is present.
Unless there is no possible ambiguity in interpreting a situation, conflict may be present and result in a breaking down of the interaction,
but more often what happens is a renegotiation of meaning that brings
about a common understanding of the situation. Verbal communication
is very important in this respect, and the convergence to a shared perception of what constitutes appropriate behavior that accompanies it is
probably one of the reasons why, in many experimental settings, allowing individuals to communicate about the experimental game results in
higher levels of cooperation, as well as a greater concern for fairness and
reciprocity.

The only systematic evidence presently available about which cues
make people focus on pro-social norms are the results of experiments

on Ultimatum, Dictator, Trust, and Social Dilemma games. Though the experiments I shall discuss in the next two chapters were not meant to test hypotheses about norms, they are consistent with a theory of script activation. Furthermore, some behavioral discontinuities that have baffled investigators can become comprehensible in light of the view of norms I am proposing.

3

A Taste for Fairness

Introduction

One of the most important concepts in social exchanges and interactions is that of fairness. We can come to accept the most onerous tasks if we are convinced that the decision procedure was fair, and, conversely, we may reject even a profitable exchange if we feel treated unfairly. Since the dawn of philosophy, a concern with fairness – what it is and how to define it – has been central to the philosopher's quest. Philosopher's concern, however, is more with finding reasons to justify and lend consistency to our intuitions about fairness than with the actual fairness judgments that people express. My interest here is to understand how people form fairness judgments and the nature of the cognitive dynamics involved in the process. Within a given culture, there is usually a great deal of agreement as to how given goods, positions, and opportunities ought to be allocated, and what properties of the claimants matter to the allocation. Every culture has developed a number of shared scripts about the fair allocation and distribution of various goods in different circumstances. Norms of fairness, in turn, are just an essential part of such shared scripts. Our fairness judgments are thus never completely subjective, independent of what our group or society considers fair given the circumstances. When we assess a situation or judge or decide about the fairness of an allocation, we apply scripts and obey norms that successfully coordinate our expectations and behaviors with the expectations and behaviors of other people. This does not mean that people always *agree* on what a fair distribution is, given a set of circumstances.

Disagreement, however, typically occurs when the situation is ambiguous and open to different interpretations. A typical example is the tension between equality and equity concerns in deciding how a given good or opportunity should be allocated. Interestingly enough, within a culture there usually exist agreed-upon justifications for deviating from equality. Reasons of merit or need are, depending on the nature of what has to be allocated, collectively judged to be acceptable or unacceptable, and typically disagreement occurs on the weight that different parties are prepared to give to some acceptable justifications.[1] As we shall discuss later on, *self-serving biases* are just the natural tendency of individuals to cast more weight, in ambiguous situations, to an interpretation of fairness that favors them.

To say that people follow shared scripts and obey fairness norms differs from assuming that they have a 'preference' for fairness. To follow a fairness norm, one must have the right kinds of expectations. One must expect others to follow the norm, too, and also believe that there is a generalized expectation that one will obey the norm in the present circumstances. The preference to obey a norm is *conditional* upon such expectations.[2] Take away some of the expectations, and behavior will significantly change. A conditional preference will thus be stable under certain conditions, but a change in the relevant conditions may induce a predictable preference shift. The predictions of a norm-based theory, as we shall see, are thus testable and quite different, at least in some critical instances, from the predictions of other theories that postulate a preference for fairness or a concern for reciprocity.

When economists postulate fairness preferences, they make two related, important assumptions. The first is that what matters to an agent is the final distribution, not the way the distribution came about (Fehr and Schmidt 1999). This is a *consequentialist* assumption. The second assumption is that preferences are *stable*. Both assumptions are easy to test. When falsified, however, it is less clear who the culprit is. For example, if a person has a stable preference for fair outcomes, we would expect her cross-situational behavior to be consistent and insensitive to the circumstances surrounding the specific distributive situation. Whether you

---

[1] In our culture, for example, it is usually agreed that transplant organs should not be allocated according to the merit or income of the potential recipient, whereas we tend to believe that merit is the most important criterion in allocating scholarships.

[2] The conditions for following a norm were formally described in Chapter 1.

are the Proposer in an Ultimatum or a Dictator game should not matter to your choice of how much money to give to a Responder. Similarly, information about *who* the Proposer is – a real person or a random
device – should not have an effect on one's propensity to accept or reject
its offer. What is observed instead is cross-situational inconsistency. The
reason for this inconsistency is not obvious. It is possible that people do
care about how a distribution came about, that the process itself matters.
For example, one might accept an unequal share of the pie if it comes
from a lottery but would reject it if it results from an auction. Preferences
could still be assumed to be stable, but in this case what one would prefer is a combination of goods and processes to distribute/allocate those
goods. On the other hand, we may take a different direction and go as far
as saying that preferences are context-dependent. Change the context,
or the context's description, and you have a noticeable preference shift.
In the latter case, however, to be able to make any prediction we would
need a mapping from contexts to preferences. But no such mapping has
ever been provided.

   In what follows I will examine some of the most common games studied by experimental economists. Ultimatum and Dictator games come in
many flavors and variants, but the simplest, bare versions of both games
are in some sense ideal, since they offer a very simplified allocation problem. The good to be allocated (or divided) is money, and the situation is
such that most familiar contextual clues are removed. It is thus possible
to introduce in this rarefied environment simple contextual information
and control for its effects on the perception of what constitutes a fair division. The results of such experiments consistently defy the predictions
of traditional rational choice models. Agents are clearly not solely concerned with their monetary payoffs: They care about what other agents
get and how they get it. The big challenge has been to enrich traditional rational choice models in such a way that they can explain (and
predict) behavior that is not just motivated by material incentives in a
variety of realistic contexts. I will compare some of the most interesting and influential new models with my norm-based approach and show
that the hypothesis that people obey fairness norms offers a more complete explanation for the phenomena we observe. Where my predictions
differ from those of alternative theories, the data seem to vindicate my
model. However, we need many more experiments to test the effects
that manipulating expectations (and thus norm compliance) have on
behavior.

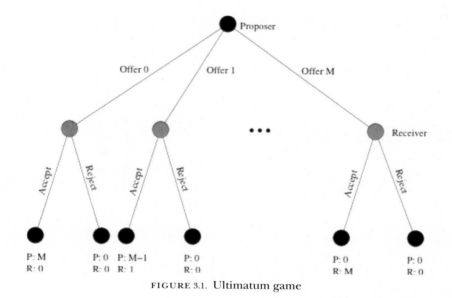

FIGURE 3.1. Ultimatum game

The Ultimatum Game

In 1982, Guth, Schmittberger, and Schwarze published a seminal study in which they asked subjects to play what is now known as an Ultimatum bargaining game. Their goal was to test the predictions of game theory about equilibrium behavior. Their results instead showed that subjects consistently deviate from what game theory predicts. To understand what game theory predicts, and why, let us look at a typical Ultimatum game (Figure 3.1).

The structure of this game is fairly simple. Two people must split a fixed amount of money M according to the following rules: the Proposer (P) moves first and offers a division of M to the Responder (R), where the offer can range between M and zero. The Responder has a binary choice in each case: to accept the offer or to reject it. If the offer is accepted, the Proposer receives $M - x$ and the Responder receives x, where x is the offer amount. If the offer is rejected, each player receives nothing. If rationality is common knowledge, the Proposer knows that the Responder will always accept any amount greater than zero, because Accept dominates Reject for *any* offer greater than zero. Hence P should offer the minimum amount guaranteed to be accepted, and R will accept it. For example, if $M = \$10$ and the minimum available amount is 1¢, the Proposer should offer it and the offer should be accepted, leaving the Proposer with $9.99.

When experiments are conducted, what one finds is that nobody offers one cent or even one dollar. Note that such experiments are always one-shot and anonymous; that is, subjects play the game only once with an anonymous partner and are guaranteed that their choice will not be disclosed. The absence of repetition is important to distinguish between generous behavior that is dictated by a rational, selfish calculation and genuine generosity. If an Ultimatum game is repeated with the same partner, or if one suspects that future partners will know of one's past behavior, it may be perfectly rational for a player who is only interested in his material payoff to give generously, if he expects to be on the receiving side at a future time. On the other hand, a Receiver who might accept the minimum in a one-shot game might want to reject a low offer at the beginning of a repeated game, in the hope of convincing future Proposers to offer more.

In the United States, as well as in a number of other countries, the modal and median offers in one-shot experimental games are 40 to 50% of the total amount, and the mean offers are 30 to 40%. Offers below 20% are rejected about half the time.[3] These results are robust with respect to variations in the amount of money that is being split and cultural differences (Camerer 2003). For example, we know that raising the stake from $10 to $100 does not decrease the frequency of rejections of low offers (those between $10 and $20), and that in experiments run in Slovenia, Pittsburgh, Israel, and Tokyo the modal offers were in the range of 40 to 50% (Roth et al. 1991; Hoffman et al. 1998).

If by rationality we mean that subjects maximize expected utility *and* that they only value their monetary outcomes, then we must conclude that a subject who rejects a nonzero offer is acting irrationally. However, individuals' behavior across games suggest that money is not the sole consideration, and instead there is a concern for fairness, so much so that subjects are prepared to punish those who behave in inequitable ways at a cost to themselves.[4]

---

[3] Guth et al. (1982) were the first to observe that the most common offer by Proposers was to give half of the sum to the Responder. The mean offer was 37% of the original allocation. In a replication of their experiments, they allowed subjects to think about their decision for one week. The mean offer was 32% of the sum, which is still very high.

[4] We know that Responders reject low offers even when the stakes are as high as three months' earnings (Cameron 1995). Furthermore, experiments in which third parties

A concern for fairness is just one example of a more general fact about human behavior: We are often motivated by a host of factors of which monetary incentives are one, and often not the most important. We act out of love, envy, spite, generosity, desire to imitate, sympathy, or hatred, to name just a few of the 'passions' and desires that move us to act. When faced with different possible distributions, we usually care about how we fare with respect to others, how the distribution came about, who implemented it, and why. Experiment after experiment has demonstrated that individuals care about others' payoffs, that they may want to spend resources to increase or decrease such payoffs, and that what they perceive to be the (good or bad) intentions of those they interact with weigh in their decisions. Unfortunately, the default utility function in game theory is a narrowly selfish one: It is selfish because it depicts people who care only about their own outcomes, and it is narrow because motivations like altruism, benevolence, guilt, envy, or hatred are kept out of the picture. Such motives, however, can and should be incorporated into a utility function, and economists have recently started to develop richer, more complex models of human behavior that try to explain what we have always known: People care about other people's outcomes. Thus a better way to explain what is observed in experiments (and real life) is to provide a richer definition of rationality: People still maximize their utilities, but the arguments of their utility functions include other people's utilities.

The obvious risk of such models is their ad hocness: One may easily explain any data by adjusting the utility function to reflect what looks like envy, or altruism, or a preference for equal shares. What we need are utility functions that are general enough to subsume many different experimental phenomena and specific enough to make falsifiable predictions. In what follows I will look at some proposed explanations for the generous distributions we observe in Ultimatum games and test them against some interesting variations of the game. Such testing is not always easy to conduct, though. The problem is that we still have quite rudimentary theories of how motives affect behavior. And to test a hypothesis about what sort of motives induce us to act one way or another, we have to be very specific in defining such motives, and the ways in which they influence our choices. Let me clarify this statement with an example.

Observing the results of Ultimatum games, someone might argue that subjects in the Proposer's role are behaving altruistically. Others would

have a chance to punish an 'unfair' Proposer at a monetary cost to themselves show that (moderately) costly punishment is frequent (Fehr and Fishbacher 2004).

deny that, saying that people like to give because of the "warm glow" their actions induce in them (Andreoni 1990, 1995), and yet others would say that what we observe is just benevolence, nothing else. Now, to make sense at all, such concepts need to be made as specific as possible, and operational. Take for example a distribution (x_1, x_2) of, say, money between two people. Being an altruist would mean that 1's utility is an increasing function of 2's utility, that is, $U_1 = f(x_2)$ and $\delta U_1/\delta x_2 > 0$. That is, a true altruist would not care about his own share; he would only care about how much the other gets (and the more, the better). A Proposer who is a pure altruist would 'donate' all the money to the Responder, provided he believes the Responder only cares about money.[5] Being benevolent instead means that one cares about one's own payoff *and* the other's, that is, $U_1 = f(x_1, x_2)$. In this case, the first partial derivatives of $U_1 = f(x_1, x_2)$ with respect to x_1, x_2 are strictly positive, meaning that the utility of a benevolent player 1 increases as the utility of player 2 increases. Depending on one's degree of benevolence, one will turn out to be more or less generous, but a benevolent attitude on the part of the Proposers might explain, *prima facie*, the results of experimental Ultimatum games.

The results of typical Ultimatum games eliminate the 'pure altruist' hypothesis, since people almost never give more than 50%, but do not eliminate the benevolence hypothesis. If benevolence is a stable character disposition, however, we would expect a certain behavioral stability or consistency in any situation in which a benevolent Proposer has to offer a division of money to an anonymous Responder. A variant of the Ultimatum game is the Dictator game, in which the Proposer receives a sum of money from the experimenter and decides to split the money any way in which she chooses; her decision is final in that the Responder cannot reject whatever is offered. If we hypothesize that the Ultimatum game results reveal that a certain percentage of the population has a benevolent disposition, we should expect to observe roughly the same percentage of generous offers in all those circumstances in which one of the parties, the Proposer, is all-powerful. In most of the experiments, however, the modal offer is one in which the Proposer keeps all the money to himself, and in double-blind experiments 64% of the participants give

---

[5] I am not sure such characters exist, and if they do, how much liked they would be. In the Cloven Viscount Calvino (1951), depicts the whereabouts of a totally virtuous half nobleman who, because he took virtue to the extreme, was feared and disliked as much as his totally evil half-counterpart.

nothing. Still, it must be mentioned that although the most frequent offer is zero, the mean allocation is 20% (Forsythe et al. 1994). These results suggest that people are not totally selfish, but it would be hard to argue they are benevolent, unless we are prepared to presume that benevolence is a changeable disposition, as mutable as the circumstances that we encounter.

Social Preferences

Altruism and benevolence are just two examples of *social preferences*, whereas by social preference I refer to how people rank different allocations of material payoffs to self and others. If we stay with the Ultimatum game as an example, we can think of other, slightly more complex ways to explain the results we discussed before. The uniformity of the Responders' behavior suggests that people do not like being treated unfairly. That is, if subjects perceive an offer of 20 or 30% of the money as unfair, they may reject it to "punish" the greedy Proposer, even at a cost to themselves. It is important to repeat that the experiments I am referring to were all one-shot, which means that the participants were fairly sure of not meeting again; therefore, punishing behavior cannot be motivated as an attempt to convince the other party to be more generous the next time around. Similarly, Proposers could not be generous because they were expecting reciprocating behavior in future interactions. One possibility is to assume that both Proposers and Responders are showing a preference for fair outcomes, or an aversion to inequality. We can thus try to explain the experimental results with a traditional rational choice model, where the agents' preferences take into account the payoffs of others.

In models of inequality aversion, players prefer both more money and that allocations be more equal. Though there are several models of inequality aversion, perhaps the best known and most extensively tested is the model of Fehr and Schmidt (1999). This model intends to capture the idea that people may be uneasy, to a certain extent, about the presence of inequality, even if they benefit from the unequal distribution. Given a group of L persons, the Fehr-Schmidt utility function of person i is

$$U_i(x_1, \ldots, x_L) = x_i - \frac{\alpha_i}{L-1} \sum_j \max(x_j - x_i, 0)$$

$$- \frac{\beta_i}{L-1} \sum_j \max(x_i - x_j, 0),$$

where x_j denotes the material payoff person j gets. α_i is a parameter that measures how much player i dislikes disadvantageous inequality (an 'envy' weight), and β_i measures how much i dislikes advantageous inequality (a 'guilt' weight).[6] One constraint on the parameters is that $0 < \beta_i < \alpha_i$, which indicates that people dislike advantageous inequality less than disadvantageous inequality. The other constraint is $\beta_i < 1$, so that an agent does not suffer terrible guilt when she is in a relatively good position. For example, a player would prefer getting more without affecting other people's payoffs even though that results in an increase of the inequality.

Applying the model to the game in Figure 3.1, the utility function is simplified to

$$U_i(x_1, x_2) = x_i - \begin{cases} \alpha_i(x_{3-i} - x_i) & \text{if } x_{3-i} \geq x_i \\ \beta_i(x_i - x_{3-i}) & \text{if } x_{3-i} < x_i \end{cases} \quad i = 1, 2.$$

Obviously, if the Responder rejects the offer, both utility functions are equal to zero, that is, $U_{1reject} = U_{2reject} = 0$. If the Responder accepts an offer of x, the utility functions are as follows:

$$U_{1accept}(x) = \begin{cases} (1 + \alpha_1) M - (1 + 2\alpha_1) x & \text{if } x \geq M/2 \\ (1 - \beta_1) M - (1 - 2\beta_1) x & \text{if } x < M/2 \end{cases}$$

$$U_{2accept}(x) = \begin{cases} (1 + 2\alpha_2) x - \alpha_2 M & \text{if } x < M/2 \\ (1 - 2\beta_1) x + \beta_2 M & \text{if } x \geq M/2. \end{cases}$$

The Responder should accept the offer if and only if $U_{2accept}(x) > U_{2reject} = 0$. Solving for x we get the *threshold for acceptance*: $x > \alpha_2 M/(1 + 2\alpha_2)$. Evidently, if α_2 is close to zero, which indicates that player 2 (R) does not care much about being treated unfairly, the Responder will accept very mean offers. On the other hand, if α_2 is sufficiently big, the offer has to be close to a half to be accepted. In any event, the threshold is not higher than $M/2$, which means that hyperfair offers (more than half) are not necessary for the sake of acceptance.

Note that for the Proposer, the utility function is monotonically decreasing in x when $x \geq M/2$. Hence a rational Proposer will not offer more than half of the money. Suppose $x \leq M/2$; two cases are possible, depending on the value of β_1. If $\beta_1 > 1/2$, that is, if the Proposer feels sufficiently guilty about treating others unfairly, the utility is monotonically increasing in x, and his best choice is to offer $M/2$. On the other hand, if

---

[6] The term $\max(x_j - x_i, 0)$ denotes the maximum of $x_j - x_i$ and 0; it measures the extent to which there is disadvantageous inequality between i and j.

$\beta_1 < 1/2$, the utility is monotonically decreasing in x, and hence the best offer for the Proposer is the minimum one that would be accepted, that is, (a little bit more than) $\alpha_2 M/(1 + 2\alpha_2)$. Lastly, if $\beta_1 = 1/2$, it does not matter how much the Proposer offers, as long as it is between $\alpha_2 M/(1 + 2\alpha_2)$ and $M/2$. Note that the other two parameters, α_1 and β_2, are not identifiable in Ultimatum games.

As noted by Fehr and Schmidt, the model allows for the fact that individuals are heterogeneous. Different α's and β's correspond to different types of people. Although the utility functions are common knowledge, the exact values of the parameters are not. The Proposer, in most cases, is not sure what type of Responder she is facing. Along the Bayesian line, her belief about the type of the Responder can be formally represented by a probability distribution P on α_2 and β_2. When $\beta_1 > 1/2$, the Proposer's rational choice does not depend on what P is. When $\beta_1 < 1/2$, however, the Proposer will seek to maximize the expected utility:

$$EU(x) = P(\alpha_2 M/(1 + 2\alpha_2) < x) \times ((1 - \beta_1) M - (1 - 2\beta_1)x).$$

Therefore, the behavior of a rational Proposer in the Ultimatum game is determined by her own type (β_1) and her belief about the type of the Responder. The experimental data suggest that, for many Proposers, either β is big ($\beta > 1/2$) or they estimate the Responder's α to be large. The choice of the Responder is only determined by his type (α_2) and the offer. Small offers are rejected by Responders with a positive α.

The positive features of the above-described utility function are that it can rationalize both positive and negative outcomes, and that it can explain the observed variability in outcomes with heterogeneous types. One of the major weaknesses of this model, however, is that it has a consequentialist bias: Players only care about the final distributions of outcomes, not about how such distributions come about.[7] As we shall see, more recent experiments have established that how a situation is framed matters to an evaluation of outcomes, and that the same distribution can be accepted or rejected depending on 'irrelevant' information about the players or the circumstances of play. Another difficulty with this approach is that, if we assume the distribution of types to be constant in a given population, then we should observe, overall, the same proportion of 'fair' outcomes in Ultimatum games. Not only does this not happen,

---

[7] This is a *separability* of utility assumption: What matters to a player in a game is her payoff at a terminal node. The way in which that node was reached and the possible alternative paths that were not taken are irrelevant to an assessment of her utility at that node. Utilities of terminal node payoffs are thus separable from the path through the tree and from payoffs on unchosen branches.

but we also observe individual inconsistencies in behavior across different situations in which the monetary outcomes are the same. If we assume, as is usually done in economics, that individual preferences are stable, then we would expect similar behaviors across Ultimatum games. If, instead, we conclude that preferences are context-dependent, then we should provide a mapping from contexts to preferences that indicates in a fairly predictable way how and why a given context or situation changes one's preferences. Of course, different situations may change a player's expectation about another player's envy or guilt parameters, and we could thus explain why a player may change her behavior depending on how the situation is framed. In the case of Fehr and Schmidt's utility function, however, experimental evidence that I shall discuss later implies that a player's *own* β (or α) changes value in different situations. Yet nothing in their theory explains why one would feel consistently more or less guilty (or envious) depending on the decision context.

Reciprocity

Theories of inequality aversion only include other players' material payoffs in the calculation of utility. What other players did, and why they did it, do not play any role in a player's utility. Yet we tend to take into account what we believe are the intentions of those we interact with, and respond accordingly. Reciprocity is a common phenomenon in human interaction: We tend to be kind to kind persons and punish the mean. By leaving reciprocity out, the previous model gains simplicity and tractability. But, as Matthew Rabin (1993) forcefully argued, in order to model reciprocity we have to include beliefs and intentions in our models. In Rabin's model, utilities do not just depend on terminal-node payoffs but also on players' beliefs. As a result, his model builds on the framework of what is called psychological game theory (Geanakoplos et al. 1989).

Consider a two-person game of complete information. According to Rabin's model, a player's utility is not only determined by the actions taken, but it also depends on the player's beliefs (including second-order beliefs, viz. beliefs about beliefs). Specifically, player i will evaluate her "kindness" to the other player, f_i, by the following scheme:

$$f_i(a_i, b_j) = \begin{cases} \dfrac{\pi_j(b_j, a_i) - \pi_j^c(b_j)}{\pi_j^h(b_j) - \pi_j^{\min}(b_j)} & \text{if } \pi_j^h(b_j) - \pi_j^{\min}(b_j) \neq 0 \\ 0 & \text{otherwise} \end{cases}$$

$$i = 1, 2; \ j = 3 - i,$$

where a_i is the strategy taken by player i, b_j is the strategy that player i *believes* is chosen by player j, π_j is j's material payoff that depends on both players' strategies, $\pi_j^h(b_j)$ is the highest material payoff, and $\pi_j^{\min}(b_j)$ is the lowest payoff that player j can potentially get by playing b_j. In other words, they denote respectively the highest and lowest payoffs player i can grant player j given the latter is playing b_j. A key term here is $\pi_j^c(b_j)$, which represents a "fair" material payoff player j "should" get by playing b_j and is defined by Rabin as:

$$\pi_j^c(b_j) = \frac{\pi_j^h(b_j) + \pi_j^l(b_j)}{2}.$$

$\pi_j^l(b_j)$ is the worst payoff player j may incur given that players do not play Pareto dominated strategies. Obviously we have $\pi_j^l(b_j) \geq \pi_j^{\min}(b_j)$. Thus a positive $f_i(a_i, b_j)$ means player i has been kind to j, because j got a payoff higher than the fair one, and a negative value signifies i was mean to j, who got a lower than fair payoff.

Similarly, player i can estimate player j's kindness towards her, denoted by

$$\tilde{f}_j(b_j, c_i) = \begin{cases} \dfrac{\pi_i(c_i, b_j) - \pi_i^c(c_i)}{\pi_i^h(c_i) - \pi_i^{\min}(c_i)} & \text{if } \pi_i^h(c_i) - \pi_i^{\min}(c_i) \neq 0 \\ 0 & \text{otherwise,} \end{cases}$$

where c_i is i's belief about j's belief about the strategy taken by i, a second-order belief. The meanings of other terms are obvious given the previous explanations. Clearly this estimated kindness is just a conjecture about player j's intentions, and to form this conjecture player i must make a guess about what player j believes that i will do.

Finally, the utility function of player i depends on her strategy, (first-order) belief, and second-order belief:

$$U_i(a_i, b_j, c_i) = \pi_i(a_i, b_j) + \tilde{f}_j(b_j, c_i) + \tilde{f}_j(b_j, c_i) f_i(a_i, b_j).$$

The first term tells us that player i cares about her material payoff, the second term tells us that it matters to i whether she is treated nicely or not, and reciprocity lies in the last interaction term (the product of the kindness i expects and of her own kindness). Intuitively, it satisfies a player to be kind to kind players and tough to tough ones. An equilibrium of the game, called a *fairness equilibrium*, occurs when every belief turns out to be correct and each player's utility is maximized.

A problem with this approach is that there can be many fairness equilibria, depending on the beliefs the players happen to have. Since this

model applies no constraint on possible beliefs, it becomes impossible
to predict which equilibrium will be played. Furthermore, though it is
certainly more realistic to assume that players care about other players'
intentions, we do not attribute good or bad intentions in a vacuum.
An intention is only good or bad against a background of expectations.
Such expectations are often dictated by the situation one is in, and thus
they are quite homogeneous among players. As we shall see, a theory of
social norms can predict the beliefs and expectations the players will have
in a particular setting, and thus predict that a specific equilibrium will
obtain.

Norms Matter

Rule-based approaches are not completely new. Guth (1995), for example, interpreted the results of the Ultimatum game as showing that people have rules of behavior such as sharing money equally, and they apply
them when necessary. The problem with such solutions is that we need
a plausible story about how people change their behavior in response to
changes in payoffs and framing. If rules are inflexible, but we observe
flexible compliance, there must be something wrong with a rule-based
approach. Indeed, a common understanding of norms, one that I have
tried to dispel in my definition (see Chapter 1), is that they are inflexible behavioral rules that one would apply in any circumstance that calls
for them. But nothing could be farther from the truth. To be effective,
norms have to be *activated* by salient cues.[8] As I discussed in Chapter 1, a
norm may exist, but it may not be followed simply because the relevant
expectations are not there, or because one might be unaware of being
in a situation to which the norm applies. Recall that I said that people
have *conditional preferences* for conformity to a norm, in that they would
prefer to follow it on condition that (a) they expect others to follow it and
(b) they believe that, in turn, they are expected by others to abide by the
norm. Both conditions have to be present to generate conformity. Indeed,
there is plenty of evidence that manipulating people's expectations has
an effect on norm compliance (Cialdini et al. 1990). Thus I would argue
that belief elicitation in experiments is crucial to determining whether a
norm will be perceived as relevant and then followed. We already know,

[8] Cues that activate or 'bring to mind' a norm may involve a direct statement or reminder
of the norm, observing others' behavior, similarity of the present situation to others in
which the norm was used, as well as how often or how recently one has used the norm.

for example, that telling subjects how others have behaved in a similar game has a profound effect on their choices, and that allowing people to communicate before playing the game often results in a cooperative outcome.[9]

Furthermore, some norms are more *local* than others, in the sense that their interpretation is highly context-dependent. Fairness is a case in point. To be fair means different things in different contexts. In some situations being fair means sharing equally, while in others it may mean giving more to the needy or to the deserving. Ultimatum games are in some sense ideal, because they offer a very simplified allocation problem. The good to be allocated (or divided) is money, and the situation is such that most familiar contextual clues are removed. It is thus possible to introduce in this rarefied environment simple contextual information and control for its effects on the perception of what constitutes a fair division. In the Ultimatum game, the salience of the equal-split solution is lost if subjects are told that offers are generated by a random device (Blount 1995) or if it is believed that the Proposer was otherwise constrained in her decision. In both cases, Responders are willing to accept lower offers. This phenomenon is well known to consummate bargainers: If an unequal outcome can be credibly justified as a case of *force majeure*, people can be convinced to accept much less than an equal share. Also, variations in the strengths of 'property rights' alter the shared expectations of the two players regarding the norm that determines the appropriate division. In the original Ultimatum game, the Proposer receives what amounts to a monetary *gift* from the experimenter. As a consequence, he is perceived as having no special right to the money and is expected (at least in our culture) to share it equally with the Responder. Because the fairness norm that is activated in this context dictates an equal split, the Proposer who is offering little is perceived as mean, and consequently he gets punished. Note that the Proposer who was constrained in his decision is not seen as being intentionally mean, since intentions matter only when the choice is perceived as being freely made. To infer another person's intention or motive, we consider not only the action chosen, but also the actions that were not chosen but, as far as we know, *could* have been chosen.

Because what counts as fair is highly context-dependent, a specific context gives reasons to expect behavior appropriate to the situation. It also gives a clue as to the Proposer's intention, especially when the offer

---

[9] I discuss these results and the relevant literature in the next chapter.

is different from what is reasonably expected in that context. Subjects approach resource sharing or, for that matter, any other situation with implicit knowledge structures (scripts) that detail conditions that are prototypically associated with sharing tasks. Once we have categorized the particular decision task we face, we enact scripts that tell us how people typically behave and what they expect others to do. However, it must be emphasized that people will display expected, appropriate behavior to the extent that crucial environmental cues match those of well-known prototypical scripts. An interesting question to ask is, under which conditions will an equal sharing norm be violated? I shall discuss this point more extensively later on, but for now let me say that my hypothesis is that a deviation from equal sharing will be mainly due to (a) the presence of appropriate and acceptable justifications for taking more than an equal share or (b) the shift to a very different script that involves different roles and expectations. An example of the second reason is when the Proposer is labeled "seller" and the Responder "buyer"; in this case the Proposer offers a lower amount than in the control and Responders readily accept (and expect) less than an equal share (Hoffman et al. 1994). The interaction is perceived as being market-like, and in a market script it is deemed equitable that a seller earns a higher return than a buyer. An example of the first reason is when the Proposer has "earned" the right to the money by, for example, getting a higher score on a general knowledge quiz (Frey and Bohnet 1995; Hoffman and Spitzer 1985). In this case, the Proposer has an available, acceptable justification for getting more than the equal share. Doing better than someone else in a test is a common and reasonable mechanism, at least in our society, for determining differential access to a shared resource. It thus seems appropriate to many Proposers to choose equity versus equality in such conditions even if, as we shall see, this self-serving rule is not shared by the Responder.[10]

There is continuity between real life and experiments with respect to how 'rights' and 'entitlements,' considerations of merit, need, desert, or sheer luck shape our perception of what is fair and what kinds of reasons count as acceptable justifications for violating a fairness norm. Cultures differ in their reliance on different allocative and distributive rules, because such rules depend on different forms of social organization.

---

[10] Kahneman et al. (1986) describe different norms of fairness, including situations in which unfair behavior is commonly accepted and "excused."

Within a given culture, however, there usually is a consensus about how different goods and opportunities should be allocated or distributed. Cross-cultural studies of Ultimatum and Dictator games in 15 small-scale societies show quite convincingly that the behavior displayed in such games is highly correlated with the economic organization and social structure of each society (Henrich et al. 2004). Furthermore, because experimental play is presumably categorized according to the specific sociocultural patterns of each society, the experimental results showed much greater variability than the results of typical Ultimatum and Dictator games played in modern Western (or westernized) societies.[11] These results lend even more support to the hypothesis that social norms, and the accompanying shared expectations, play a crucial role in shaping behavioral responses to experimental games.

A norm-based explanation of the results of experiments with Ultimatum and Dictator games predicts that – whenever Proposers are focused on the relevant expectations – they will behave in a norm-consistent way. In the traditional Ultimatum game, the expected opportunity cost of not following an equal division rule may be enough to elicit fair behavior. In asking herself what the Responder would accept, the Proposer is forced to look at the situation and categorize it as a case in which an equality rule applies. This does not mean that the person who follows the norm is in fact fair, or casts a high value on equitable behavior. As I made plain in my definition of what it takes to follow an existing norm, if a player assesses a sufficiently high probability to her opponent's following the norm, and expects to be punished for noncompliance, she will prefer to conform to a norm even if she has no interest in the norm itself.

The general utility function I introduced in Chapter 1 can now be applied to the Ultimatum game. Let π_i be the payoff function for player i. Recall that the norm-based utility function of player i depends on the strategy profile s and is given by

$$U_i(s) = \pi_i(s) - k_i \max_{s_{-j} \in L_{-j}} \max_{m \neq j} \{\pi_m(s_{-j}, N_j(s_{-j})) - \pi_m(s), 0\},$$

where $k_i \geq 0$ is a constant representing i's sensitivity to the relevant norm. Such sensitivity may vary with different norms; for example, a person may be very sensitive to equality and much less sensitive to equity

---

[11] In some groups, rejections were extremely rare, even when the offers were very low, whereas in other groups, 'hyperfair' offers were frequently rejected, pointing to very different (but interculturally shared) interpretations of the experimental situation.

considerations. However, I take a person's sensitivity to a particular norm to be a fairly stable disposition. The first maximum operator takes care of the possibility that a strategy profile instantiates a norm for several players simultaneously (as would be the case, for example, in a Social Dilemma with three players). The second maximum operator ranges over all the players other than the norm violator. In plain words, the discounting term (multiplied by k_i) is the maximum payoff deduction resulting from all norm violations.

The model is motivated by people's apparent respect (or disregard) for social norms regarding fairness. In the traditional Ultimatum game, the norm usually prescribes a 'fair' amount the Proposer ought to offer. The norm functions that represent this norm are the following: N_1 is a constant N function, and N_2 is nowhere defined.[12] If the Responder (player 2) rejects, the utilities of both players are zero:

$$U_{1\,reject}(x) = U_{2\,reject}(x) = 0.$$

Given that the Proposer (player 1) offers x and the Responder accepts, the utilities are

$$U_{1\,accept}(x) = M - x - k_1 \max(N_1 - x, 0)$$
$$U_{2\,accept}(x) = x - k_2 \max(N_2 - x, 0),$$

where N_i denotes the amount player i thinks he should get/offer according to some social norm applicable to the situation, and k_i is nonnegative. Note that k_1 measures how much player 1 dislikes to deviate from what he takes to be the norm. To obey a norm, 'sensitivity' to the norm need not be great, nor be due to an appreciation for what the norm stands for. Fear of retaliation may make a Proposer with a "low" k behave according to what fairness dictates, but, absent such risk, his attitude to deviations may lead him to be unfair. For the moment, I assume it is common knowledge that $N_1 = N_2 = N$, which is not too unreasonable in the traditional Ultimatum game. Again, the Responder should accept the offer if and only if $U_{2\,accept}(x) > U_{2\,reject} = 0$, which implies the following *threshold for acceptance*: $x > k_2 N/(1 + k_2)$. Notice that an offer larger than the norm dictates is not necessary for the sake of acceptance.

For the Proposer, the utility function is decreasing in x when $x \geq N$; hence a rational Proposer will not offer more than N. Suppose $x \leq N$.

[12] Intuitively, N_2 should proscribe rejection of fair (or hyperfair) offers. The incorporation of this consideration, however, will not make a difference in the formal analysis.

If $k_1 > 1$, the utility function is increasing in x, which means that the best choice for the Proposer is to offer N. If $k_1 < 1$, the utility function is decreasing in x, which implies that the best strategy for the Proposer is to offer the least amount that would result in acceptance, that is, (a little bit more than) the threshold $k_2 N/(1 + k_2)$. If $k_1 = 1$, it does not matter how much the Proposer offers provided the offer is between $k_2 N/(1 + k_2)$ and N.

It should be noted that k_1 plays a very similar role as that of β_1 in the Fehr-Schmidt model. In fact, if we take N to be $M/2$ and k_1 to be $2\beta_1$, the two models agree on what the Proposer's utility is. It is equally apparent that k_2 in this model is analogous to α_2 in the Fehr-Schmidt model. There is, however, an important difference between these parameters. The α's and β's in the Fehr-Schmidt model measure people's degree of aversion toward inequality, which is a very different disposition than the one measured by the k's, that is, people's sensitivity to different norms. The latter may be a stable disposition, and behavioral changes may be due to changes in focus or in expectations. A theory of norms can explain such changes, whereas a theory of inequity aversion does not. I will come back to this point later.

It is also the case that the Proposer's belief about the Responder's type figures in her decision when $k_1 < 1$. The belief can be represented by a joint probability over k_2 and N_2, if the value of N_2 is not common knowledge. The Proposer should choose an offer that maximizes the expected utility

$$EU(x) = P(k_2 N_2/(1 + k_2) < x) \times (M - x - k_1(N_1 - x)).$$

As will become clear, an advantage this model has over the Fehr-Schmidt model is that it can explain some variants of the traditional Ultimatum game more naturally. However, it shares a problem with the Fehr-Schmidt model: They both entail that fear of rejection is the only reason why people offer almost fair amounts rather than lower sums. This prediction, however, could be easily refuted by a parallel Dictator game where rejection is not an option.

Variations on the Ultimatum Game

So far I have only considered the basic Ultimatum game, which is not the whole story. There have been a number of interesting variants of the

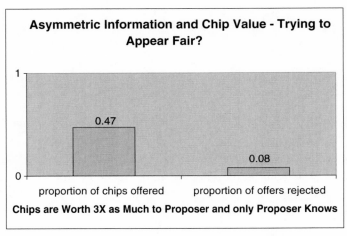

FIGURE 3.2. Asymmetric information

game in the literature, to some of which I now apply the models to see if they can tell reasonable stories about what happens in those experiments.

Ultimatum Game with Asymmetric Information and Payoffs
Kagel et al. (1996) designed an ultimatum game in which the Proposer is given a certain amount of chips. The chips are worth either more or less to the Proposer than they are to the Responder. Each player knows how much a chip is worth to her, but she may or may not know that the chip is worth something different than the other. Participants play an Ultimatum game over 10 rounds with changing opponents, and this is public knowledge. The particularly interesting setting is one in which the chips have higher (three times more) values for the Proposer, and only the Proposer knows it. It turns out that in this case the offer is (very close to) half of the chips and the rejection rate is low. A popular reading of this result is that people merely prefer to *appear* fair, as a really fair person is supposed to offer about 75% of the chips. As Figure 3.2 shows, Proposers offered close to 50% of the chips, and very few such offers were rejected.[13]

---

[13] In the condition in which only Proposers know the chips' value, when the Proposers' chips were worth less, offers declined to a mean of 31.4 chips and rejections increased to 21%. Note that in the condition in which only the Responders know the chips' value, the Proposers who had a higher chip conversion offered a mean of 45.7 chips over ten bargaining periods. However, the chips are worth less to the Responder, who knows both values, and hence the rejection rate was 34%. When the Responder had a high

To analyze this variant formally, we only need a small modification to our original setting. That is, if the Responder accepts an offer of x, the Proposer actually gets $3(M - x)$, though, to the Responder's knowledge, she only gets $M - x$. In the Fehr-Schmidt model, the utility function of player 1 (the Proposer), given the offer gets accepted, is now

$$U_{1\,accept}(x) = \begin{cases} (3 + 3\alpha_1)M - (3 + 4\alpha_1)x & \text{if } x \geq 3M/4 \\ (3 - 3\beta_1)M - (3 - 4\beta_1)x & \text{if } x < 3M/4. \end{cases}$$

The utility function of the Responder upon acceptance does not change, as to the best of his knowledge, the situation is the same as in the simple Ultimatum game. Also, if the Responder rejects the offer, both utilities are again zero. It follows that the Responder's threshold for acceptance remains the same: He accepts the offer if $x > \alpha_2 M/(1 + 2\alpha_2)$. For the Proposer, if $\beta_1 > 3/4$, her best offer is $3M/4$; otherwise, her best offer is the minimum amount above the threshold. An interesting point is that even if someone offers $M/2$ in the simple Ultimatum game, which indicates that $\beta_1 > 1/2$, she may not offer $3M/4$ in this new condition. This prediction is consistent with the observation that almost no one offers 75% of the chips in the real game.

At this point, it seems the Fehr-Schmidt model does not entail a difference in behavior in this new game. But Proposers in general do offer more in this new setting than they do in the usual Utimatum game, which naturally leads to the lower rejection rate. Can the Fehr-Schmidt model explain this? One obvious way is to adjust α_2 so that the predicted threshold increases. But there is no reason in this case for the Responder to change his attitude toward inequality. Another explanation might be that, under this new setting, the Proposer believes that the Responder's distaste for inequality increases, for after all it is the Proposer's belief about α_2 that affects the offer. This move sounds as questionable as the last one, but it does point to a reasonable explanation. Because the Proposer is

conversion rate, Proposers offered less (mean $= 29.7\%$). The authors of the study did not report if the offers lower than 50% were those rejected, but they concluded that rejections were due to inequality aversion. Rejections were 21%. Note that the mean offer is close to the money-equalizing split. When both players knew the chips' value, Proposers with a high conversion rate offered a mean of 54.4 chips over the first three rounds. Rejections in these rounds were high at 52%. This brought the offer up to 63.7 chips by round 10, and the overall rejection rate lowered to 39%. Unfortunately, the overall mean offer was not reported in the paper. When the chips were worth more to the Responder, the mean offers stayed close to 25.5, the money-equalizing split, throughout the game. Rejection rates were low at 14%.

uncertain about what kind of Responder she is facing, her belief about α_2 should be represented by a nondegenerate probability distribution. She should choose an offer that maximizes her expected utility, which in this case is given by

$$EU(x) = P(\alpha_2 < x/(M - 2x)) \times ((3 - 3\beta_1)M - (3 - 4\beta_1)x).$$

The main difference between this expected utility and the one in the simple Ultimatum game is that it involves a bigger stake. Hence it is likely to be maximized at a bigger x unless the distribution (her belief) over α_2 is sufficiently odd. Thus the Fehr-Schmidt model can explain the phenomenon in a reasonable way.

If we apply my model to this new setting, again the utility function of player 2 does not change. The utility function of player 1 (the Proposer), given acceptance, is changed to

$$U_{1\,accept}(x) = 3(M - x) - k_1 \max(N_1' - x, 0).$$

I use N_1' here to indicate that the Proposer's perception of the fair amount, or her interpretation of the norm, may have changed due to her awareness of the informational asymmetry.[14] My model behaves quite similarly to the previous one. Specifically, the Responder's threshold for acceptance is still $k_2 N_2/(1 + k_2)$. The Proposer will/should offer N_1' only if $k_1 > 3$, so people who offer the "fair" amount in the simple Ultimatum game ($k_1 > 1$) may not offer the "fair" amount under the new setting. That means that even if $N_1' = 3M/4$, the observation that few people offer that amount does not go against my model. The best offer for most people ($k_1 < 3$) is the least amount that would be accepted. However, because the Proposer is not sure about the Responder's type, she will choose an offer to maximize her expected utility, and this in general leads to an increase of the offer given an increase of the stake. Although it is not particularly relevant to the analysis in this case, it is worth noting that N_1' is probably less than $3M/4$ in the situation as thus framed. This point will become crucial in games with obvious framing effects.

The Rabin model, as it stands, has several difficulties. The primary trouble still centers on the kindness function. It is not hard to see that, according to Rabin's definition of kindness, the function that measures the Proposer's kindness to the Responder does not change at all, while the

---

[14] It is important to note that, because norms are very dependent on expectations, informational asymmetries will almost certainly affect norm-following behaviors.

function that measures the other way around does change.[15] This does not sound plausible. Intuitively, other things being equal, the only thing that may change is the Proposer's measure of her kindness to the other. There is no reason to think that the Responder's estimation of the other player's kindness to him will change, as the Responder does not have the relevant information. Strictly speaking, Rabin's original model cannot be applied to the situation where asymmetric information is present, because his framework assumes the payoffs being common knowledge.

It is, however, worth noting that if the kindness functions all remain the same [as is the case under the definition of kindness in Bicchieri and Zhang (2004)], the arguments available to Rabin to address the new situation are very similar to the ones available to the previous models. One move is to manipulate α's, which is unreasonable, as already pointed out. Another move is to represent beliefs with more general probability distributions (than a point mass distribution) and to look for Bayesian equilibria. The latter move will inevitably further complicate the already complicated model, but it does seem to match the reality better.

Ultimatum Game with Different Alternatives
There is also a very simple twist to the Ultimatum game, which turns out to be quite interesting. Falk et al. (2000) introduced a simple Ultimatum game where the Proposer has only two choices: either offer 2 (and keep 8) or make an alternative offer that varies across treatments in a way that allows the experimenter to test the effect of reciprocity and inequity aversion on rejection rates. The alternative offers in four treatments are (5/5), (8/2), (2/8), and (10/0). As Figure 3.3 shows, when the (8/2) offer is compared to the (5/5) alternative, the rejection rate is 44.4%, and it

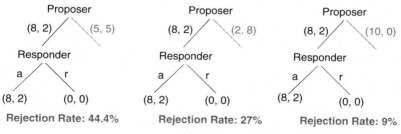

FIGURE 3.3. Alternatives matter

---

[15] By Bicchieri and Zhang's definition of kindness, both functions remain the same as in the simple setting.

is much higher than the rejection rates in each of the alternative three treatments. In fact, it turns out that the rejection rate depends a lot on what the alternative is. The rejection rate decreases to 27% if the alternative is (2/8) and further decreases to 9% if the alternative is (10/0).[16]

Is it hard for the Fehr-Schmidt model to explain these results? In this consequentialist model there does not seem to be any role for the available alternatives to play. As the foregoing analysis shows, the best reply for the Responder is acceptance if $x > \alpha_2 M/(1 + 2\alpha_2)$. That is, different alternatives can affect the rejection rate only through their effects on α_2. It is not entirely implausible to say that "what could have been otherwise" affects one's attitude toward inequality. After all, one's dispositions are shaped by all kinds of environmental or situational factors, to which the 'path not taken' seem to belong. Still it sounds quite odd that one's sensitivity to fairness changes as alternatives vary, and, in particular, it is not compatible with the assumption of independence of irrelevant alternatives, a common assumption in decision theory.

The norm-based model, by contrast, seems to have an easier time. For one thing, my model can explain the data by telling a story about how the norm's perception might change, and the story, unlike in the previous case, can be quite plausible. Recall that my definition of what it takes to follow a norm relies heavily on expectations, both empirical and normative. As I discussed in the previous chapter, how we decide and act in a situation depends on how we interpret, understand, and encode it. Once a situation is categorized as a member of a particular class, a schema (or script) is invoked. Such a script allows us to make inferences about unobservable variables, predict other people's behavior, make causal attributions, and modulate emotional reactions. The script we invoke is the source of both projectible regularities and the legitimacy of our expectations. If, as I argued, social norms are embedded into scripts, then the particular way a situation is framed will have a large effect on our expectations about others' behavior and what they expect from us. Thus a change in the way a situation is framed will induce a change in expectations and have an immediate effect on our focusing on the norm that has (or has not) been elicited.

As the possible alternatives vary, the player may no longer believe that the same norm applies, and it is quite reasonable to conjecture that

---

[16] Note that 30% of the subjects proposed (8,2) when the alternative was (5,5), 70% proposed (8,2) when the alternative was (2,8), and (100)% proposed (8,2) when the alternative was (10,0). Each player played four games, presented in random order, in the same role.

different alternatives point the Responder to different norms (or lack thereof). In the (8,2), (5,5) situation, players are naturally focused on the equal split. The Proposer who could have chosen it but did not is sending a clear message about his disregard for fairness. If the expectation of a fair share is violated, the Responder will probably feel outraged, attribute a mean intention to the Proposer, and punish him accordingly. If the alternatives are (8,2) or (2,8), few people would expect a Proposer to 'sacrifice' for the Responder. In real life, situations like this are decided with a coin toss. In the game context, it is difficult to see that any norm would apply to the situation. This is why 70% of the subjects choose the (8,2) split and only 27% reject it. Finally, the choice of (8,2) when the alternative is (10,0) appears quite nice, and indeed the rejection rate is only 9%. When the alternative for the Proposer is to offer the whole stake, there is little reason for the Responder to think that the norm is still (50%, 50%) or something close to this. Thus a natural explanation given by my model is that N_2 changes (or may be empty) as the alternative varies.

The results of this experiment tell us that most people do not have selfish material preferences, in which case they would always accept the (8,2) division. But they also tell us that people are not simply motivated by a dislike for inequality, otherwise we would have observed the same rejection rate in all contexts.

Ultimatum Game with Framing

Framing effects, a topic of continuing interest to psychologists and social scientists, have also been investigated in the context of Ultimatum games. Hoffman et al. (1994), for example, designed an Ultimatum game in which groups of 12 participants were ranked on a scale 1–12 either randomly or by superior performance in answering questions about current events. The top six were assigned to the role of "seller" and the rest to the role of "buyer." They also ran studies with the standard Ultimatum game instructions, both with random assignments and assignment to the role of Proposer by contest. The exchange and contest manipulations elicited significantly lowered offers, but the rejection rates were unchanged as compared to the standard Ultimatum game.[17]

Figure 3.4 shows that the 'exchange' framing significantly lowered offers, but the fact of being the winner of a contest in the traditional

---

[17] Rejections remained low throughout, about 10%. All rejections were on offers of $2 or $3 in the exchange instructions; there were no rejections in the contest entitlement/divide $10, and there was 5% rejection of the $3 and $4 offers in the random assignment/ divide $10.

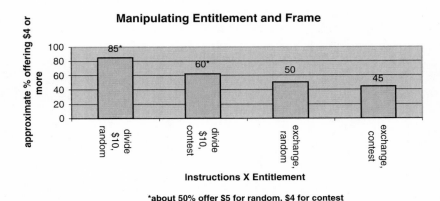

FIGURE 3.4. Entitlements matter

Ultimatum game also had an effect on the Proposers' offers. Several other experiments have consistently shown that when the Proposer is a 'contest winner' (Frey and Bohnet 1995), or has 'earned the right' to that role (Hoffman and Spitzer 1985), offers are lower than in the traditional Ultimatum game. As I suggested before, in the presence of prototypical, acceptable justifications for deviating from equality, subjects will be induced to follow an equity principle. Framing in this case provides salient cues, suggesting that an equity rule is appropriate to the situation.

Because, from a formal point of view, these situations are not different from that of a traditional Ultimatum game, the previous analysis remains the same. Hence, within the Fehr-Schmidt model, one has to argue that the framing of the game decreases α_2. In other words, the role of a "buyer" or the knowledge that the Proposer was a superior performer or had simply earned the right to his role lowers the Responder's concern for fairness. This does not sound intuitive and demands some explanation. In addition, the Proposer has to actually *expect* this change in order to lower his offer. It is equally if not more difficult to see why the framing can lead to different beliefs the Proposer has about the Responder.

In my model, the parameter N plays a vital role again. Although we need more studies about how and to what extent framing affects people's expectations and perceptions of what norm is being followed, it is intuitively clear that framing, like the examples mentioned previously, will change the players' conception of what is fair. The 'exchange' framework is likely to elicit a market script where the seller is expected to try to get as much money as possible, whereas the entitlement context has the effect of focusing subjects away from equality in favor of an equity rule. In both cases, what has been manipulated is the perception of the situation, and thus the expectations of the players. An individual's sensitivity and concern for norms may be unchanged, but the relevant norm is clearly different from the usual 'fairness as equality' rule.

Games with Computers

To better understand the impact of norms on behavior in Ultimatum games, it is useful to look at experiments in which expectations are irrelevant. Such games are typically played against a computerized opponent. Blount (1995) performed a one-shot Ultimatum game experiment in which Responders played against a computer making random offers as well as against human Proposers. In these games, the subjects knew when they were paired with computers or humans. The subjects rejected, as usual, low offers from humans but rarely rejected low offers coming from the computer. The computer has no expectation that its human opponent will follow a norm, and the player has no reason to expect that the computer will follow a norm, be fair, or have any intention whatsoever. As a result, human players quickly begin to play as predicted by the standard theory.

Dictators with Uncertainty

In a theory of norms, the role of expectations is crucial. Norms and expectations are part of the same package. Focusing people on a norm usually means eliciting certain expectations, and, in turn, when people have the right empirical and normative expectations they will tend to follow the relevant norm. In the traditional Ultimatum game, at least in Western societies, the possibility of rejection forces the Proposer to focus on what is expected of her.[18] In the absence of information about the Responder, and without a history of previous games and results as a guide, equal (or almost equal) shares become a focal point. Eliminate the possibility of rejection, and equality becomes much less compelling: for example, we know that when the Dictator game is double blind, 64% of the Proposers keep all the money. The Dictator

---

[18] I do not want to imply that sanctions are crucial to norm following. They may just reinforce a tendency to obey the norm and serve the function – together with several other indicators – of focusing individuals' attention on the particular norm that applies to the situation.

game is particularly interesting as a testing ground for the study of how norms influence behavior, because it illustrates in a clear manner how sensitive we are to the presence, reminder, or absence of others' expectations.

Because I always thought that it was not at all obvious what one should choose in a Dictator game, and I did not find an 'equal share' compelling, I was curious to know what people perceive as the 'normal' thing to do in such games, and whether it is different from what they think the 'right' thing to do is. I thus ran a questionnaire on 126 undergraduate students at Carnegie Mellon University (see the appendix). The students were all enrolled in Philosophy 80-100, a course that almost every student takes, irrespective of his or her major. What the answers would do, I thought, was to define a baseline perception of the Dictator game. Interestingly, there was no overall consensus about what to do and what 'most people' were expected to do. Almost 56% of the students thought that 10–0 would be the most common allocation, and only 13% thought 5–5 to be the norm. Furthermore, 46 of the 70 (65.7%) who thought that 10–0 would be the most common allocation also felt that such an allocation was not unfair. When explicitly asked about the 'fair' allocation, 68% felt that 5–5 was fair, but a sizable 21.4% thought 10–0 to be fair. As for the unfair question, almost 56% felt that nothing was unfair or greedy. The Dictator game seems thus to be a situation in which there is no obvious norm to follow, and, because of that, it is an excellent testing ground for the role expectations (and their manipulation) can play in the emergence of a consensual script and, consequently, a social norm.

A recent experiment done by Dana, Weber, and Kuang (2003) enlightens this point. The basic setting is a Dictator game where the allocator has only two options. The game is played in two very different situations. Under the "Known Condition" (KC), the payoffs are unambiguous, and the allocator has to choose between option A, (6, 1), and option B, (5, 5), where the first number in the pair is the allocator's payoff and the second number is the receiver's payoff. Under the "Unrevealed Condition" (UC), the allocator is to choose between option A, (6, ?), and option B, (5, ?), where the receivers' payoff is 1 with probability 0.5 and 5 with probability 0.5 (Figure 3.5). Before the allocator makes a choice, however, she is given the option to privately find out at no cost which game is being played and thus know what the receiver's payoff is. It turns out that 74% of the subjects choose B, (5, 5), in KC, and 56% choose A, (6, ?), without revealing the actual payoff matrix in UC.

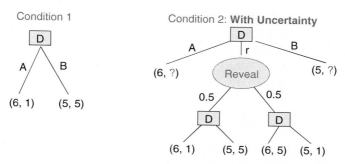

Condition 1

Condition 2: **With Uncertainty**

? is 1 with probability 0.5 and 5 with probability 0.5

FIGURE 3.5. Uncertainty matters

This result, as Dana et al. point out, stands strongly against the Fehr-Schmidt model. If we take the revealed preference as the actual preference, choosing (5, 5) in KC implies that $\beta_1 > 0.2$, while choosing (6, ?) without revealing the actual payoff matrix in UC implies that $\beta_1 < 0.2$.[19] Hence, unless a reasonable story could be told about β_1, the model does not fit the data. If a stable preference for fair outcomes is inconsistent with the above results, can a conditional preference for following a norm show greater consistency? Note that, if we were to *assume that N_i is fixed* in both experiments, a similar change of k would occur in my model, too.[20] However, the norm-based model can offer a natural explanation of the data through an interpretation of N_i. In KC, subjects have only two, very clear choices. There is a 'fair' outcome (5,5) and there is an inequitable one (6,1). Choosing (6,1) entails a net loss for the receiver and only a marginal gain for the allocator. A similar situation, and one that we frequently encounter, is giving to the poor or otherwise disadvantaged. In Dana's example, what is \$1 more to the allocator is \$4 more to the receiver, mimicking the multiplier effect that money has for a poor person. In this experiment, what has probably been activated is a norm of

[19] In KC, choosing option B implies that $U_1(5,5) > U_1(6,1)$ or $5 - \alpha_1(0) > 6\beta_1(5)$. Hence, $5 > 6 - 5 - \beta_1$ and therefore $\beta_1 > 0.2$. In UC, not revealing and choosing option A implies that $U_1(6, (.5(5), .5(1))) > U_1(.5(5,5), .5(6,5))$, because revealing will lead to one of the two 'nice' choices with equal probability. We thus get $6 - .3(\beta_1) > 2.5 + .5(6 - \beta_1)$, which implies that $\beta_1 < 0.2$.

[20] According to my model, if we were to keep N_i constant, choosing option B in KC means that $U_1(5,5) > U_1(6,1)$, and hence $5 > 6 - k_1(4)$. It follows that $k_1 > 0.25$. In UC, not revealing and choosing option A implies that $U_1(6, (.5(5), .5(1))) > U_1(.5(5,5), .5(6,5))$, and hence $6 - k_1(2) > 5.5$, which implies that $k_1 < 0.25$.

beneficence, and subjects uniformly respond by choosing (5,5). Indeed, when receivers in Dana's experiment were asked what they would choose in the allocator's role, they unanimously chose the (5,5) split as the most appropriate. Interestingly, in a related experiment (Dana et al. 2003), in the presence of uncertainty all of the receivers believed that the most frequently chosen option would be the most unfavorable to them, indicating that there is a consensus about when equal shares are to be expected and when they are not.

A natural question to ask is whether we should hold N fixed, thus assuming a variation in people's sensitivity to the norm (k), or if instead what is changing here is the perception of the norm itself. I want to argue that what changes from the first to the second experiment is the perception that a norm exists and applies to the present situation, as well as expectations about other people's behavior and what their expectations about one's own behavior might be. Recall that in my definition of what it takes for a norm to be followed, a necessary condition is that a sufficient number of people expect others to follow it in the appropriate situations *and* believe they are expected to follow it by a sufficient number of other individuals. People will *prefer* to follow an existing norm *conditionally* on entertaining such expectations. In KC, the situation is transparent, and so are the subjects' expectations. If a subject expects others to choose (5,5) and believes she is expected so to choose, she might prefer to follow the norm (provided her k, which measures her sensitivity to N, is large enough).[21] In UC, on the contrary, there is uncertainty as to what the receiver might be getting. To pursue the analogy with charitable giving further, in UC there is uncertainty about the multiplier ("am I giving to a needy person or not?") and thus there is the opportunity for *norm evasion*: As we saw with the Ik thatching their roofs in the middle of the night,

---

[21] A similar example of focusing on the 'fair' outcome is provided by a two-part experiment conducted by Kahneman et al. (1986). In the first task, subjects in a Dictator game had to choose between two possible allocations of $20: Either one could keep $18 and give $2 to an anonymous Responder, or one could split $20 evenly. A lottery selected eight pairs (out of 80) to actually be paid. The subjects chose to divide the money evenly 76% of the time. In the second part of the experiment, the same subjects were presented with another choice. This time the subjects had to decide between splitting different amounts of money with one of two subjects who had previously played the game with somebody else. Either the subjects could split $12 evenly with another subject, who had chosen to keep $18 in the first part of the experiment, or they could halve $10 with a subject who had divided equally the sum of money in the first part of the experiment. Most (74%) of the subjects preferred to split the money with the person who had previously acted fairly. They were clearly condemning unfair behavior by preferring to lose $1 rather than splitting a greater sum with someone who had acted unfairly.

the player can avoid activating the norm by not discovering the actual payoff matrix. Though there is no cost to see the payoff matrix, people will opt to not see it in order to avoid having to adhere to a norm that could potentially be disadvantageous. So a person who chooses (5, 5) under KC may choose (6, ?) under UC with the same degree of concern for norms. Choosing to reveal the actual payoff matrix looks like what moral theorists call a *supererogatory* action. We are not morally obliged to perform such actions, but it is awfully nice if we do. Indeed, I believe few people would expect an allocator to choose to reveal, and similarly I would expect few people would be willing to punish an allocator who chooses to remain in a state of uncertainty.[22]

A very different situation would be one in which the allocator has a clear choice between (6,1) and (5,5), but she is told that the prospective receiver *does not even know* he is playing the game. In other words, the binary choice would focus the allocator, as in the KC condition, on a norm of beneficence, but she would also be cued about the absence of a crucial expectation. If the recipient does not expect her to give anything, is there any reason to follow the norm? This is a good example of what I have extensively discussed in Chapter 1. A norm exists, the subject knows it and knows she is in a situation in which the norm applies, but her preference for following the norm is conditional on having certain empirical and normative expectations. In our example, the normative expectations are missing, because the recipient does not know that a Dictator game is

---

[22] It should be stressed here that there are several ways in which a person might be focused on expectations that induce more generous behavior. For example, we know that being able to look at one's partner, or to communicate with him, has an effect on how much is allocated. In experimental variations in which the allocator can look the prospective receiver in the face or is allowed to talk to him, an offer of half the money is the norm. For example, Frey and Bohnet (1997) describe three Dictator game experiments in which allocators were given CHF 13 to keep or share with a receiver. In each experiment, a different level of interpersonal identity was made salient. In the first experiment, the allocator and receiver were unknown to one another and the mean amount of money given by the allocator to the receiver was CHF 3.38. In the second experiment, the partners faced one another but were not allowed to communicate. Allocators gave an average of CHF 6.25 to recipients. In the third experiment, subjects were given the choice of whether to communicate with each other. The majority (75%) chose communication; the mean allocation from allocators in this majority was CHF 5.70. Interestingly, when allocators in the third experiment answered a questionnaire concerning the reasons for their decisions, most cited binding agreements or commitments with their partner as the reason for their choice of allocation. A face-to-face encounter, or the possibility of communication, evidently generates a cognitive and emotional shift of attention. As social distance between the parties dwindles, one is forced to focus on the reasonable expectations of the other party.

being played and his part in it. In this case, I predict that a majority of allocators will choose (6,1) with a clear conscience. This prediction is different from what a 'fairness preference' model would predict, but it is also at odds with theories of social norms as 'constraints' on action. One such theory is Rabin's (1995) model of moral constraints. Very briefly, Rabin assumes that agents maximize expected utility subject to constraints. Thus our allocator will seek to maximize her payoffs but experience disutility if her action is in violation of a social norm. However, if the probability of harming another is sufficiently low, a player may 'circumvent' the norm and act more selfishly. Since in Rabin's model the norm functions simply as a constraint, beliefs about others' expectations play no role in a player's decision to act. Because the (6,1) choice does in fact 'harm' the recipient, Rabin's model should predict that the number of subjects who choose (6,1) is the same as in the KC of Dana's experiment. In my model, however, the choices in the second experiment will be significantly different from the choices we observed in Dana's KC condition.

To summarize, the norm-based model explains the behavioral changes observed in the above experiments as due to a (potentially measurable) change in expectations. An individual's propensity to follow a given norm would remain fixed, as would her preferences. However, since preferences in my model are conditional on expectations, a change in expectations will have a major, predictable effect on behavior.

Evasions and Violations

The results of experiments on Ultimatum games show the importance of framing and context in determining what is perceived as a 'fair' allocation. They do not control, however, for individual (or group) biases in deciding what 'fair' means in situations in which the choice of the dimension on which a fair allocation or distribution should be established is indeterminate. For example, equality as a rule of fairness presupposes that individuals are the same in all relevant aspects and therefore deserve the same outcomes. The rule of equity instead holds that individuals should receive in proportion to their inputs. The affirmative action controversy is an example of the perennial tension between these two poles. The disadvantaged groups, usually minorities, tend to focus on preexisting differences (in income, access to education, etc.) that favor the advantaged group unfairly. Affirmative action is perceived as a means to bring the disadvantaged group closer to equality. Members of the advantaged group instead tend to perceive affirmative action as an unfair advantage. Both sides can provide acceptable justifications, but the weights attributed to such justifications by each group will differ. So far, I have assumed that the social norm, N, is the same for all the parties involved, and this fact is common knowledge. A different and not uncommon case is one in which more than one norm might apply, so that a player must assess a probability distribution over the range of the possible norms that the other players may adopt. In an Ultimatum game in which $10 is to be divided, but players are focused on considerations of merit (as when the Proposer won a contest), the values of N_2 may range from (5,5) to (7,3). The Proposer's expected utility function will now have to include the probabilities of the Responder adopting one or another norm. In this case, we observe a deviation from the equality rule (5,5), but only a minority of Proposers offers less than $4. My interpretation is that Proposers will be keen to justify a deviation from equality in favor of equity but will also be aware that this justification carries less weight with the Responder. In this case, a higher probability mass will be cast on (6,4), a division that rewards merit but is not too far from equality. A norm-based model can thus explain (and predict) deviations from equality in Ultimatum games, as well as their direction, without having to assume that players change their preference for fairness or believe others to undergo such a change.

There are a few good examples in the experimental literature that show how, in ambiguous situations, *self-serving biases* occur. It is interesting to note, however, that such biases seem to be tempered by a concern for the expectations of the other party.[23] I do not see how, in the absence of shared norms, a player would be able to assess others' expectations and condition her behavior on them. Moreover, there are several ways to test the role played by expectations on decision making; for example, if a subject were made aware that *no one* expects her to obey a particular norm, then my prediction is that we will observe behavior that significantly deviates from what a relevant norm would dictate in favor of more selfish outcomes.

Messick and Sentis (1983) report the results of a series of experiments aimed at testing the hypothesis that one tends to select the fairness rule that best conforms to one's preferences. Perhaps the most interesting experiment is Van Avermaet's (1974) double-blind study of how a

---

[23] In Ultimatum games players who, because of reasons of 'merit,' choose an equitable (as opposed to equal) allocation almost never award themselves 70 or 80% of the money. In turn, recipients keep rejecting offers lower than 30% at the same rate as the controls.

group of 94 undergraduate students decided to divide some money they 'earned' in an experimental session. Van Avermaet manipulated both the length of time worked and the number of questionnaires to be filled. One-third of the students worked for 90 minutes filling out a set of personality questionnaires and were told that they were working independently with another student who was in a different room and they would never see. They were told the other student worked 90 minutes, too (90, 90). Another third of the students worked 90 minutes and was told that the other student only worked 45 minutes (90, 45). The last group worked 45 minutes and was told that the other student worked 90 minutes (45, 90). The subjects were given either three or six questionnaires to complete and were led to believe that the other student had filled either three or six questionnaires in the given time. The questionnaire combinations were (6, 3), (3, 3), and (3, 6). After the test was completed, each student was given $7 for his help and was told that his 'partner' had to leave in a hurry. The students were also made aware that their 'partner' did not expect a payment but was given an envelope with the address of the other student, in case they decided to send the other a share of the money. Note that, in this case, though one's partner is not believed to expect a share, the fact that one is given an envelope addressed to the partner strongly suggests that the experimenter expects the student to give something. In other words, those whom I believe expect me to follow a norm need not be the target of a fair division. To give me a reason to conform, it is only necessary that I believe that *some people* expect and prefer me to follow a norm.

Indeed, only 2 out of 94 students did not mail some money, but the amount of money given to the 'partner' was a function of the perceived importance of one's input in relation to the other's. For example, in all those cases in which either the student worked a longer time (90, 45) or had more questionnaires to fill (6, 3), the subjects kept more than half of the money, irrespective of the fact that the other dimension favored their partner [e.g., one such combination could be (90, 45) and (3, 6)]. When the subjects were equal in one dimension, but the other dimension favored the other [e.g., (90, 90) and (3, 6)], the subjects kept half of the money. When the subjects deserved less, because both dimensions were unfavorable [e.g., (45, 90) and (3, 6)], the mean amount kept was $3.3, only slightly inferior to an equal share. However, a student in the opposite position [i.e., (90, 45) and (6, 3)] would keep a mean amount of $4.68. These data are consistent with the results of several other studies that show the tendency among lower input persons to prefer equal division of the group's outcome, whereas higher input people prefer an equitable division of the rewards.

Messick and Sentis interpret the data as showing that, most of the time, when they face an allocative decision people try to strike a difficult balance between self-interest and fairness. Specifically they maintain that, in ambiguous situations, individual preferences over outcomes will determine the interpretation of fairness that one adopts. The process they depict is one of "constrained optimization" of preferences: First, one would rank the allocative options in terms of personal desirability, and then one would find plausible arguments that bolster one's claim to, say, more than an equal share of the resources. There is little evidence, however, to suggest that the self-serving bias is a conscious one, in the sense that individuals are aware of the foregoing process. There are of course circumstances in which one consciously tries to find good arguments to justify one's choice in an allocative task. If I am expecting to be held accountable for my choices, I will make an effort to find good, compelling reasons to support my actions. Similarly, if I am questioned about my choice after the fact, I will try to rationalize my actions by appeal to an interpretation of fairness that supports my allocation.

In most circumstances, however, biases tend to steer our choices in one or another direction without much thought or control on our part. A self-serving bias will have the effect of eliciting a particular script, of focusing subjects on a specific interpretation of fairness. When several interpretations are possible, we will perceive one of them as salient because it favors us, but I view the entire process as mostly automatic and unreflective. Self-interest lends salience to a particular rule of fairness, as much as an in-group bias makes people choose to favor their own group in an allocative task. In the latter case, the fact that allocators are unaffected by their choices and, moreover, have no information about the relative contributions of different groups, lends credibility to the hypothesis that biases act as salience pointers in an almost automatic way. If several norms could justifiably apply to a situation, a person will tend to lend more weight to the one that favors oneself or one's group. However, as the following well-known experiment illustrates, self-serving biases are always tempered by the knowledge (of which we might not always be fully conscious) that others' expectations might differ from our wishes, so that the final outcome turns out to be a balancing act between equity and equality concerns.

I am referring here to Henry Tajfel's early experiments on the effects of meaningless categorization on intergroup discrimination (Tajfel, 1970). A typical experiment would start with a visual judgment task, which was devised to divide the participants into two groups, or categories, on an arbitrary basis. The subjects would observe dots on a screen and then estimate their numbers. They were subsequently told that people have the tendency to consistently underestimate or overestimate the number of dots, but such tendencies were not related to accuracy, and they were then grouped based on their performance in estimating the number of dots.[24] The second part of the experiment consisted of a different task involving the allocation of money to other participants, only identified by their label (group membership) and code. Every subject was given 18 pages of allocation matrices like the following:

Allocation to:											
Subject x	16	15	14	13	12	11	10	9	8	7	6
Subject y	7	8	9	10	11	12	13	14	15	16	17

In each matrix, each vertical pair of numbers is an alternative allocation of money, with the upper number going to subject x and the lower number going to subject y. Subjects x and y could both be overestimators, or both could be underestimators, or they could belong to different categories. Note that the allocator was aware that he was allocating money to two other participants, hence he would be unaffected, and both the allocator and the participants were anonymous, the code of each participant only showing to which group he belonged. Given these preconditions, one would expect fairness to dictate an allocation as close to an equal amount of money as possible. Indeed, when subjects x and y belonged to the same group (i.e., they were both underestimators or both overestimators), the tendency was to allocate equal shares; in our example, it would be either (12, 11) or (11, 12). However, when the two target individuals belonged to two different groups, 90% of the allocators assigned more money to the in-group member. In our example, participants allocated an average of 13 to the member of their own group and only 10 to the out-group member. Not unlike the experiments that show a self-serving bias, here

---

[24] Another group of subjects was explicitly told that some people are more accurate estimators than others, to control for the impact of value judgments on in-group biases (Tajfel, 1970).

too individuals try to strike a balance between being fair to both groups and favoring their in-group.

The in-group bias observed in Tajfel's experiments could not apparently be justified by material self-interest, because the anonymous allocator would not benefit from or be penalized by his choice. It could not be rationalized on the basis of relative ability either, because the subjects were explicitly told that roughly 50% are underestimators and 50% are overestimators; thus both biases are equally common, and the resulting estimates are equally inaccurate. Tajfel's conclusion was that the gratuitous discrimination was the result of simply categorizing individuals into two separate groups, even if the categorization is totally arbitrary. Categorization, in Tajfel's view, would have the effect of producing a more favorable evaluation of in-group members, and this evaluation in turn would be motivated by the need to give oneself a positive social identity. That is, if one perceives one's group to be 'better' than other groups, one feels better about oneself. The link between self-esteem, favorable assessment of the in-group, and categorization is quite weak. But even if we could show that there is a strong relation among those variables, it would not follow that favorable assessment of the in-group will lead to discrimination in its favor. To 'like better' does not necessarily translate into 'treating better.' There could be other, more compelling reasons for in-group favoritism. The latter could be due to "mutual fate control," a situation in which each member's payoff depends on other group members' choices but is independent of her own choice (Yamagishi et al. 1999). Indeed, experiments by Jin et al. (1996) show that there is a difference between in-group boasting and favoritism. Boasting seems to be produced by simple categorization, but it is not enough, alone, to produce in-group favoritism. The latter only appears in the presence of mutual fate control. In a condition of mutual fate control, one favors the in-group member because one *expects reciprocation*. Because all these experiments involve anonymity, one's favor to the in-group cannot be detected, so expected reciprocation does not appear to be rational or grounded in the nature of the relationship.[25] Indeed, the expectation amounts to what Jin et al. call an "illusion of control."

Yet if we consider expectations to be part of a script that has been brought about by how the experimental situation is presented, then

---

[25] Jin et al. (1996) gave post-experiment questionnaires to their subjects asking questions like: Did you think your own group members would give you more if you gave more to an in-group member? Only those who responded positively practiced in-group favoritism.

they seem much less irrational and unjustified. My hypothesis is that expected reciprocity is normative. We know that people tend to perceive in-group members as more honest, trustworthy, and cooperative than the out-group, even (or especially) if the grouping is arbitrary and anonymous. We may have evolved generic norms of group behavior that have served us well since before we became *Homo sapiens*. Individuals living in small bands or groups punished free-riders and practiced reciprocity as a means of survival. Although we live in far less close-knit groups, there are still many groups to which we belong – families, neighborhoods, and work groups – that teach us the importance of group solidarity and allegiance. In large, anonymous groups, or in a situation of complete anonymity, group solidarity makes little sense, but such circumstances are relatively 'new' (evolutionarily speaking), and we do not seem to be endowed with the psychological mechanisms that would allow us to 'fine tune' our responses and effortlessly switch them from one situation to another. What I am saying does not imply, however, that default expectations will be completely insensitive to information that may steer us in other directions. In an in-group/out-group context, I would expect the default expectation to be one of generalized reciprocity within the in-group. Because of that, one will tend to favor one's own group by moving away from an equal share.

What would happen if we get the allocators focused on the fact that the recipients of their allocation *do not know* they are in-group members? In this case we would have eliminated *mutual knowledge* of group membership. My prediction is that, though multilateral dependence might be *prima facie* assumed by the allocators, it would become irrelevant if mutual knowledge of group membership is absent. Indeed, there is some experimental evidence that subjects act differently depending on whether there is unilateral or mutual knowledge of group membership (Yamagishi 1998). Like all situations to which norms apply, we need to have the right kinds of expectations in order to conform to a norm. If the default expectation of generalized reciprocity is not removed, a norm of fairness as equity will be justified by acceptable reasons to give more to the in-group. One gives more to the in-group because one expects more from them and less from the out-group, *and* one believes in-group members expect such behavior from each other. Yet I believe that the complementary expectation that the out-group will reason in a similar way and might display negative reciprocity if treated poorly tempers favoritism and is the reason why deviations from equality are not too large. Absent those reasons, we should expect equality to rule.

Appendix to Chapter 3

With the help of Jason Dana, I conducted the following survey in five sections of 80–100. The sections ranged in size from 20 to 30 respondents. We had 126 responses (one person did not answer what was the most common allocation, and two did not answer what was the fairest allocation).

Imagine that the conductors of this survey give a survey respondent (call them person A) ten $1 bills and the following instructions: "Another survey respondent (person B) has been paired with you randomly. This pairing is anonymous, meaning that we will not inform you who you are paired with, nor will we inform the person you are paired with who you are. Your task is to distribute the ten dollars between yourself and the person you are paired with in any way that you want. That means that you may keep or give away all of the bills, or take any action in between. Your choice is final; you keep as many of the bills as you want and the rest are given to the other person."

Now please answer the following questions:

What is the thing that person A ought to do in this situation? That is, what action would you consider fair and reasonable? Please indicate below:
Keep __ bills   and give away __ bills
(these numbers should add up to 10)

Are there any actions that person A could take that you would consider excessively greedy or unfair? If so, how many bills would he/she have to keep to be greedy? Please indicate below:
Keep __ bills and give away __ bills   or circle: any action is fair

What do you expect that most people in the position of person A would do? That is, which division would be most common? Please indicate below:
Keep __ bills   and give away __ bills

Now consider two people involved in such a situation. Imagine that you, as a third party, are allowed to look at a proposed division of $10 like the one above, between two people anonymous to you. In this situation, you have the right to inspect the offer and **accept** or **reject** it. If you **accept** the offer, the two people get the amounts of money proposed by person A. If you **reject** the offer, *both* people will receive zero dollars. You neither gain nor lose money by accepting or rejecting. Thus, you have no personal monetary stake in the outcome. For the divisions listed below, indicate which, if any, you would reject.

(please circle accept or reject – accept means divide as proposed, reject means both get zero)

Person A keeps 5 dollars, and gives 5 to B.	Accept	Reject
Person A keeps 2 dollars, and gives 8 to B.	Accept	Reject
Person A keeps 1 dollar, and gives 9 to B.	Accept	Reject
Person A keeps 10 dollars, and gives 0 to B.	Accept	Reject
Person A keeps 8 dollars, and gives 2 to B.	Accept	Reject
Person A keeps 6 dollars, and gives 4 to B.	Accept	Reject
Person A keeps 3 dollars, and gives 7 to B.	Accept	Reject
Person A keeps 9 dollars, and gives 1 to B.	Accept	Reject
Person A keeps 7 dollars, and gives 3 to B.	Accept	Reject
Person A keeps 4 dollars, and gives 6 to B.	Accept	Reject
Person A keeps 0 dollars, and gives 10 to B.	Accept	Reject

Here is a summary of the results of the survey.

For the "common" response, a strong mode of almost 56% felt that 10–0 would be the most common allocation. The rest of the responses were spread fairly evenly between 5–9, with the next biggest bump being almost 13% choosing 5–5 as the most common. Forty-six of the 70 (65.7%) who thought that 10–0 would be most common allocation also felt that nothing was unfair.

For the "ought to" or fair question, a strong mode of 68.3% felt that 5–5 was fair. A smaller bump of 21.4% felt that 10–0 was what ought to be done; very few people indicated anything but these two responses.

As for the unfair question, almost 56% felt that nothing was unfair. Of these 70 who felt that nothing was unfair, 46 (65.7%) thought that 10–0 would be the most common answer. Almost 20% felt that 10–0 was unfair, and about 15% felt that keeping 6 or more was unfair. Of those 56 who did think that some actions were greedy, 43 (76.8%) went on to punish at least some allocation choice. Of the 70 who thought nothing was unfair, 24 (34%) still punished at least some allocation.

For the punishment option, 54% chose to punish at least one allocation. More than 48% would punish a 10–0 offer, 31.7% would punish a 9–1 offer, and 26.9% would punish an 8–2 offer. Nineteen percent displayed some pure inequity aversion, preferring to punish some offers keeping more than 5 as well as some keeping less than 5. Four of the 126 respondents would punish only for giving money away, but not for keeping 10.

Whether some offers were judged greedy was most strongly related to punishment. Of interest is that a logistic regression of a dummy punish/no punish variable on both common and fairest variables shows that common is a significant predictor while fairest is not. Thus, people are more likely to punish an offer that they think violates a descriptive norm than one that violates their sense of what is fair.

4

Covenants Without Swords

Introduction

A social dilemma is, by definition, a situation in which each group member gets a higher outcome if she pursues her individual interest, but everyone in the group is better off if all group members further the common interest. Overpopulation, pollution, Medicare, public television, and the depletion of scarce and valuable resources such as energy and fish-rich waters are all examples of situations in which the temptation to defect must be tempered by a concern with the public good. There are several reasons why some individuals might not contribute to the provision of public goods or refrain from wasting common resources. Usually these resources are used by or depend on very large groups of people for their continued maintenance. It is easy, therefore, for an individual to consider her contribution to a public good or her personal consumption of a common resource as insignificant. Furthermore, in social dilemmas there is a huge difference between the costs and benefits accruing to an individual. Gains go to the individual, but the costs are shared by all. Given the structure of social dilemmas, rational, self-interested individuals are predicted to defect always. Yet almost 50 years of experiments on social dilemmas show cooperation rates ranging from 40 to 60%, and everyday experience shows people making voluntary contributions to public goods, giving to charities, volunteering, and refraining from wasting resources.

There is plenty of evidence that most people are *conditional cooperators*: They cooperate when they expect others to cooperate and defect otherwise. In other words, most people are neither pure altruists nor selfish brutes: They rather tend to condition their choices on what they expect other choosers to do, and, in cases in which such choices have a cost, they also take into account what others expect them to do. As I already argued, different people will have different attitudes to others' preferences and expectations: Some will recognize them as legitimate and will strive to meet them; others will need the threat of retaliation to be induced to cooperate. Be it as it may, for most people expectations about others' behavior and beliefs will be an important determinant in the decision to cooperate or defect.

Empirical (and normative) expectations need not be grounded on actual knowledge of how the people one interacts with have behaved in the past or what their expectations have been. We know that, in the absence of evidence about the past behavior of their partners, individuals tend to base their expectations on their own dispositions, cooperative or else (Dawes and Thaler 1988). When people use their own behavior as a cue in predicting others' choices, and expect cooperation, they tend to follow through with seemingly redundant contributions. In the framework of a rational choice model that takes material self-interest to be the driving force behind behavior, there appears to be an inconsistency between such beliefs and the resulting choices: If one expects others to cooperate, one should defect. This apparent inconsistency disappears, however, if we interpret the situation as one in which a social norm is known to apply. In this case, if one has the right kind of empirical and normative expectations, one will also prefer to conform to the norm that is made salient in the specific decision context.

If we take expectations to be critical in determining the choice to contribute in a social dilemma, we would anticipate their experimental manipulation to have a major effect on decisions to cooperate or defect. For example, observing a history of defections on the part of one's group would probably dampen the cooperative drive, while letting subjects discuss the dilemma before making a choice is likely to influence their expectations about others' behavior and thus their choices. Indeed, one variation in social dilemma experiments that dramatically increases cooperation rates is to allow subjects to discuss the dilemma. In what follows I will consider two possible explanations for this "communication effect." One is that communication enhances group identity, and the other is that communication elicits social norms. Though group identity may focus people on group norms, such as in-group loyalty and trust, I want to argue that the group in this case is only an instrument for the deployment of a norm and not its cause. I shall argue that the main reason for cooperative behavior is the working of norms. Discussion, when successful, involves commitments and promises and the intervening expectation that promises will be kept. A collective commitment to cooperate changes subjects' beliefs about what others will do and expect one to do and is a powerful encouragement to behave in a way that benefits the collective.

Experiments

To examine how group members make their decisions in social dilemmas, two different research paradigms are used. In a public goods dilemma, such as contributing to the maintenance of a public space or funding public television, individuals must contribute resources to insure the provision of the public good. Because one can enjoy public broadcasting without making a financial contribution, groups run the risk that members will not contribute, and that the public good will not be provided at all. In a resource dilemma, such as making use of common grazing land or clean air, groups share a scarce resource from which individual members can harvest. Because individuals' use of the resource, while beneficial to them, has negative effects on others, the group runs the risk of excessive harvesting, leading to depletion of the resource.

A typical social dilemma experiment uses the mixed-motive structure of the Prisoner's Dilemma to study choice behavior. Like Prisoner's Dilemma games, both public goods and resource dilemmas have the property that the individual rational choice is always defection, but if all refuse to cooperate, all are worse off.[1] The usual experimental procedure involves subjects previously unknown to one another, who may receive a monetary payoff or points, and form one or two groupings, depending on the experimental design. The subjects are given instructions and are presented with a payoff matrix describing the monetary consequences of their actions. It is individually best for each to keep his money or to appropriate a large amount of a common resource (to defect), but all are better off if everyone makes a cooperative decision

---

[1] Another class of social dilemmas is the "step-level" public goods problem, in which, after a threshold number of contributions is reached, the public good is provided. These dilemmas involve a coordination element, as less than the total number of participants is needed to provide the public good. Moreover, if one believes that one is the critical person who will 'make or break' the public good, one has an incentive to cooperate. However, in experiments with a step-level public goods provision, subjects behave as if they were involved in a pure social dilemma (Dawes et al. 1986).

TABLE 4.1.

Number of givers	Payoff to keep	Payoff to give
5	–	$12
4	$20	$9
3	$17	$6
2	$14	$3
1	$11	$0
0	$8	–

to contribute to the public good or take little of the common resource. When two separate groups are formed, subjects are given the choice between allocating money to the in-group or to the out-group; if there is only one group, individuals must choose between giving money to their group or keeping it themselves.[2] Choices are made privately, interactions may be one-shot or repeated, and discussion before playing may or may not be allowed. I shall consider here mainly one-shot interactions, because repeated interactions allow opportunities for reciprocation or reputation formation. In a repeated game, it might work to the advantage of a rational, self-interested player to develop a reputation for being a "nice guy." In this case cooperation is not surprising, and it is easily explained by the traditional rational choice model. Only when there is no apparent incentive to cooperate does pro-social behavior become really interesting.

As an example of what experimental subjects may face, consider the following "Give some" game (Dawes 1980), which is an example of a public goods dilemma. There are five players, and each receives $8 from the experimenter. The choice is between keeping the money or giving it away, in which case every other player gets $3. What a player gets depends on his choice and the choice of the other players:

Table 4.1 shows that it is always better for any individual player to keep the money, at least in terms of monetary payoffs, but the outcome of everyone giving is much better than the outcome of everyone keeping ($8 versus $12).

An example of a resource dilemma is the following "Take some" game (Dawes 1980). There are three players, and each has to decide whether to pick a red chip, in which case he gets $3 and all three players are fined

[2] I am referring to the experiments discussed in Orbell et al. (1988).

TABLE 4.2.

Number picking blue chip	Payoff to red chip	Payoff to blue chip
3	–	$1
2	$2	$0
1	$1	–$1
0	$0	–

$1, or pick a blue chip, in which case he gets $1 and there is no fine (Table 4.2). Again, the individual outcome depends on one's choice, as well as the other players' choices. In this situation, too, it is better to defect (hold the red chip), but the collective outcome of defection is worse than the cooperative outcome.

What we know from years of social dilemma experiments is that a significant baseline of cooperation is found in all experimental conditions, contrary to the prediction of rational choice theory. Even more interesting, we also know that in one-shot games in which subjects are allowed a short period of communication about the dilemma, cooperation increases well above the baseline. Indeed, a meta-analysis of social dilemma experiments conducted from 1958 to 1992 (Sally 1995) shows that the mean cooperation rate across conditions was 47.4%, that communication increased cooperation by 40%, and commitment and promising increased cooperation by 30%. Similar conclusions are drawn by Gerry Mackie (1997), who summarized the results of several social dilemma experiments devoting particular attention to the role of communication and commitment. His conclusions can be thus summarized:

- Discussion about the dilemma (but not 'irrelevant' discussion) increases cooperation rates.
- The primary content of discussions about the dilemma is promises and commitments to cooperate.
- To be effective, promising must be unanimous.
- Overhearing spoken commitments from another group does not increase cooperation.
- When subjects are instructed that pledges are 'nonbinding,' they treat them as such and pledges have no effect on cooperation.
- Commitments tend to be kept even if the beneficiary is a computer.
- Commitments made on the initial belief of benefit to the in-group tend to be kept when the locus of benefit unexpectedly switched to the out-group (carryover effect).

- Discussion improves contribution to a step-level public good even when it is confined to subgroups smaller than the critical number necessary to attain the cooperative payoff.
- Cooperation declines over repetitions.

A number of suggestions have been advanced to explain the effectiveness of communication in increasing cooperation rates in one-shot games. For example, communication may help subjects to understand the game, facilitate coordinated action, alter expectations of others' behavior, promote group solidarity, elicit generic norms of cooperation, or result in commitments to cooperate (Kerr and Kaufman-Gilliland 1994). However, as it is now common experimental practice to make sure the subjects understand the game they are going to play, even in the absence of communication, this cannot adequately explain the effects of communication on cooperation rates. Attaining coordination, in turn, is a necessary but not a sufficient condition for cooperation, and it remains to be explained how expectations of others' cooperative behavior induce subjects to cooperate instead of tempting them to defect. As to the elicitation of 'generic' norms of cooperation, I do not believe such generic norms exist.[3] What we have are specific, contingent norms that apply to well-defined situations. Thus communication may indeed focus subjects on some norms, but they will be specific to the context in which communication takes place. Finally, commitments to cooperate certainly play an important role in increasing cooperation rates, but it remains to be explained why and under which conditions pledges to cooperate in one-shot games in which one's action will remain anonymous do work. Why communication successfully increases cooperation rates is still an open question, but among the former suggestions, only group identity and social norms have not been eliminated by experimentation as possible explanations.

At the heart of the controversy between the group identity and social norms explanations of the effects of communication on cooperation rates lie two different views of the relation between an individual and the groups to which she belongs. In a reductionist perspective, the basic explanatory unit is the individual, and the group is just the aggregate of its members. Group behavior is thus explained in terms of properties of the individuals that make up the group. Individuals may be motivated by rational considerations, social norms, or be "driven" to behave in given ways by

---

[3] Cf. the definition of social norms given in Chapter 1 and the discussion of 'local' norms in Chapter 2.

automatic, unconscious processes. Communication in this view increases cooperation rates by making individuals focus on particular social norms, such as a norm of promise-keeping. A holistic perspective instead views the group as a primitive, distinct explanatory unit. Group membership has important cognitive consequences as to how we perceive ourselves and others, how we process and filter information, and how we represent other collectives. Thinking of oneself as a group member causes major shifts in motives and behavior. A basic tenet of social identity theory is that individuals incorporate groups into their self-concepts, and this internalization precipitates motivational changes, so that often behavior contrary to self-interest is activated. As far as I know, few have tried to merge the two perspectives.[4] It is entirely possible, however, to view group identity as a trigger for norm-abiding behavior. When we represent a collection of individuals as a group, we immediately retrieve from memory roles and scripts that "fit" the particular situation, and access the relevant empirical and normative expectations that support our conditional preference for following the appropriate social norm, if one exists.[5] Thus we have seen that in an in-group/out-group situation, individuals have the tendency to favor the in-group members if they have reason to expect 'generalized reciprocity,' and this expectation in turn is justified by norms of group solidarity that are easily triggered by casting people in a 'we' versus 'them' framework. Though group identity can be a motivating force, it may be less compelling in a situation in which the alternative is 'me' versus 'us,' as is the case in the social dilemmas I will discuss. When the choice is between doing something for the group and doing something for oneself, we do not have much evidence to suggest that group identity alone is sufficient to produce cooperative behavior, unless it prompts expectations that support conformity to a preexisting norm. I shall return to this important point later.

Group Identity

Dawes et al. (1988) are among the leading proponents of the social-identity explanation of cooperation in social dilemmas. They reasoned that if individuals incorporate groups into their self-concept, a

---

[4] An example of such merging is found in Jetten et al. (1996).

[5] For a discussion of norms and scripts, cf. Chapter 2. Also see Bicchieri (2000). Hertel and Kerr (2001) have provided some evidence for the quick retrieval (via priming) of social norms.

motivational shift would occur, and group welfare would matter more than individual welfare. They detail two experiments designed to investigate the role of discussion in increasing cooperation rates via a group identity effect. During each session, multiple groups of 14 subjects were randomly divided into subgroups of 7 persons each; afterwards, they went to separate rooms. Each subject was given a promissory note worth $6, which he could keep or give away. If they chose to give the money away, six other subjects would each receive $2. If everyone cooperated, each would get $12. In half of the subgroups, the subjects were told that contributions benefited six out-group members, whereas in the remaining half, the subjects were told that contributions benefited the other six in-group members. Half of the subgroups could discuss the dilemma for 10 minutes before playing. At the end of the discussion period, half of the subgroups who were allowed to discuss were informed that the beneficiaries of their contribution had changed. If the subjects were originally told that their contributions would benefit the in-group, they were now told that the out-group would receive the money, and vice versa. All experimental discussions were taped, and I shall examine them later to argue that it is not group identity, but norms of promise keeping, that explain the high rate of cooperation after a period of discussion.

Subjects contributed much more when both the dilemma was discussed and they initially believed that their contribution would go to the in-group, as Table 4.3 shows. Since increases in cooperation rates were not uniform across conditions, but appeared only when discussion of the dilemma was allowed, the authors reject the hypothesis that general norms of cooperation motivate contribution. If a general norm of cooperation were at work, they argued, subjects would not have discriminated between groups (as they would not have cared about the recipients of their money). Their conclusion is questionable. If norms are interpreted

TABLE 4.3.

| | Initial belief that money goes to in-group | | Initial belief that money goes to out-group | |
| | Belief at time of decision | | Belief at time of decision | |
	In-group	Out-group	In-group	Out-group
No discussion	37.5%	30.4%	44.6%	19.6%
Discussion	78.6%	58.9%	32.1%	30.4%

as generic imperatives, always readily available and invariably followed by those who hold them, then of course Orbell et al. are right. But norms, as I stated in Chapter 1, are often context-specific, and subjects have to be focused on them in order to conform. The choice to follow a social norm is conditional upon one's beliefs about how many other people are following it and whether one is expected to follow it by a sufficient number of people. Discussion may reveal a general willingness to cooperate, and so change one's expectations about others' behavior, but it may also reveal a potential discontent with defectors, thus engendering normative expectations.[6] The effect of discussion on cooperation rates might precisely be due to the fact that discussing the dilemma often involves an exchange of pledges and promises, and the very act of promising focuses subjects on a norm of promise-keeping, as well as that it fosters expectations that a sufficient number of subjects will fulfill their promises.

Social norms can be thought of as default rules that are activated in the right circumstances.[7] More often than not the activation process is unconscious; it does not involve much thinking or even a choice on the part of subjects.[8] We may thus expect that, once a norm has been activated, it will show some inertia, in the sense that unless a major change in circumstances occurs, people will keep following the norm that has been primed. This absence of fine tuning might explain an interesting finding from this experiment: When a group initially believed themselves to be the beneficiaries of their contributions, but were subsequently told prior to their decision that the out-group would benefit instead, 58.9% still cooperated. This carryover effect of discussion suggests that cooperation results from the activation of a norm of promise-keeping. Such a norm would only become salient in the context of in-group giving but, once activated, would show some inertia and still be followed even if the beneficiaries have changed. If instead the commitments and pledges exchanged during the discussion period were just contracts with particular people (the in-group), then knowing that the money will go to the out-group should decrease cooperation rates. Identification with one's own group may encourage cooperative behavior, but once it becomes

---

[6] For a discussion of the difference between empirical and normative expectations, cf. Chapter 1.

[7] See, for example, Bicchieri (1997, 2000).

[8] Recall that, even if I use a belief/desire framework to describe social norms, this does not imply that people must be aware that they hold certain beliefs. In experiments in which beliefs are manipulated, subjects are usually *not* aware of the effect that such manipulation has on their choices.

apparent that the money would go to the out-group, the motivation to give should disappear.

There is some other indirect evidence supporting a norm-based explanation. The carryover effect is also present in a very different experiment by Isaac and Walker (1988). In it, subjects played a two-period game with 10 trials per period. The experiment had three conditions: (1) no discussion in either period; (2) no discussion in period one but discussion in period two; (3) discussion in period one but not in period two. The results were as follows: In condition (1), cooperation in period one started at 50% but then declined to 10%. In period two it started at 40% and then declined to zero. In condition (2), cooperation in period one went from an initial 50% to 10%. In period two, it started at 60% and then went to 90%. In condition (3), cooperation remained close to 100% in period one. There was a carryover effect in the second period (no discussion), since cooperation started at 100% but eventually decreased to 85%. These data seem to indicate that groups quickly agreed on a behavioral norm, which was then adhered to through the trials. In condition (1), for example, subjects observed their partners' behavior and could then form empirical expectations about their future behavior. A descriptive norm (defined in Chapter 1) favoring defection quickly emerged and stabilized in both periods. In condition (2), the descriptive norm that emerged in period one was initially 'carried over' into the second period of interaction: Low rates of cooperation carried over into the second period, and cooperation only increased toward the end of the next 10 trials. A plausible explanation is that, initially, there might have been some conflict between the previously established descriptive norm and a social norm of cooperation that people focused on through discussion. But inertia, and anchoring to previously established behavior, were eventually taken over (if slowly) by the agreed upon cooperative behavior. In condition (3), discussion in period one immediately induced full cooperation. Discussion, I want to suggest, focused subjects on socially desirable behavior and induced both empirical and normative expectations of compliance. Interestingly, such expectations also stayed high in the second period, where no discussion occurred, and transgressions were not enough to significantly bring down cooperation levels. These results are in line with my hypothesis about the relative strength and stability of social norms, as opposed to descriptive norms. Recall that a descriptive norm coordinates individual actions, and, if coordinating with others' behavior is the main goal, it is not contrary to self-interest. For example, observing generalized cooperation will often induce cooperative behavior, even if one might be tempted to reap greater gains from defection. On the other hand, observing generalized defection induces similar behavior not only because defection is perceived as the norm, but also because cooperation in such an environment would be extremely costly. The desire to imitate, coordinate, or just behave like the others may trump other material incentives, but the tension between the desire to act like others and the advantage that *not* acting like others may confer could contribute to the relative instability of some descriptive norms. Whereas a 'good' descriptive norm is vulnerable to small threshold effects, in that few defections may lead to the norm's decline [as exemplified in the outcome of condition (1), where cooperation is quickly taken over by defection], a 'bad' descriptive norm is harder to displace. In the first case, it takes a few defectors to tilt the cost/benefit balance of cooperation in favor of costs, whereas in the second case it takes a large number of cooperators to tilt the balance in favor of benefits. When a 'bad' descriptive norm is in place, an effective way to eliminate it is to focus people on beneficial social norms, and this is precisely what the initial discussion period did. As the results of condition (3) exemplify, even in the presence of defections (in period two) normative expectations will stay high. As I will discuss later (and my definition of social norms makes clear), people need not expect universal compliance in order to follow a norm: What matters to them is the belief that enough people comply, where 'enough' may vary from person to person.

The purpose of the second experiment by Orbell et al. (1988) was to clarify the relationship between promise-making and cooperation. This time all groups of 14 subjects participated in an initial discussion of the dilemma. Afterward they were divided into subgroups of seven as in the first experiment. Half of the subgroups were allowed to discuss the dilemma for another 10 minutes. Subjects could make one of three possible choices: They could keep their $5; they could give it to their in-group, in which case the other six members would each receive $2; or they could give it to the out-group, in which case all seven out-group members would receive $3 each. Because the initial discussion took place before each group of 14 subjects was split into two subgroups, and the best choice for the whole group of 14 was to give to the out-group, promises to cooperate were exchanged among all the participants, with the understanding that – once they were split into two subgroups – the money would go to the out-group. To investigate the relationship between promise-making and cooperation, the experimenters stratified the groups into three categories: (1) groups in which everyone promised to cooperate with the out-group; (2) groups in which some promised to cooperate with the out-group and others didn't; and (3) groups in which the subjects decided to make their own independent choices. In more than half of the groups there was unanimous promising, and in that case 84% cooperated with the out-group. Without universal promising, cooperation was a meager 58%.

Though this second experiment led Orbell et al. to reject the hypothesis that higher rates of cooperation occurring after discussion are due to 'generic' norms of cooperation, one cannot exclude the possibility that more specific norms are at work. The data indicate that individuals are more likely to cooperate when everyone in the group promises to cooperate, that is, when a consensus on how to behave is reached and an informal social contract is established. But, one might argue, if a specific norm of promise-keeping is responsible for cooperative behavior, we should observe a linear relationship between the number of subjects who promise and the number of cooperators in each group, and no such relationship is shown by the data. This objection presupposes that the norm of promise-keeping is a personal (and almost unconditional) norm, because in the absence of external sanctions of any kind (choices are one-shot and anonymous) only a personal system of values would have sufficient motivational power to induce subjects to cooperate. Then, if discussion is allowed and promises to cooperate are exchanged, those who promised should fulfill their obligations irrespective of how many others in the group promised. If the data show otherwise, cooperation cannot be imputed to the working of personal norms.[9]

The above-mentioned objection presupposes an unduly restrictive view of how norms work. People may not have a personal norm prescribing a given behavior, yet they may display that behavior if a social norm encouraging it is made salient (Cialdini et al. 1990).[10] Not unlike Cialdini's littering experiments, unanimous promising points to a consensually held norm. Subjects are faced with an empirical expectation

[9] I take personal norms to be unconditional (or nearly so), as opposed to social norms. The main difference between a social and a personal norm is that expectations of others' conformity play a crucial role in the former and much less so in the latter. There is a difference between conforming to a norm because one expects others to conform (and believes others expect one to conform) and conforming because one is convinced of its inherent value. In the first case, the preference for conformity is conditional on expecting others to conform; in the second case, one's preference for conforming is (almost) unconditional. I discuss this point in detail in Chapter 1.

[10] See, for example, Chapters 1 and 2.

("most people will cooperate, because most of those who promised to cooperate will keep their word") and a normative expectation ("keeping one's promise is the appropriate thing to do, and I am expected to follow through with cooperation"), and will thus be prompted to conform. In fact, my definition of social norms can explain why, in a group where only *some* promise to cooperate, the outcome may turn out to be dismal. A promise to perform a potentially costly action will be kept *if* it is expected that a substantial number of other group members will contribute to the socially desirable outcome. The evidence that some subjects did not promise makes one expect them to defect. Since norm compliance is conditional on expectations of others' compliance, it may be that, unless a sufficiently high number of people openly commit to cooperate, cooperation will not occur. In this case, even those who promised may decide to defect.

Note that if unanimous promising prompts a subject to cooperate, less than unanimous promising may not necessarily induce complete defection. The data from Orbell et al. (1988) suggest that the rate of cooperation is not completely discontinuous, with high cooperation under unanimity and almost no cooperation otherwise. However, apart from the unanimity case, there seems to be no correlation between the number of promisors and subsequent cooperation. As I already mentioned, an individual will follow an existing norm if, among other things, she expects a *sufficient* number of people to follow it *and* she believes a sufficient number of people expect her to follow it. People, however, differ as to their thresholds for conformity. Someone may need 100% promising to be induced to cooperate, whereas another may think that 50% of the group exchanging pledges to cooperate is a sufficient number. Because each group is a composite of heterogeneous individuals, it is not surprising that no correlation is found between number of people promising and number of cooperators. Barring the case of unanimity, each group will differ in cooperation rates. This consideration, nonetheless, does not preclude a norm-based explanation of the effect of communication on cooperation rates. Orbell et al. (1988), however, maintain that discussion has an effect on cooperative behavior mainly because it creates group identity. Though the data do not refute their hypothesis, there are several difficulties with it. For one, it is never independently tested, and, as we shall see momentarily, the very concept of group identity needs clarification. Furthermore, an analysis of the taped discussions that occurred in the first expriment of Orbell et al. (1988) lends support to a norm-based explanation.

Cheap Talk

Though each group had a unique personality and discussion style, there are common themes and concerns that arose in almost all of the groups that provide insights into the causes of cooperation.[11] Many groups had leaders who dominated the discussion. They advocated a particular strategy and asked the rest of the group to concur. In the absence of group leaders, subjects found it difficult to reach an agreement and often opted to end their discussion period early. Recall that in the first experiment discussion took place after the two subgroups were formed, and the subjects had to choose whether to keep their money or, depending on the experimental condition, to give it either to the in-group or the out-group. The content of these discussions is quite different, though, depending on whether the potential beneficiary of the money is the in-group or the out-group.

Groups sometimes wanted to talk with the out-group to check if they planned to cooperate. The implication seemed to be that – if they were to make a commitment – they would be considered more trustworthy. The question of whether to trust the out-group frequently arose, and those groups who initially thought of cooperating with the out-group were worried about being cheated by them. Many groups concluded that most out-group members would defect.[12] This conclusion was reached by projection: If we were in their place, it was argued, we would certainly defect. Group members evidently considered themselves to be a statistically representative sample; knowing their own propensity to defect led them to predict with some confidence the out-group behavior. The predictability of the out-group's behavior was grounded on an expectation that they would behave 'normally,' given the circumstances. Why would most groups consider defection on the part of the out-group a normal choice?

It seems that competitiveness, mistrust, discrimination, and even aggression toward out-groups are deeply rooted attitudes, ready to emerge even in relatively neutral situations such as those encountered in

---

[11] Robyn Dawes was kind enough to make the tapes available to me, so that my student, Colleen Baker, was able to carefully analyze their content. Colleen recorded, for each group, who spoke first and what he/she said, how the subjects responded and how many responded, whether there was unanimous agreement on the strategy proposed, and how the conclusion about the out-group's expected behavior was reached.

[12] For a discussion of how intergroup schemas that are based on learned expectations about the competitive nature of intergroup relations influence a group's assessment of the out-group behavior and intentions, see Insko and Schopler (1987).

experiments. In 1948, the Sherif's Robber's Cave experiment, in which young boys selected for good psychological adjustment and sociability were separated into two rival groups, showed how quickly hostility and aggression can develop among groups that have no cultural or status differences between them. Tajfel's 'minimal group paradigm' (1973) is even more disturbing, as it shows how the mere grouping of individuals on the basis of arbitrary category differences is sufficient to produce group behavior. Group loyalty and a preference for group members are common effects of arbitrary categorization, as is the tendency to exaggerate the similarities with the in-group and the differences with the out-group. Note that these effects occur in situations in which subjects know almost nothing about the other group members, apart from the fact that they all share a common group membership. For example, one may just know that one's group is made of "overestimators of dots" as opposed to another group of "underestimators of dots" (after having quickly judged how many dots there are on a wall screen).[13]

Precisely when there is only limited personal information on other subjects, categorization alone can generate impersonal attraction (or preference) for the other group members, as well as a sense of cohesion. This is a particularly interesting observation, because it has been commonly assumed that group cohesiveness is linked to the degree of personal attraction among group members, as well as to how well the group satisfies individual needs. According to Tajfel's theory, group behavior is ultimately induced by a cognitive effect. The moment we think of ourselves as members of a group, however randomly determined, our perceptions and motives change. We start perceiving ourselves and our fellow group members along impersonal, 'typical' dimensions that characterize the group to which we belong. The generic attraction felt for in-group members is precisely this sense of being similar in those dimensions that make us a group and not an unrelated set of individuals. In

---

[13] There are several possible explanations for in-group bias. Tajfel et al. (1971) originally proposed a generic social norm of group behavior, according to which people should treat in-group members more favorably than out-group members. Later, however, he favored a different explanation based on social identity (Tajfel 1982). He assumed that, because people are motivated to maintain a positive social identity, they tend to make their social group positively distinct from other groups. As I discussed in Chapter 3, experiments conducted by Yamagishi et al. (1999) lend support to a different explanation: In-group favoritism is based on the expectation that favors made to in-group members are more likely to be reciprocated than favors made to out-group members. Expectations of generalized reciprocity seem to be based on a 'generic norm' of group behavior. Such a norm is, in turn, sustained by in-group favoritism.

well-established ethnic, gender, or professional-based groups, there will
be a shared understanding of what the similar traits are. But it is remarkable that even in newly formed and anonymous groups subjects tend to
believe that in-group members are more similar to them than out-group
members along a series of broad traits, in the absence of any evidence
supporting this assumption. If no well-established similarities are accessible, some similarity will nevertheless be presumed. Generic attraction,
again, is brought forth by perceived or presumed similarity, and the latter seems to be a consequence of group formation rather than its cause.
When more personal information is available, however, for example due
to a longer period of interaction, attraction becomes less impersonal and
group behavior is less likely to occur.

Negative and positive stereotyping is the result of our quick, almost
unconscious mental habits of categorizing people and groups. A stereotype is nothing but the prototypical descripton of what members of a
given category are (or are believed to be). It is a cluster of physical, mental, and psychological characteristics attributed to a 'typical' member of
a given group. Stereotyping, like any other categorization process, activates scripts or schemata, and what we call group behavior is nothing
but scripted behavior. For example, interpreting a situation as "we" versus "them," as frequently occurs even in the minimal group paradigm
studied by Tajfel, may activate interactive scripts that contain norms
such as "take care of one's own," which could explain the preferential
treatment accorded to in-group members.[14] In one-shot Social Dilemma
experiments, where exposure to one's or another group is minimal, we
should observe uncontaminated, basic group behavior such as loyalty and
cooperation with one's group and mistrust and hostility toward the out-
group. Indeed, in "two groups social dilemmas" (Bornstein 1992) subjects
tended to support their own group, to the detriment of the other group
and ultimately of themselves.

In the taped discussions of the experiments by Orbell et al. (1991),
when subjects were discussing with members of their group, and in situations in which in-groups benefited from their own decisions, commitments to cooperate with the in-group were frequently made. This choice
was often seen as a gamble. Discussion probably decreased the perceived
risk of a monetary loss, and this did not happen just because one was able
to assess the trustworthiness of other members by looking at their facial
expressions and body language. An important reason why cooperation

[14] Cf. Hertel and Kerr (2001).

was perceived as less risky was the exchange of pledges and commitments that took place during the discussion. Such commitments are, in
economic parlance, just "cheap talk." In a one-shot interaction, given
the assurance of anonymity, the temptation to defect is strong. In the
absence of a binding mechanism, it may be to one's advantage to make
a public pledge to cooperate, but then defect in private. Commitments
and promises to the in-group, however, were generally trusted. Is this an
effect of categorization alone, or is it mediated by some implicit normative implication produced by categorization? We must not think of an
experiment as an isolated, unique situation. Many times, in the course
of our lives, we have made promises to people we know, to members of
one group or another to which we belong. We usually keep our promises,
and we expect others to keep theirs. The experimental circumstances
are similar, in several respects, to many real-life situations subjects have
experienced.[15] Categorizing a situation as 'we' versus 'them' is bound
to activate well-rehearsed scripts about in-group loyalty and trust. If, as I
claim, norms are embedded into scripts, the categorization process will
lead one to think that one 'ought to' trust in-group members and, if
promises are made, trust that they will be kept.

Precisely because they do not know the other group members well, and
have only limited exposure to them, subjects are free to categorize their
interaction as typical. In a typical group interaction, one would trust and
cooperate with members of one's own group. The default presumption is
that they will not cheat on us, that they will be nice and helpful. This may
be the reason why betrayal by an acquaintance is much more devastating
than betrayal by a stranger. We do not expect the first to occur. Thaler
(1992) noted that well-established groups are often less cooperative than
newly formed ones. If group identity were the ultimate cause of cooperation, we would expect much higher rates of cooperation in established
groups. What may happen instead is that, after an initial period in which
a newly formed group adopts cooperative norms by default, "deviant"
behavior may lead members to reconsider the context of interaction and
their understanding of the situation, and possibly reach the conclusion
that the dominant behavior is defection. Similarly, in repeated Social
Dilemma trials with no communication, it has been observed that cooperation rates are high in the initial periods and then steadily decline over
trials. This pattern is probably due to the fact that subjects are initially
uncertain as to what constitutes appropriate behavior. Hence they rely

[15] A similar argument is made by Hertel and Kerr (2001) in their study of how social norms
that favor the in-group are primed in the right circumstances.

on default social norms they deem appropriate to the situation. If, as trials continue, some group members defect, cooperators will revise their expectations and start defecting, too.

Another belief shared by many subjects was that cooperating with the in-group was not that risky.[16] When *all* group members committed to cooperate, some subjects held the belief that at least half of them would keep their word. In this case, a cooperator would not lose her money. Many were even more optimistic, and voiced the belief that more than half of those promising to cooperate would keep their word. Notice that the subjects did not naively expect everyone to keep their promise; rather, they realistically expected *most* people to keep their commitments most of the time. The subjects were focused on a shared norm of promise-keeping, and unanimous promising was likely encouraging them to believe that enough other people were keeping their promises, making it worthwhile to follow the norm.[17] Unanimity therefore should not be interpreted as fostering the expectation of universal compliance, nor as an indication that everybody "buys into the cooperative solution," thereby creating an obligation on the part of the promisor.[18] Note that unanimous promising also signals that there is a consensus on the appropriateness of cooperation, and that the group is highly cohesive in its judgment. This high cohesiveness might in itself be sufficient to create strong conformity pressures.

Creating Identities

When it is suggested that solutions to social dilemmas may be facilitated by exploiting the solidarity and bonding arising from a shared group identity (Brewer 1979), a big open question remains to be answered: How can we arouse group identification in such a way that group interest is promoted? For the proponents of the social identity explanation, inducing a salient group identity will cause a blurring of the boundaries between personal and group welfare, a change in preferences and perception that is ultimately responsible for the increased rate of cooperation we witness after discussion of the dilemma. It is therefore important to know what makes

[16] I am referring here to the systematic analysis of the taped discussions done by my student Colleen Baker (cf. footnote 11).
[17] Indeed, my definition of social norm says that a subject will follow a norm provided she expects a sufficiently high number of people to follow it, and expect her to follow it, in the relevant circumstances. Of course, what 'sufficiently high' means differs for different people.
[18] Orbell et al. (1991, p. 121).

group identity salient not just in an experimental context, but especially in the large, anonymous groups that are a common setting for social dilemmas.

There are some minimal conditions for a collection of individuals to constitute a psychological group – a state of affairs where they feel to be a group and act as one. A prominent traditional theory defines a psychological group as a collection of individuals characterized by mutual attraction, reflecting the members' interdependence and mutual need satisfaction. This definition is severely limited, though, because it applies only to small groups, whereas some of our most important group memberships refer to large-scale social affiliations such as nationality, gender, race, religion, and so on. Members of a nation are not usually united around a single common goal; they interact only with small subsets of people and not always amicably, and they obey different norms, depending on the organizations and subcultures to which they belong. National membership is not usually chosen – we are born into it – and the moments in which we are most likely to feel psychological membership are not ones in which our individual needs are satisfied. Indeed, our loyalty to our nation may be fiercest in circumstances, such as a war, that require sacrifice and deprivation. Similarly, the fact that some groups of people are treated in a homogeneous way by others due to the color of their skin, religious background, or otherwise may give them a sense that they belong to a group, even if the grouping is not the result of their choice and membership into the group may involve discrimination and abuse by the rest of society. It is often reported that during the Nazi period, many German Jews felt for the first time an identification with their fellow Jews. They had been completely integrated and considered themselves to be Germans first and foremost, but finding themselves associated with other European Jews in a common fate gave them, for the first time, a sense of their separate identity.

It is the realization that there can be psychological group membership without interdependence, need satisfaction, personal attraction, social structure, or common norms and values that led Tajfel, and later Turner and Brewer, to design experiments in the context of the minimal group paradigm. In these experiments, people were divided into distinct groups on the basis of meaningless criteria (such as estimation of the number of dots on a screen), group membership was anonymous, and there were no group goals or any apparent link between group membership and self-interest. I discussed some of these experiments in Chapter 3, observing how a default expectation of generalized reciprocity leads individuals to systematically discriminate in favor of in-group and against out-group members. The data collected by Tajfel and his colleagues imply that group behavior and group membership can exist in the absence of any social contact, social structure, or interdependence between members. It was concluded that the minimal (sufficient) condition for psychological group formation is the recognition and acceptance of some self-defining social categorization. Social interaction, common fate, proximity, similarity, common goals, or shared threats are not necessary for group formation, even if they usually increase the cohesiveness of an existing group. It is an open question whether they can be sufficient conditions for group formation, in the absence of an explicit categorization of people into groups. Presumably the answer will lie in assessing how efficiently and under which conditions such variables function as cues to the formation of social categorizations.

Group behavior, as opposed to individual behavior, is characterized by distinctive features such as perceived similarity between group members, cohesiveness, the tendency to cooperate to achieve common goals, shared attitudes and beliefs, and conformity to group norms. If social categorization is sufficient for group formation, by which mechanisms does it produce group behavior? According to Turner's (1987) 'self-categorization theory,' group behavior depends on the effects of social categorization on the definition and perception of the self. Self-perception, or self-definition, is defined as a system of cognitive self-schemata that filter and process information and output a representation of the social situation that guides the choice of appropriate behavior. This system has at least two major components, social and personal identity. Social identity refers to self-descriptions related to group memberships. Personal identity refers to more personal self-descriptions, such as individual character traits, abilities, and tastes.

Though personal and social identity are mutually exclusive levels of self-definition, this distinction must be taken as an approximation. There are many interconnections between social and personal identity, and even personal identity has a social component. It is, however, important to recognize that sometimes we perceive ourselves primarily in terms of our relevant group memberships rather than as differentiated, unique individuals. Depending on the situation, personal or group identity will become salient.[19] For example, when one makes interpersonal comparisons between self and other group members, personal identity will become salient, whereas group identity will be salient in situations in

---

[19] Brewer (1991) has developed a theory of "optimal distinctiveness" to explain under which conditions we make personal (or social) identity relevant.

which one's group is compared to another group. Within a group, all those factors that lead members to categorize themselves as different and endowed with special characteristics and traits are enhancing personal identity. If a group is solving a common task, but each member will be rewarded according to his contribution, personal abilities are highlighted and individuals will perceive themselves as unique and different from the rest of the group. Conversely, if the reward for a jointly performed task is shared equally by all group members, group identification is going to be enhanced. When the difference between self and fellow group members is accentuated, we are likely to observe selfish motives and self-favoritism against other group members. When instead group identification is enhanced, in-group favoritism against out-group members will be activated, as well as behavior contrary to self-interest.

According to Turner, social identity is basically a cognitive mechanism whose adaptive function is to make group behavior possible. Whenever social identification becomes salient, a cognitive mechanism of categorization is activated that produces perceptual and behavioral changes. For example, the category "Asian student" is associated with a cluster of behaviors, personality traits, and values. We often think of Asian students as respectful, diligent, disciplined, and especially good with technical subjects. When thinking of an Asian student solely in terms of her group membership, we attribute her the stereotypical characteristics associated with her group, so she becomes interchangeable with other group members. When we perceive people in terms of stereotypes, we depersonalize them and see them as 'typical' members of their group. The same process is at work when we perceive ourselves as group members. Self-stereotyping is a cognitive shift from perceiving oneself as unique and differentiated to perceiving oneself in terms of the attributes that characterize the group. It is this cognitive shift that mediates group behavior.

The feature of group behavior most relevant to Social Dilemma experiments is the tendency to cooperate with the in-group even when such behavior is contrary to self-interest. Through common group membership, individuals share the same self-stereotypes and perceive themselves as 'depersonalized' and similar to other group members in the stereotypical dimensions linked to the relevant social categorization. Insofar as group members perceive their interests and goals as identical – because such interests and goals are stereotypical attributes of the group – self-stereotyping will induce a group member to embrace such interests and goals as his own, and act to further them. The dark side of this process is the shared perception of group members that their interests are in conflict with those of other groups or of unaffiliated individuals. A prediction of social identity theory is thus that the more salient group membership becomes, the greater will be the tendency to display cooperative behavior toward the in-group and discrimination against out-groups.

How can group identification be aroused in social dilemmas in such a way that cooperation is promoted? In a multi-trial commons dilemma, Kramer and Brewer (1984) showed that subgroup categorization of a six-person group decreased cooperation when compared with a condition in which the group was not subdivided.[20] Kramer and Brewer interpreted the result as an instance of in-group favoritism and in-group/out-group competition: The defectors in the subgroup categorization condition wanted to gain as much as possible for their own subgroup in comparison with the other subgroup. However, if we examine the payoff structure, it appears that the benefits of defection accrued only to the individual, not the subgroup, whereas the costs of defecting were spread out over the whole group. The choice was thus either to serve one's private interest (to defect) or to serve the interest of the whole six-person group (to cooperate). There was no possibility to differentially benefit one's own subgroup. Also, from the additional results of a questionnaire that was filled out after the experiment, it appears that categorization manipulation did not affect the subjects' perceptions of their fellow subgroup members and of the members of the other subgroup, contrary to the prediction of social identity theory. However, because the subjects received feedback about the other group members' choices after each trial, they may have used this information in their post-trial perception ratings of the other group members, thus mitigating the effects of the induced categorization.

In a subsequent series of experiments, Brewer and Kramer (1986) showed that when the subgroup identity was made salient, and subjects received feedback suggesting the existence of a descriptive group norm (the group could be made of "high users," who took large amounts of common resources, or "low users," who took small amounts), they tended to follow the group norm. When instead a collective identity was made

[20] The experimenters manipulated the salience of the collective or subgroup identity. In some conditions the subjects were told the experimenters were interested in the choices of psychology students vs. economics students, who were the remotely located members of the collective group. Such instructions aimed to elicit a subgroup identity. In other conditions, the experimenters told the students that they were interested in the decisions of students at their particular university vs. students at other universities, to elicit a collective group identity.

salient, and it was clear that resources were rapidly dwindling, individuals belonging to groups of "high users" restrained themselves most. It is not clear, however, that this behavior results from group identification. Subsequent analysis of subjects' expectations of other group members' behavior revealed no effect of categorization, nor was an in-group bias apparent from the data. The abandonment of the "high use" subgroup norm in the superordinate identity condition may be due to a perceived conflict between a descriptive subgroup norm and an opposite social norm prescribing restraint. The superordinate identity could have made the social norm salient, and we know from the work of Cialdini et al. (1990) that when there is a conflict between these two kinds of norms, and the social norm is made salient, people tend to follow the latter. The identity manipulation in this case would have mediated the effect of a cooperative social norm (mandating restraint) through the cognitive salience of group membership.

In a typical Social Dilemma experiment, there is no imposed or suggested categorization on the part of the experimenter. Subjects do not know each other and, in one-shot experiments, do not expect to play or meet again. The minimal group paradigm was successful in producing group behavior because it created an explicit in-group/out-group categorization that, even in the absence of conflicting interests, induced in-group favoritism. In a typical social dilemma, however, the choice is between favoring oneself and favoring the group. We know that the mere realization that universal cooperation is in the group's interest does not induce cooperative behavior, but the social identity hypothesis predicts that making group membership salient will induce a cooperative orientation. Common fate, perceived similarities, and verbal interactions, among other things, should contribute to the process of perceptual group formation, inducing people to categorize themselves as part of a more inclusive unit. We would then expect a period of discussion, especially on a theme close to the subjects' lives, to engender cooperative behavior, as would the experience of sharing a common fate. From the viewpoint of creating group identity, there is no reason to expect discussion of the dilemma to be more effective than any other discussion of a relevant topic, or the experience of a common fate.

Keeping Promises

There are now a handful of experiments aimed at directly testing the group identity hypothesis in social dilemmas. None of them explicitly considers the possibility that social norms are responsible for the increase in cooperation rates observed after a period of discussion of the dilemma, though the data can be interpreted as supporting a norm-based explanation. Because the behavioral effects of group identity might be indistinguishable from the effects of other variables, such as perceived consensus or commitment, these studies introduced an independent measurement of group identity, defined as a sense of belonging or a feeling of membership in a group.

Kerr and Kaufman-Gilliland (1994) used *self-efficacy* as a variable to differentiate between group identity and commitment explanations of the effect of communication on cooperation rates. They proposed a distinction between cooperation-contingent remedies and public good remedies. The former increase the value one puts on the cooperative choice; they include side payments, sanctions, and feelings like pride and guilt. The latter increase the value one puts on the group's welfare, and they include altruism and enhanced group identity. They reasoned that if cooperation was motivated by a public good remedy, then as the efficacy of one's contribution declines, it becomes less likely that one cooperates. Stay the group identity explanation of the effects of discussion assumes that communication works by increasing the value one puts on group welfare, discussion is a public good remedy. Hence, whenever it is evident that one's action is less efficacious, discussion should not be expected to matter much to one's choice. An explanation based on commitments instead assumes that discussion increases the value of the committed choice itself. Hence efficacy of one's action should not matter: Committed subjects would cooperate no matter what.

The experiment consisted of groups of five subjects playing an "investment game." Each player was given $10 and an allocation of points. In each play, 100 points were randomly assigned among the five players. Each player only knew her share; but the larger one's share, the more effective one's choice would be in providing for the public good. If choosing to give, a player would donate $10 plus her allocated points. If 51 or more points were contributed to a step-level public good, then each group member would obtain $15. The game was to be played 16 times, and half of the subjects were allowed a period of discussion before making their (anonymous) choices.[21] The discussion effect was replicated, with

[21] The experiment also tested anonymity conditions, showing that anonymity has no effect on the behavior of subjects. A later study by Kerr et al. (1997) extended the anonymity condition to the experimenters and also found it not to be a significant factor.

74.2% cooperation in groups that discussed and only 56.8% cooperation in groups in which no discussion was allowed. Cooperation, however, was stable across levels of efficacy, suggesting that the perception of personal significance in providing for the public good was not an important factor in the choice to contribute. As in other experiments, group discussion contained frequent promises to cooperate, and groups varied in the agreements they reached. Some groups achieved unanimous promising, and in those groups cooperation rates were highest and the minimal efficacy level at which subjects were willing to cooperate was lower than in other groups. Some groups agreed to conditionally cooperate depending on each subject's level of efficacy, and other groups decided instead that each individual would make his or her own independent choice.

Different groups thus seemed to develop their own norms, such as "contribute only if you have a reasonable share" or "contribute no matter what." Yet there was no apparent difference in the respective levels of perceived group identity, as measured by the Hinkle et al. (1989) Group Identity Scale. The conclusion drawn by the experimenters is that group identity is not a good explanation of discussion-induced cooperation. Commitments, and the norm of promise-keeping that supports them, are the most likely candidates. I must hasten to add that, though I sympathize with the conclusions, I find them too swift. The assumption that group identity entails the desire to enhance group welfare overlooks the possibility that many actions we take also have a "symbolic" value. In some of Tajfel's experiments with allocations, if given the choice, subjects tended to maximize the difference between in-groups and out-groups, and in so doing were ready to sacrifice their own group's welfare. For example, between an equal allocation of $10 to a member of each group and an allocation of $6 to a member of one's own group and $2 to an out-group member, many subjects would choose the second. It is a choice that penalizes both groups but hurts the out-group more. If actions have a symbolic value for the actor, she might perform them irrespective of their efficacy or contribution to in-group welfare.

A better way to test the group identity hypothesis is to check whether several presumably equivalent ways to create or enhance group identity produce the same results in terms of cooperation. The group identity explanation predicts that *any* manipulation arousing group identity will be sufficient to induce cooperation. Bouas and Komorita (1996) ran a series of experiments to test whether discussion or common fate would have an effect on cooperation rates. If discussion of the dilemma has an effect on cooperation, but discussion of an irrelevant topic has no effect (Dawes et al. 1977), we cannot rule out the group identity

TABLE 4.4. *Group identity prediction*

	Common fate	No common fate
Control condition	–	Defect
No discussion	Cooperate	Defect
Discussion of relevant topic	Cooperate	Cooperate
Discussion of dilemma	Cooperate	Cooperate

TABLE 4.5. *Perceived consensus prediction*

	Common fate	No common fate
Control condition	–	Defect
No discussion	Defect	Defect
Discussion of relevant topic	Defect	Defect
Discussion of dilemma	Cooperate	Cooperate

explanation, because an insignificant discussion topic may not be sufficient to elicit group identity. Discussing a relevant issue, such as an increase in students' tuition when the experimental subjects are college students, should instead create a bond among them, as this topic touches their lives and they can sympathize with each other's concerns. Another way to induce group identity is common fate. Common fate may not involve a common objective or shared needs. It may simply mean that certain categories of people are treated in a homogeneous manner by others on the basis of their sex, color of skin, language, and many other attributes. And it may be as tenuous as participating in a lottery that will determine the monetary worth of the points owned by each subject. Though participating in a common lottery does not strike me as a strong inducement to social identity formation, there is some evidence about its effects on cooperation rates (Kramer and Brewer 1984, 1986).

The alternative explanation of discussion-induced cooperation that Bouas and Komorita favor is not one based on norms. In their view, discussion has an effect because it creates consensus and consequently reduces risk and fosters the expectation that other group members will cooperate. Because the only discussion that can create a meaningful consensus is a discussion about the dilemma, the perceived consensus explanation predicts that only discussions of the dilemma will increase cooperation rates. To compare the different predictions generated by the social identity and the perceived consensus explanations, it is helpful to compare Tables 4.4 and 4.5.

TABLE 4.6.

	Control	Common fate	Discussion	Discussion of dilemma
Mean cooperation	.13	.13	.17	.81
Group identity[22]	5.1	5.1	6.1	6.3
Consensus perception	2.25	2.40	5.45	6.65
Expected cooperation	1.05	1.20	1.25	2.47

Bouas and Komorita's experiment consisted of groups of four subjects facing a typical social dilemma and had four conditions: a control condition in which there was no discussion or common fate manipulation; a second condition in which the subjects were allowed to discuss a relevant issue and were then exposed to a common fate manipulation; a third condition in which the dilemma was discussed and a common fate was present; and, finally, a common fate condition in which no discussion was allowed. The common fate manipulation meant that the subjects' payoffs were determined by a lottery. In this experiment, too, group identity was independently measured through Hinkle et al.'s Group Identity Scale, after the decisions were taken. Consensus perception and expectations of the group members' cooperation were also independently measured. The results are reported in Table 4.6.

Whereas 81% of the subjects involved in discussion of the dilemma and common fate cooperated, only 17% did so after discussing a relevant issue (an increase in tuition), and common fate manipulation alone did not even raise cooperation rates above the baseline. Group identity, however, was higher in both discussion conditions, while common fate had no effect on group identity. What seemed to matter was perceived consensus, which was highest under discussion of the dilemma but was also quite high in the relevant discussion condition. These results led Bouas and Komorita to reject the group identity explanation.

A few comments on common fate and the effect of perceived consensus are in order. Common fate is introduced here as a chance event (a lottery). As such, it has no effect on cooperation rates. However, Kramer and Brewer (1984) claimed that common fate induces group identity when such an identity is superimposed on a preexisting subgroup identity. In

---

[22.] Social identity and perceived consensus were measured on a nine-point scale. Expectation of cooperation refers to the number of others (zero to three) expected to cooperate.

this case, they show that common fate is in fact salient. If there is no prior group identity, perhaps the notion of common fate has to be strengthened to do its job. For example, it would be interesting to see what happens if common fate were to entail interdependence among the parties, as when subjects are involved in a common task, however briefly, before the Social Dilemma experiment proper.

Perceived consensus increased after discussing the dilemma, but it was also high when another relevant topic was discussed. Note that consensus is weaker than universal promising, in that it does not require unanimous agreement and does not elicit normative expectations. Bouas and Komorita (1996) argue that perceived consensus is what causes greater expectations of cooperative behavior; hence it presumably lowers the risk of losing money. However, because discussion of the dilemma often entails promises to cooperate, we cannot rule out as an explanation of risk reduction the expectation that others will keep their commitments because of a shared norm of promise-keeping. If norms were responsible for the increase in cooperation rates we observe after a period of discussion of the dilemma, the prediction of a norm-based explanation would be like the one in Table 4.5. Because this prediction is fulfilled, we cannot exclude that it is norms, and not just perceived consensus, that cause higher cooperation rates. Moreover, perceived consensus in not in conflict with a norm-based explanation. Discussion of the dilemma, with the intervening exchange of promises and pledges, can trigger both an empirical expectation (most people keep their word, hence most people will contribute) and a normative expectation (I am expected to contribute, because others expect me to keep my word). What is perceived is that the group reached a consensus on what the appropriate course of action should be. Reaching a consensus on, say, how unfair an increase in university tuition is does not increase cooperation rates. I want to add that consensus, in my view, may only be useful in generating empirical expectations about 'common' behavior, but would not be sufficient to engender normative expectations. Suppose a group of people were to discuss whether cooperation is better than defection in a public goods dilemma and agree that cooperation is better, or even that cooperation is the most frequent behavior. However, if no pledges or promises are exchanged, it is difficult to imagine how individuals would come to expect other group members to be cooperative, or even come to believe that others expect them to cooperate. In this case, people would be focused on a descriptive norm ("most people cooperate"), but there would be little incentive to follow it, and expecting others to cooperate might have the opposite effect of tempting an individual to defect.[23] If instead promising is allowed, group members may not only agree on a course of action, but they may actively promise each other to follow it. The promise indicates a willingness to perform a potentially costly action, a commitment to forego narrow self-interest in favor of a collective gain. Individuals are now focused on a social norm. But for promise-keeping to be effective, we know that it must be supported by the expectation that enough people are going to keep their promises. Bouas and Komorita (1996) do not tell us how many people promised, but, because consensus and expectations were pretty high, I suspect promising was widespread. In conclusion, if consensus alone is not sufficient to motivate giving to the group, it must be that the norms activated during discussion are responsible for the perception of reduced risk that accompanies the expectation of cooperative behavior on the part of other group members.

Talking to Machines

Sometimes support for a hypothesis is found in unexpected places. The norm-based explanation I favor says that norms are like default rules that are triggered in the right circumstances but not otherwise. Because this process is largely unconscious, we do not expect individuals to be very discriminating or strategically oriented in their norm-following behavior.[24] Whenever a norm is made salient by the situation one is in, the first reaction is to follow the norm, unless something unexpected occurs that forces reconsideration and possibly reinterpretation of the situation. The field of human–computer interaction is particularly interesting in this respect because it studies, among other things, the reactions people have to various kinds of computer interfaces and the rules, if any, that people adopt in interacting with computers.

Kiesler, Sproull, and Waters (1996) examined human–computer interaction in a Social Dilemma experiment. Subjects were presented with an "investment game" that was in fact a common Prisoner's Dilemma in which the choice to cooperate was dubbed "project green" and the

---

[23] Cooperation becomes a social norm when there are both empirical and normative expectations that support it. In the case of discussion without commitment, normative expectations would typically be absent.

[24] Cf. Chapter 1.

choice to defect was dubbed "project blue," to devoid choices of any evaluative undertone. Subjects played six rounds against one of the following
types of partners: a human confederate, a computer that communicated
through written text, a computer that communicated with speech, and a
computer that communicated with a synthesized face and speech. Subjects knew whether the partner was a human or a computer.

The partner used the same strategy across conditions:

Round 1: The partner asks the subject to make a proposal and then
cooperates.

Round 2: The partner proposes cooperation and then cooperates.

Round 3: There is no discussion and the partner cooperates.

Round 4: The partner asks the subject to make a proposal and then
defects.

Round 5: The partner proposes cooperation and then cooperates.

Round 6: There is no discussion and the partner defects.

After each round, the choices of the players were revealed.

The results are surprising, because they show that discussion and commitment have a strong effect on cooperation, regardless of the nature of
the discussion partner.[25] In the first round, 80% of the subjects proposed
cooperation to the human confederate, and 94% of them kept their commitment. In the same round, 59% of the subjects proposed cooperation
to the computer, and 62% of them kept their commitment. Cooperation
was consistently high in rounds 1, 2, 4, and 5, that is, when there was
discussion with the partner. Even in round 5, after observing a defection in the preceding round, the subjects were willing to cooperate with
a partner who proposed cooperation. Evidently they trusted their partner's willingness to cooperate despite their previous experience, and this
occurred even if the partner was a computer. In this case, discussion had
the effect of discounting previous defection. In rounds 3 and 6, there was
a sharp drop in cooperation under all conditions; these were the rounds
in which there was no communication, and hence no commitment to
cooperate.

If group identity were elicited through discussion, we would have not
observed a drop in cooperation in round 3, because previous discussions
and commitments to cooperate should have carried over to this round.

---

[25] It is possible that people expect a computer to be programmed to follow simple social
norms or rules like keeping one's commitments.

At the very least, we should not have observed a drop in cooperation with the human confederate, as identification with a computer may be harder than with another human being. The results offer a strong support for the hypothesis that discussion enhances cooperation rates because of its content: promises to cooperate are made and subsequently kept. Less individuals propose cooperation to the computer than to a human partner, but of those who do, most fulfill their pledge. These individuals seem to be adopting the same social rules to interact with computers as they do with other human beings, which lends credibility to the hypothesis that we are witnessing the operation of default social norms. If commitments are pledges to behave in accordance with the object of the commitment, regardless to whom the commitment is made, we can easily explain the former results. When a powerful norm of promise-keeping is activated, most individuals will obey it, whether the promisee is another person or a machine.

Cognitive Misers

To explain what happens in an experimental situation, and to assess the accuracy of the general conclusions we draw about behavior in social dilemmas, it helps to briefly summarize the cognitive processes (described in Chapter 2) that result in a cooperative choice on the part of so many subjects. The methods we use to make inferences are far from ideal. Social inference is heavily schema-driven, we disregard regression effects and base-rate information, and we are prone to perceive illusory correlations. We store information in long-term memory and retrieve scripts/schemata to interpret and understand our environment, as well as to make inferences and explain and predict others' behavior. Such schemata, as discussed in Chapter 2, are cognitive structures that represent knowledge about people, events, and the self. Most of the time, they work reasonably well, though they bias all aspects of information processing and inference toward conservative, schema-confirming inferential practices. To apply schematic knowledge, one first needs to be able to categorize the person or situation one encounters as fitting a particular schema/script.

When confronting a new experimental setup, an individual will first search for cues to categorize, and thus interpret, the present situation as an instance of a well-known schema or script. The fact that the experimental situation is strange and unnatural, because choices are typically anonymous and there may be no prospect of future interaction, is overlooked in favor of an interpretation biased toward what we know well and have frequently experienced. When we retrieve a script (or a schema), it comes with expectations attached. Even if we do not have any information about the people we will be interacting with, our script tells us what to expect. For example, we know that in experiments in which subjects are given the choice to opt out, besides cooperating or defecting, cooperators typically decide to play and defectors instead opt out more frequently.[26] This happens because cooperators expect cooperation from their partners and defectors instead expect defection. Frequent cooperators activate a cooperative script, which increases their confidence that they will encounter kindred spirits.

When we have to deal with a new collection of individuals, this collection will be mentally compared to past groupings, and this comparison process will provide us with behavioral cues appropriate to the new situation. Categorizing a social situation as fitting a particular schema/script will typically elicit behavioral roles and norms. In similar, previously experienced contexts we had a role and expectations that we import into the new situation. As I already mentioned, interpreting a situation as "we" versus "them," as frequently occurs even in the minimal group paradigm studied by Tajfel, may activate interactive scripts that contain norms such as "take care of one's own," "be loyal," and "trust your group," which would explain the preferential treatment accorded to in-group members. Similarly, when a subject must choose between keeping the money or giving it to the in-group or the out-group, the way she represents the situation will influence her subsequent choice. Indeed, we know that expecting the out-group to benefit from one's contribution consistently dampens the impulse to give, whereas if it is the in-group that benefits from one's act of giving, there is much more willingness to part with one's money.

Depending on how a situation is interpreted, different scripts and thus different norms will be activated. Because our interpretation and understanding of a situation will depend both on a frame of reference and on past experience, different people may interpret the same situation differently. In Chapter 3 I discussed how ambiguity may lead to self-serving biases in judgments of fairness. In the case of social dilemmas in which discussion of the dilemma is allowed, discussion itself may perform a disambiguating role, shaping individuals' perception of the situation they face and allowing a uniform interpretation of the situation to emerge.

[26] Cf. Orbell and Dawes (1993).

Discussion of the dilemma may thus perform several functions, all of them important in increasing cooperation rates. When people face a new situation, they often turn to each other for cues as to how to interpret it. In this context, the role of a leader is substantial, because she provides an interpretation of the situation, or suggests a schema, that other group members can recognize as both familiar and relevant. Unanimous agreement on appropriate behavior is usually reached only with the help of leaders, who are instrumental in lending salience to a specific descriptive norm (i.e., "what is normally done" in such situations). A 'leader' in this case is simply a person who convincingly argues in favor of interpreting the current situation in a specific way. In the taped discussions we analyzed, leaderless groups were typically groups in which no common agreement emerged, and where subjects' behavior was similar to the behavior of control groups, where no discussion was allowed.

Yet discussion also involves promises, and the act of promising has the effect of focusing people on the social norm of promise-keeping by representing the situation as an instance of situations we have experienced in the past, when we made commitments we usually honored and expected others to do likewise. As I already mentioned, promises will be kept (and thus the norm followed) if subjects believe that a sufficiently high number of other subjects will keep their promises, and also believe that a sufficiently high number of subjects expect them to fulfill their commitment. Unanimous promising generates precisely that expectation, as well as the belief that a sufficient number of subjects expect promises to be kept and strongly disapprove of betrayals.[27]

Note that discussion of the dilemma, when successful, points to several norms at once: a descriptive cooperative norm that might come to be perceived as prescriptive, or "the right thing to do," and a social norm of promise-keeping. Disentangling their respective effects on behavior is very difficult, and we will have to wait for further experiments to provide answers. We already have, however, some scattered evidence hinting at the consequences of making descriptive norms salient in social dilemmas. Schroeder et al. (1983), for example, investigated the effects of observing the behavior of others in simulated social dilemmas. They found that subjects quickly conformed to the behavior of the observed players, regardless of whether it was cooperation or defection. Pillutla and Chen

---

[27] Interestingly, subjects in Orbell et al.'s experiments also exchanged threats, even if it was clear to all that choices would be anonymous and that there would be no chance of recognizing and punishing transgressors.

(1999) found similar results in a study on the effects of context (economic or noneconomic) and feedback on cooperative behavior. Information about the other members' behavior was the sole variable influencing cooperation rates. Similarly, Allison and Kerr (1994) found that individuals behaved consistently with the perceived group norm, which was inferred from information about past group performance. These data are interesting because they contradict some other results that indicate how viewing or listening to other groups' taped pledges to cooperate had no effect on cooperation rates. One wonders whether the positive effect reported in the former studies was due to the fact that subjects observed the behavior of *their own* group members. If so, individuals were conforming to what they perceived as the 'normal' behavior of their group. Unanimous promising may play the same role as observing past behavior, indicating the group's convergence on a behavioral rule. Because conformity to norms is correlated with the perceived cohesiveness of the group (which supports the expectation that *most* individuals will conform), it should come as no surprise that only under unanimous promising do we observe almost universal cooperation.

We may now come back to our original question of whether explaining cooperation in social dilemmas as due to the working of norms is compatible with the social identity hypothesis. As we have seen, there are cases in which group identification and social norms are inextricably connected. Often groups develop their own special norms; in that case, group members believe that certain patterns of behavior are unique to them and use their distinctive norms to *define* group membership. Many close-knit groups, such as the Amish or the Hasidic Jews, enforce norms of separation proscribing marriage and intimate relationships with outsiders, as well as specific dress codes and a host of other prescriptive and proscriptive norms that make the group unique and differentiate it from out-groups. In this case, once an individual perceives herself as a group member, she will adhere to the group prototype and behave in accordance with it. Hogg and Turner (1987) called the process through which individuals come to conform to such group norms *referent informational influence*. Group-specific norms have, among other things, the twofold function of minimizing perceived differences among group members and maximizing differences between the group and outsiders. Once formed, such norms are internalized as cognitive representations of appropriate behavior as a group member. Social identity is built around group characteristics and behavioral standards; hence any perceived lack of conformity to group norms is seen as a threat to the legitimacy of the group.

Self-categorization accentuates the similarities between one's behavior and that prescribed by the group norm, thus causing conformity as well as the disposition to control and punish in-group members who transgress group norms. In this view, group norms are obeyed because one identifies with the group, and conformity is mediated by self-categorization as an in-group member.

Experimental groups, however, have had no time to develop their unique norms, and even if discussion succeeds in eliciting the empirical and normative expectations that support a given norm (such as promise-keeping), one can hardly claim that such a norm is special to the group, make it unique, or differentiate it from other groups. We are thus back to square one: In experimental groups, perceiving oneself as a group member, when such perception is successfully induced, does not guarantee that one will conform to norms that are not group-specific. Eliciting group identity, as is explicitly done in some of the previously discussed experiments, is never sufficient to induce cooperation. It does not hurt, but it may not help. At most, we know that inducing group identification in experimental contexts will generate behavior favoring one's group in situations in which an allocative choice has to be made between in-group and out-group members. To explain the biased allocation results he obtained after having grouped his subjects into different (but meaningless) categories, Tajfel concluded that in minimal groups a generic norm prescribing in-group favoritism is at work (Tajfel 1970). Yamagishi et al. (1999), however, convincingly explained such favoritism as being due to an expectation of 'generalized reciprocity,' an expectation that occurs only in those situations in which group membership is common knowledge. Otherwise, group identification will produce boasting, not favoritism (Jin et al. 1996). It is important to realize that the *group schema* that presumably induces the expectation of generalized reciprocity is being activated in experiments that consist of separate groups, and it may well involve social norms that prescribe cooperation and trust within one's group. In such cases, what one is focused on is a 'we' versus 'them' situation, and trust and greater cooperativeness with the in-group might be enhanced by being constantly reminded of the presence of another group that will presumably have different interests at heart. Yet, as Yamagishi's experimental work made clear, even in an in-group/out-group context, greater trust and cooperation should only be expected in those situations in which there is common knowledge of group membership and thus an expectation that trust or cooperation will be reciprocated by in-group members.

At this point, we may wonder if such group schemata could be primed even in situations in which there is no 'we' versus 'them' but still some form of group identification might be induced. For example, we know from Bouas and Komorita's (1996) experiment that subjects will identify with the group if they are allowed to discuss a topic that matters to them and reach a consensus on it. Discussion should also help in making subjects aware of a shared group membership, a crucial condition, in Yamagishi's view, for expecting reciprocation of whatever pro-social behavior one engages in. Yet we do not observe higher cooperation rates in all circumstances in which group identity is made salient, but only when discussion of the dilemma *and* unanimous promising occur. We may conclude that a norm-based explanation of cooperation, although it recognizes the importance of group identity in making certain group norms salient, cannot rely on group identification as a crucial mechanism for ensuring norm compliance, especially in those cases in which such norms are not specific to the group. We know instead that even without identifying with a group, an individual may get sufficient cues from the environment (signaling that a descriptive and/or social norm is in place) to induce cooperative behavior. Discussion of the dilemma, when it produces a collective agreement as to the appropriate behavior, is sufficient to generate both the empirical and normative expectations that lead conditional cooperators to act on them.

Hobbes may thus have been wrong when saying that "covenants without swords are nothing but words." Covenants are made and kept even in the absence of obvious sanctions. The very act of promising, 'cheap talk' of no consequence, might be enough to induce many of us to behave contrary to narrow self-interest. A social norm has been activated, and, under the right circumstances, we are prepared to follow it.

5

Informational Cascades and Unpopular Norms

Introduction

The discussion of the effects of communication in social dilemmas points to the emergence of a shared understanding of the situation among participants, and their convergence to a common script. Group communication, when successful, generates common beliefs and expectations, which in turn make possible coordinated action. I have previously stressed how the norms that people focus on *influence* their behavior. It is also important to study how norms *form* in the first place. This question is tantamount to asking how certain beliefs originate and how we come to believe that a behavioral regularity exists that applies to certain types of situations Bettenhausen and Murnighan (1985, 1991) were the first to study experimentally norm formation in small groups.[1] In their experiments on the allocation of research money among coalitions, they report that groups rapidly formed norms about resource sharing, but each group displayed a unique character and developed unique norms. Their research provides evidence that norm formation is a step-by-step process. In a newly formed group, all members will initially anchor the current situation to what they perceive are previously experienced situations. Each group member will have a sense of which behavioral scripts may be appropriate to the new situation because they resemble behaviors adopted in similar social contexts. As they interact, group members

---

[1] M. Sherif (1996) studied the emergence of perceptual norms in autokinetic experiments. Though there are similarities between his and Bettenhausen and Murnigham's experiments, the latter were the first to study the formation of pro-social norms in an experimental setting.

trade scripts, and, through discussion, they come to form a shared perspective of what the 'appropriate behavior' is. Once a new, local script has been informally adopted, people will interact according to the script and will even tend to apply the same script to new situations in which they are matched with different group members. When a script is agreed upon, a local norm is formed, and usually attempts to alter the behavior it controls will be met by sanctions. What Bettenhausen and Murnighan's experiments illustrate so well is that, since we are not a *tabula rasa*, every new group norm will be the result of a process of importing and reshaping old scripts to new situations. We look for analogies with past experiences to guide us, and the final outcome of this collective search will be something new that we can still recognize as familiar.

Communication, I hasten to add, does not necessarily result in the formation of a socially beneficial norm. Somebody once told me of an experimental group in which a student had just completed an economics course. He immediately recognized the social dilemma as a version of the Prisoner's Dilemma he had studied and successfully convinced his fellow group members to do the unique rational thing. All group members defected. Through communication, subjects may agree to behavior that is ultimately damaging for the entire group, and such behavior may even persist for a long time. Several factors could contribute to the formation and persistence of 'negative' norms. People may wrongly believe that such norms have a positive effect, or they may lack an understanding of what is in the group's best interest. I want to argue, however, that we may contribute to the emergence and persistence of a norm even when we dislike it and know it to be damaging or inefficient, and we do so in a perfectly rational fashion. I will later argue that lack of communication, or lack of transparent communication, is one of the main reasons why inefficient and unpopular norms arise and persist among rational agents.

If you go back to the existence conditions for social and descriptive norms that I presented in Chapter 1, you will notice that in both cases I said that it must be true that a behavioral rule *R exists* for a certain type of situation, and also that a sufficiently large subset of the relevant population (to which the norm would apply) *knows* that *R* exists and applies to that type of situation. From now on, when I talk of norm formation, I will refer to a situation in which people *do not know whether a behavioral rule R exists* in a certain type of situation, but they expect one to exist and try to find out what it is. This condition is different from one in which someone *learns* about an already existing norm. All of us have experienced situations in which we come into a new environment or a new culture and try to understand what the standing norms are. Either someone teaches us, or we learn by trial and error. The subjective experiences of learning about an already existing norm versus trying to find out if a behavioral rule exists and what it is can be similar, but the outcome is quite different. In the latter case, those who look for a regularity may unknowingly contribute to its creation, and the outcome may turn out to be one they would have not wanted if they had a choice.

The case I want to explore is also different from one in which people learn to coordinate with each other and eventually settle on a particular equilibrium, a descriptive norm in my own language.[2] It is distinct as well from a situation in which individuals repeatedly interact for a sufficiently long time and learn, say, to cooperate with each other. If adequate monitoring and sanctions are present, such a cooperative equilibrium will become a social norm.[3] Though the games are very different, in both cases there are multiple equilibria and a story has to be told about how the players settle into one, or how their beliefs about each other's actions come to be correct. In our simple game-theoretic representations, we start by assuming that agents know each other's preferences or, if they have incomplete information, that they at least know each other's possible types. I do not want to suggest that such models are not useful in describing how some equilibria come about. In real life, however, most of the time we cannot possibly know all the potential types of players we are facing, and we have to guess their aims and preferences from observation or verbal communication that may be anything but sincere. Our lives are rife with enduring informational asymmetries.

The case of interest here is one in which several people approach a new situation believing that a behavioral rule exists, but they *do not know* what it is. In fact, no such rule exists, but in the process of searching for one people do form beliefs that induce them to behave as if such regularity existed, thus generating it and, with it, all the intervening expectations and preferences that make it a norm. Because the process of norm formation is essentially a process of belief formation (of the beliefs that support the norm's existence), at least at the micro-level at which I am analyzing it in this chapter, I shall focus upon one of the most challenging questions such a process presents us with: How can our beliefs create a reality none of us designed or desired? Part of the answer, as we shall see, is that our

[2] Vanderschraaf and Skyrms (1994).
[3] Cf. Bicchieri (1990).

wishes to coordinate with others, to be approved by them, or at least not to be disliked and scorned, direct us to observe how others behave and reach conclusions as to their values and preferences. Such conclusions, however, might be wrong. If other people's preferences matter to us, we may be influenced to choose actions that nobody likes. To use the jargon of game theory, I will be depicting situations in which people do not know whether there are different types of agents or what their preferences are, and they have to act on inferences (about others' preferences and/or beliefs) they draw from observed behavior. The story I am going to tell is a vivid example of how we can produce our social reality, where our creation may turn out felicitous or nightmarish, depending (among other things) on whether we can openly communicate with each other and, when we communicate, whether we are free to express our true beliefs and preferences.

A related question is why an unpopular norm, once emerged, may survive. Norms of discrimination against minorities, norms of revenge that are still alive in some Mediterranean countries, widespread corruption and bribery of public officials, juvenile gangs' violent behavior, and binge eating among adolescents are all examples of unpopular and inefficient norms that often persist in spite of their being disliked, as well as being obviously inefficient from a social or economic perspective. From a functionalist viewpoint, such norms are anomalous, because they do not seem to fulfill any beneficial role for society at large or even for the social groups involved in sustaining the norm. In many cases it would be possible to gain in efficiency by eliminating, say, norms of racial discrimination, in that it would be possible to increase the well-being of a racial minority without harming the rest of society. To social scientists who equate persistence with efficiency, the permanence of inefficient norms thus presents an anomaly. They rest their case on two claims: When a norm is inefficient, sooner or later this fact will become evident. And evidence of inefficiency will induce quick changes in the individual choices that sustain the norm. That is, no opportunity for social improvement remains unexploited for long. Unfortunately, all too often this is not true, and this is not because people mistakenly believe inefficient norms to be good or efficient.

Should we hasten to conclude that individuals are making irrational choices? Is the businessman who freely decides to bribe a public officer though he condemns the practice plainly irrational? Evidence gathered through several prosecutions associated with the Italian "Bribesville" scandal shows that often the parties involved in corrupt deals were not endorsing the norms they nevertheless obeyed (Bicchieri and Rovelli

1995). Similarly, interviews with gang members (Matza 1964) revealed little sympathy for the level of violence mandated by gang membership, and studies about the attitudes of prison guards (Klofas and Toch 1982) show that they systematically overestimate collective support for the 'tough' behaviors they feel compelled to display. Such individuals seem to be rational at least in the minimal sense of taking those actions that they believe best fulfill their goals. If they conform to a norm they dislike, there must be some good reason.

What is common to the gang member, the prison guard, and the briber is that they all engage in *social comparison.* If you think about that, observing other people's behavior can provide us with a host of valuable information: We may get clues as to what it is appropriate to do in a given setting, get help in interpreting a new or ambiguous situation, obtain valuable information about our environment, and, finally, we may get information about other people's preferences and attitudes. The case of social comparison I am interested in is one in which individual choices are influenced by the preferences of others, but the true distribution of preferences is not known and must be inferred from observation. If the behavior that an individual observes does not reflect the true preferences of society (or any other relevant reference group), he may be influenced to choose an action that is dispreferred both by himself and by his group (or by society at large). In the youth gang example, each gang member believes that others confer greater social status on those who display violent behavior, and the evidence that sustains this belief is the prevalence and endorsement of violent behavior. No one considers the possibility that everyone else behaves violently not because they personally think violent acts are cool, but because they think others think that violence is cool. *The social pressure to conform, however, might be more imagined than real.* When the imagined social pressure is acted on, public behavior provides further evidence of the validity of the false beliefs, and each act of violence corroborates the general belief that the group endorses and supports norms of violence. If the gang member wants to be accepted and praised by his group, he will choose an action that, given his beliefs, will be most likely to promote his goal. Violence, though disliked, is a rational choice.[4]

---

[4] Note that in cases like norms of revenge, the social pressure to conform is real, and this makes such norms particularly robust. When every group member is responsible for the conduct of every other member, a single deviation has a cost for the whole group. This creates a collective interest in compliance and strong incentives to punish transgressions.

That rational choice may ensue in suboptimal and even disastrous social outcomes is a well-known tenet of the collective action literature, exemplified by the somewhat simplistic story of the Prisoner's Dilemma. What I am telling here is a different story of mismatch between individual choices and social outcomes, one that may occur even when there is no conflict between the individual and the collective good. There are psychological factors and systematic cognitive biases that are crucial in shaping decision making: We often hold irrational beliefs and aspirations or simply have wrong beliefs about our social environment. A robust descriptive theory of choice cannot ignore the extensive empirical evidence gathered by social psychologists about how individuals interpret and model their social reality. Because of systematic biases in interpreting other people's behavior, individuals may wrongly believe that a behavior they personally condemn is widely supported in the population or group to which they belong. If they act on their wrong beliefs and conform to what they take to be the majority's position, their public behavior will provide further evidence for the validity of their beliefs. Illusory private deviance will be experienced as real as people perceive the norm to have universal support. Misperception of social reality can have dire consequences in terms of the emergence and persistence of unpopular norms.

Norms whose existence depends on a collective illusion can be fragile. Whenever the veil of collective misperception is lifted, such norms may suddenly collapse. In the last part of the chapter I show with a simple model how a norm that most people dislike can be established, and under which conditions it will break down. In my model, under the assumptions of conformism and pluralistic ignorance, a small number of trendsetters can determine the behavior of large groups or even an entire society. Agents are assumed to be rational, in that they maximize expected utility and update their information using Bayes' rule. They may rationally choose to follow the behavior of other agents and ignore their private information (or preferences) because they (wrongly) infer that others' choices are based on information (or preferences) that dominate their own. In this case, there may be quick convergence to an unpopular norm on the basis of very little information. The bright side of the story is that dissemination of even very little new public information by a reputable source can upset the established norm. For example, the government might release a public opinion poll based on the true preferences of a sufficiently large sample of the population, or it may give clear indications that some norms are inefficient and damaging.

Because the scope of this kind of model is very general, I will not attempt a specific application to any particular situation such as, for example, the case of norms of corruption.[5] The message I want to convey is that it is possible and useful to model the dynamics of unpopular norms as the product of rational choices made by individuals who misperceive their social environment. The policy conclusion one draws from this kind of model is that it might take surprisingly modest public interventions, such as the release of credible public information, to effect major changes in collective behavior.

A Few Examples and a Fairy Tale

Let us consider a few examples of fairly common behaviors that have been extensively studied by social psychologists. What they have in common is that the subjects involved manifest a marked tendency to draw wrong inferences from observing the behavior of others who, in a shared social situation, act exactly like them.

Most of us have been part of (or at least have witnessed) the following classroom dynamics. The teacher pauses during a difficult lecture to ask students if they have any questions. Silence follows. The baffled but outwardly imperturbable students try to figure out their classmates' reactions. Despite widespread confusion, no hands are raised. This feature of the dynamic is not startling, since students obviously fear asking stupid questions and embarrassing themselves in front of the classroom. What is surprising is that students infer from the silence of other students that these individuals grasp the material and that they alone are ignorant and confused (Miller and McFarland 1987). Accidents or other emergency situations are less common, but they offer a similarly puzzling picture. Bystanders to emergencies are initially afraid of embarrassing themselves by overreacting. They thus remain cool and poised while they try to figure out if there is cause for concern. They interpret correctly their own composure and inaction, but they infer from the similar behavior of others that these individuals are genuinely unconcerned and that probably there is nothing to worry about. This reluctance to respond to an emergency when other people are present has been experimentally replicated. Latane and Darley (1968) performed a series of experiments in which they tested the hypothesis that, as the number of bystanders increases,

---

[5] For an analysis of some possible dynamics of corruption norms, see Bicchieri and Rovelli (1995) and Bicchieri and Duffy (1997).

the probability that anyone will help decreases.[6] They concluded that the presence of bystanders inhibits action, and that in such situations a 'diffusion of responsibility' effect is at work.

In all circumstances in which social information is available, inhibition seems to be due to an evaluation of the emergency inferred from others' behavior: Observing the inaction of bystanders helps support the conclusion that the victim is not seriously hurt. This must have been the conclusion reached by the neighbors of Kitty Genovese the night she was murdered. Her screams and pleadings for help notwithstanding, each of the 38 witnesses who observed the attack must have inferred from the apparent inaction of others that there was nothing to worry about. Instead of a case of generalized indifference, it was probably an example of a common bias in drawing inferences from other people's behavior.

Classroom and emergency situations have something in common: They are ambiguous, in that people usually lack the information and objective criteria to make a judgment. How difficult is the question? How sick is the man lying on the road? The reactions of others provide us with some cognitive clarity, with some information about our environment. What is odd is that most people never seem to suspect that the motive behind others' composure is akin to their own; hence, in fact, their behavior conveys no information. Other people's nonchalance is not interpreted as a posture; it is rather seen as a genuine outward sign of a superior grasp of the situation. Is it the need to orient ourselves in a complex and largely unknown reality that leads us to impute different motives to others? Or is it because we are among strangers and thus feel that it would be gratuitous to credit them with our own motives? If so, we would expect this bias to disappear in all those contexts in which there is no cognitive ambiguity, and, moreover, individuals interact with each other long enough to dispel the illusion that their motives and those of others are different.

Juvenile gangs, schools, prisons, and churches are social environments in which individuals have numerous and protracted interactions with

---

[6] In some experiments, however, bystanders did not communicate or observe each other, and the 'victim' was heard but not seen. In other experiments, bystanders were face to face, but again the emergency was only heard and not directly observed. Their results have been replicated in other experiments in which the emergency was not directly observed (Schwartz and Clausen 1970). When the victim as well as other bystandres are observed, results are mixed. Piliavin et al.'s (1969) subway field study suggests that diffusion of responsibility increases as the cost of helping increases and the cost of not helping decreases.

each other. Group members typically share the in-group's values that range from the toughness and display of violent behavior common to juvenile gangs to the banning of alcohol, card games, and extramarital sex preached by many religious groups. Yet numerous studies show that group members tend to assume that their peers endorse their subculture's values more strongly than they do themselves. Matza (1964) discovered that gang members, when privately interviewed, express considerable discomfort with their anti-social behavior. But because they did not express their criticism publicly, to their peers they appeared fully committed and comfortable with the group's violent behavior. Wheeler (1961) and Kauffman (1988) found that prison guards had significantly more liberal private attitudes than those they attributed to their fellow guards. For example, Kauffman found that 78% of the guards approved of an officer defending an accused inmate in a disciplinary board hearing, but only 44% of those guards assumed that their view would be shared by other guards. Most of the school teachers interviewed by Packard and Willower (1972) believed that the majority of their colleagues supported norms enjoining strictness toward students, but actually only a small minority did support such norms. Even children are not immune from misperceiving other children's attitudes. Prentice and Miller (1996) report the results of several studies of gender stereotyping among third and fourth graders; there is ample evidence that children estimate other children's beliefs to be more sex-typed than their own.

All of these examples have a common feature: Individuals systematically underestimate the similarity of their attitudes to those of their peers. This fact, per se, does not amount to misperception. If the individuals in question had no way to observe others' behavior and to constantly compare their own actions to those of others, we might just conclude that they have a tendency to think of themselves as more liberal, sympathetic, humane, or whatever than their fellows. In all these studies, however, individuals had plenty of occasions to observe each other in action. The problem is that they typically acted in ways that did not correspond to their private preferences or beliefs, taking public positions that were in line with what they believed to be the majority stance, the norms or values shared by their group. If individuals consciously dissemble, why don't they recognize a similar gap between on-stage and off-stage behavior in their peers? Why take others' behavior at face value?

What is common to students, bystanders to an emergency, prison guards, and gang members is that, like most individuals, they are sensitive to the opinions and judgments of those around them and fear expressing views that would put them at a disadvantage, either because they show their ignorance or because they diverge from the perceived public opinion. Furthermore, individuals estimate public opinion on the basis of observable indicators, which in the preceding examples consist of the public behavior of group members. Observability may not be that direct; sometimes media reports will do, and sometimes a few active and vocal individuals suffice to create the illusion that they represent the majority opinion.

In his account of the decline of the French church in the mid-eighteenth century, Toqueville gave a striking example of how people can both publicly misrepresent their private beliefs and assume that the public behavior of others corresponds to their private beliefs. In *L'Ancien Regime* (1856), he maintained that

Those who retained their beliefs in the doctrines of the Church because of being alone in their allegiance and, dreading isolation more than error, professed to share the sentiments of the majority. So what was in reality the opinion of only a part of the nation came to be regarded as the will of all and for this reason seemed irresistible, even to those who had given it this false appearance.

(p. 155)

Alexis de Toqueville and Hans Christian Andersen are an improbable pair. What unites the historian and the novelist is a keen understanding of human psychology and of its social consequences. The covert French Catholics remind one of the courtiers in *The Emperor's New Suit* (Andersen, 1837). Here two impostors manage to convince a rather dull emperor that they have made splendid clothes for him, so beautiful and refined that only smart and discriminating men can see and appreciate them. The unfolding of the tale is well known:

The emperor marched in the procession under the beautiful canopy, and all who saw him in the street and out of the windows exclaimed: 'Indeed, the emperor's new suit is incomparable! What a long train he has! How well it fits him!' Nobody wished to let others know he saw nothing, for then he would have been unfit for his office or too stupid. Never emperor's clothes were more admired.

Until a child shouts "The Emperor is naked!" nobody has the courage to admit that he sees no clothes, and everybody takes others' admiring murmurs as genuine expressions of superior judgment and refinement. In both Andersen's tale and Toqueville's account there appears to be a perverse sequence that begins with a vocal minority creating the illusion that they are a majority. The members of the silent majority, thinking they are a minority (or even unique), assume that their dissembling peers are acting out of authentic convictions. The illusion of personal deviance persists because everyone misrepresents the conforming behavior of a majority that fears ostracism and ridicule.[7]

Pluralistic Ignorance

The individuals in the previous examples were experiencing what social psychologists call pluralistic ignorance, a psychological state character-ized by the belief that one's private thoughts, attitudes, and feelings are different from those of others, even though one's public behavior is iden-tical (Allport 1924; Miller and McFarland 1991). Perhaps the term 'igno-rance' is not the most appropriate, as the individuals concerned seem to make systematic mistakes in judging the motives, and hence the atti-tudes and beliefs, of other people. Their judgments are guided by what they observe, and, indeed, observability is always a feature of the contexts in which pluralistic ignorance arises. The problem with such judgments is that individuals wrongly infer that, unlike themselves, others must be thinking and feeling the way they are acting. The question naturally arises whether there is anything special or peculiar about the circumstances in which pluralistic ignorance occurs. Are there some contexts in which it is easier for people to interpret the similar behavior of self and others differently?

One feature common to all victims of pluralistic ignorance is that they engage in social comparison. This fact, per se, is not remarkable, given the circumstances in which they find themselves. One of the functions of social comparison is to provide us with information about a new situation, especially when we lack sufficient information or objective criteria to make a judgment, or the environment we face is ambiguous and open to several possible interpretations. Thus a bystander to an accident will look at fellow bystanders to gauge information about the seriousness of the casualty, and a student will try to guess from his classmates' expressions if the question is a difficult one. Social comparisons also help in self-evaluation, as when we try to assess our abilities or the goodness of our opinions. Finally, and most important for our topic, social comparisons help to establish one's standing as a member of a valued group. In a study of alcohol use among Princeton students, Prentice and Miller (1996) noted that excess drinking is "central to the social identity of many college

---

[7] Kuran (1995) has given a compelling account of the persistence of communism along similar lines.

students and is an important part of social life in most campuses" (p. 9). Looking at the drinking habits of their peers, students quickly infer that heavy drinking is a campus norm, and they try to adapt to what they perceive as a social trait essential to being identified as 'one of them.'

Another feature common to all contexts in which pluralistic ignorance occurs is the lack of transparent communication (or of any communication at all) among individuals. This happens when people take a public stance that does not correspond to their private attitudes or beliefs. Bystanders to an emergency may feign lack of concern, and prison guards may behave less sympathetically to inmates than they would if they were to follow their inclinations. Because there is a gap between public behavior and private attitudes or beliefs, and no way to assess other people's attitudes other than observing their overt behavior, the public expressions of others are erroneously perceived to be genuine representations of their private thoughts. A good example of how damaging a lack of communication can be is Schanck's (1932) study of the social dynamics of members of the Baptist and Methodist churches in the fictitiously named community of Elm Hollow. He found that church members supported religious values more strongly in public than in private, but that the gap between the practiced and the preached was believed to be much smaller in the case of fellow church members than it was in their own case. The fact that those individuals could not have a frank discussion about proscribed activities such as card gaming was helpful in creating the illusion of uniform compliance with church teachings. On the other hand, precisely because of the perceived conformity of church members, initiating such a discussion was feared to put one at risk of being ostracized by the community. Lack of truthful communication became self-perpetuating.

Finally, pluralistic ignorance depends on misinterpreting the similar behavior of similar (or similarly situated) others. In Toqueville's example, the covert Catholic was not comparing his position with that of the vociferous and very visible anti-religious minority. He was making comparisons with his likes, people who used to practice Catholicism and could not be suspected of revolutionary sympathies. It is their conforming to the opinions of what is to all effects a minority that is interpreted at face value. In this way, Toqueville argued, the sentiments of a small part of the nation were mistaken as the public opinion, which became irresistible even in the eyes of those who thought and felt otherwise.

To summarize, pluralistic ignorance occurs when individuals engage in social comparison and other people's behavior is observable, but there is no transparent communication, in that public stances may differ from private attitudes and preferences. Individuals, however, will assume that the observed behavior is consistent with the actors' underlying attitudes and preferences. Hence, when the observed behavior points to the existence of a shared norm, people in the grip of pluralistic ignorance will tend to conclude that the norm is widely endorsed and feel compelled to conform.

Why Misrepresentation?

Though for my purpose it is not important to dwell on the causes of pluralistic ignorance, I shall briefly examine some possible explanations of why we so often fall prey to what might be aptly called an "illusion of transparency," the systematic misrepresentation of other people's attitudes and beliefs. If the student is motivated to keep silent for fear of embarrassing himself, and the gang member conforms out of a desire to fit in with the group, why do they have such difficulty in recognizing the same motives in other people? The motives that drive students and gang members alike are social in nature: Fear of embarrassment and the desire to identify with a valued group could not exist in the absence of a reference group whose judgment one cares about. It would thus seem that people perceive social motives as more potent causes of their own than of others' behavior. It is not an inability to attribute motives or reasons for action to others that drives pluralistic ignorance; rather, it is a self/other difference in the perceived power of social motives.

It has been suggested that one possible reason for this attribution bias is that motives such as fear of embarrassment or the desire to belong and fit in are mainly defined by internal and unobservable cues (Miller and McFarland, 1987). Whereas emotions such as love, hatred, pride, or contempt are easily observable, there are others that are almost by definition much more concealed. An individual can thus easily come to believe that she experiences such emotions more strongly than others do. This view is supported by experimental evidence that individuals tend to rate themselves as more extreme than the average person on traits pertaining to social inhibition and other states mainly defined by internal cues (McFarland and Miller, 1990). It would therefore be the very unobservability of others' motives that would lead to the self/other discrepancy.

Another possible reason for the disparity is that we are subject to a cultural propensity to underestimate the power of social motives to influence behavior (Miller and Prentice, 1994). We ground our assessment of our own motives on past experiences, which usually provide evidence that we act to maintain our social standing, that we want to avoid embarrassment, ostracism, reproach, and so on. However, we base inferences about others' motives on shared cultural representations of the relative power of different motives. Such representations induce us to overestimate the extent to which others are acting on 'private' motives and to minimize the extent to which people are acting to maintain relations with their peers, to establish and retain a social identity, or to avoid feelings of shame. We fall prey, in other words, to an *attribution error* (Ross 1977): the tendency to attribute the behavior of others to an internal cause (beliefs, preferences) and our own behavior to an external cause (e.g., social pressure).

There is some merit to this interpretation, in that it fits with other studies that report the importance of cultural biases in assessing even our own reasons for action. In a comprehensive study of altruistic behavior in America (Wuthnow 1991), which is mainly expressed through voluntary caring activities such as taking meals to the elderly, visiting the sick, donating time to nursing homes and hospitals, and staffing hotlines and crisis intervention centers, it turns out that the majority of volunteers rationalize their compassionate behavior as self-interested. Altruism and compassion have to be redefined within the framework of a culture that casts a tremendous weight on self-interest in explaining behavior. Thus a volunteer in a rescue squad feels compelled to justify his seemingly self-sacrificial activities by references to 'perks' such as "being able to drive as fast as I want on the highways" and "being able to park wherever I want to," which are hardly sensible reasons to undergo the costs and risks of such an activity.

Though I do not want to deny the importance of cultural biases in assessing other people's motives, it seems that the very nature of motives such as fear of embarrassment, rejection, and ostracism presupposes a self/other disparity. To exist at all, one's fear of rejection presupposes the existence of someone who has the power and willingness to sanction one's deviant behavior. I want to conform because, among other things, I dislike the social consequences of transgressing; I would probably be less uncomfortable at the prospect of breaking the rules if I knew that everyone else complies for the same reasons I do. Those who are expected to punish cannot be presumed to share the same motives for compliance, otherwise the very threat of a sanction would become void. To recognize other people's fears would render the norm as insubstantial and volatile as the Emperor's new clothes. Thus fears of social sanctions, to be justified, need to be supported by the belief that others are committed to the norm for very different reasons.

All these explanations of motivational biases seem to presuppose that individuals are able to recognize the true causes of their own behavior. Experimental evidence, however, only supports the claim that individuals consistently report that they act in accordance with social motives, whereas they tell different stories when asked to explain other people's behavior. All we can infer is that most of us act like poor scientists, in that we discount an important piece of evidence (our own alleged motives) without apparent good reasons. This is particularly true because the victims of pluralistic ignorance are not just observers; they are participants in the group dynamics who know that their own behavior belies their internal state and cannot be taken at face value. We cannot (and should not) infer from the available experimental data that individuals have a privileged access to the true causes of their behavior. What matters to pluralistic ignorance is that the purported cause of one's behavior is not deemed to be sufficient to produce similar behavior in others. Even if we just grant that individuals know how they feel, and infer from others' observable behavior that they feel differently, this simple inference is sufficient to generate pluralistic ignorance.

Why Do People Conform?

The examples of pluralistic ignorance one finds in the literature refer to two major classes of situations in which pluralistic ignorance (PI) occurs. One is when PI yields the illusory belief that others hold the group's values more strongly than does oneself (schools, churches, prisons, etc.). We know from studies of students' drinking habits and sexual stereotyping among young children that it does not matter whether the group is transient or well established: PI will arise in the presence of both. Another class of situations where PI occurs is when individuals correctly identify the positive value a group places on a characteristic but fail to realize that other group members are just pretending to have these characteristics, like 'keeping cool' in emergencies or not looking stupid in the classroom. What is underestimated here is others' strength of motivation to avoid acting inconsistently with this value.

Given that people seem to make such huge mistakes in assessing others' motives, it remains to be explained why they choose not to raise hands, intervene in emergencies, or otherwise behave in accordance with their true preferences. That is, even if we can tell a plausible story about how PI comes about, we have not yet explained how and why beliefs about others' motives can have prescriptive power. Why would a perceived self/other difference push one to conform to what is taken to be a collective value or norm? It seems that two conditions are necessary to produce conformity to the perceived value or norm: One is that the people observed must serve as a reference group, and the second is that they are seen as uniform in their opinion.

In all those cases in which others' behavior is just taken as an indicator of a given state, people will simply choose an action that best fits their motives and information. In the case of the students or the bystanders to an emergency, other students or bystanders serve as a reference group in that one gathers information from their behavior about some piece of reality (the lecture's difficulty, the severity of the emergency), and one wants to avoid acting stupidly in public. Behavior may, however, just reflect the belief, as in emergencies, that there is nothing to worry about. Juvenile gangs and other cohesive social groups (like churches and schools) offer a more interesting perspective. Here individuals do not simply want to gather information or try not to embarrass themselves. Rather, they want to behave in accordance with what they perceive to be the group norms. The gang or the church is a valuable social group, and individuals strive to be accepted as good standing group members. It would thus seem that group identification lies at the root of many cases of pluralistic ignorance. Individuals express different views than they actually hold and act in ways they privately disapprove of because they believe those views and behaviors to be consensual within a valued group. Note that, as I discussed in Chapter 1, social norms are supported by conditional preferences for conformity. That is, an individual will conform if she expects a sufficiently high number of others to conform *and* believes she is expected to conform by a sufficiently high number of people who (she might believe) are willing to punish her if she deviates from the acceptable behavior. Suppose that, as I am assuming, most group members dislike a norm that is nevertheless universally followed. What would happen if a transgression occurs? If social pressure is more imagined than real, the norm would quickly collapse, as people would realize that no punishment follows the lapse. Yet unpopular norms are often robust because the social pressure is real, in the sense that punishment will follow a transgression. It is of course possible that, within a group, there is an active minority that embraces and likes the norm and is prepared to punish transgressions.[8] In this case even a few, exemplary sanctions will be enough to create the

---

[8] Such individuals would enforce the norm because it is in their self-interest to have it.

impression that enforcement is taken very seriously, especially if the punisher is in a leadership position. What I find interesting, however, is the pressure to enforce that is often felt even by those who dislike the norm and realize that violations do not impose a cost to the group.[9] Timur Kuran (1995) suggested that enforcing a norm may provide a low-cost way of signaling one's sincerity. His suggestion is particularly relevant in the context we are discussing here. If I believe others sincerely support a norm I privately dislike, and at the same time I care about being accepted by the group that supports such a norm, I may fear being exposed as a 'pretender.' How better to signal that I am a true believer than by actively punishing transgressors? Thus real social pressure will be produced by hypocritical enforcement: People not only comply with a norm they privately dislike, they also confer social approval on the conformists and in so doing encourage others to do the same. Identification with a valued group may thus be the first link in a chain of events whose final outcome is the persistence of an unpopular norm.

I realize that 'social identity' is an elusive concept. Here I use it in a very limited and circumscribed sense to refer, in Tajfel's own words, to "that part of an individual's self-concept which derives from his knowledge of his membership of a social group (or groups) together with the value and emotional significance attached to that membership" (Tajfel 1981, p. 255). My preoccupation is with the effects on group behavior of the significance granted by individuals to group membership. One can belong to many groups simultaneously, and some of these memberships may be more salient than others, whereas some may vary in importance with time due to changes in social and individual circumstances. A crucial feature of the concept of social identity as I use it here is that identification with a group is in some sense a conscious choice: One may accidentally belong to a group, but it is only when being a group member becomes at least partly constitutive of who one is that we can meaningfully talk of social identifications. Being born in Northern Italy, up to a few years ago, was a mere geographical accident. With the advent of the Lombard League, it has become a reason of pride and distinction for many. That social identity considerations may motivate behavior is less contentious

---

[9] Binge eating, college drinking, or a ban on pre-marital sex are examples of behaviors that may not be conceived as beneficial to the group that adopts them. Gang violence, on the contrary, may signal the group's willingness to 'fight hard' to protect their territory from the claims of rival gangs. In this case a norm transgression would damage the whole group, as it would lower its reputation for toughness, and it would be in every member's interest to sanction lapses.

than the reasons why this happens. Identifying with a particular ethnic
or geographical group, for example, might hold the promise of future
tangible rewards; the small industrial and commercial businesses that are
the political bedrock of the Lombard League stand to gain from a program of at least partial fiscal and financial separation from the rest of the
nation. Membership in the League can thus be seen as a rational choice,
strictly motivated by self-interested considerations.

At other times, however, group memberships' benefits are more
elusive: Asch's experiments on conformity (Asch, 1955) and Tajfel's 1970
study of "minimal groups" suggest that social identity effects may occur
even in the absence of the tangible or intangible rewards that membership in an established group affords. There is a crucial difference between
motives derived from self-interest and those derived from concern for the
interests and outcomes of others. Identification with a valued group can
stem from individual or collective welfare considerations: One may want
to belong to a group because of the prospect of future personal rewards,
or just because one values the group and takes the group's goals and interests as one's own, even at the cost of overlooking or restricting individual
gains. Be it as it may, I shall keep using social identity as a motivational factor, even in those cases in which it can apparently be further decomposed
into self-interested motives.

The Consequences of Pluralistic Ignorance

My goal has been that of examining some of the social consequences
of pluralistic ignorance (PI). In particular, I want to claim that PI plays a
role in the emergence and perpetuation of unpopular norms. PI explains
how individuals might wrongly believe that a certain norm, attitude, or
belief they personally condemn is widely held among a population or
group to which they belong. For example, several studies done in the
1960s and 1970s uncovered a marked tendency for white Americans to
overestimate private white support for forced racial segregation. In fact,
only 18% of those polled favored segregation, but 47% believed that
most did so (O'Gorman 1975). If the overestimators acted according to
the perceived majority opinion, a racist norm might have survived in spite
of being privately endorsed only by a small minority.

When people act on their wrong beliefs and conform to what they take
to be the majority's position, their public behavior will provide further
evidence for the validity of their beliefs. Illusory private deviance will
be experienced as real as people perceive the norm, attitude, or belief

to have universal support. In this case, if individuals come to embrace the norm or attitude they originally erroneously attributed to others, an initial wrong perception will become accurate at both the private and public levels.

Embracing a norm that is perceived as widely supported is only one of the possible ways of reducing the self/other discrepancy. To use the wording of Hirschman (1970), exit, voice, and loyalty are all potential means to solve the conflict raised by pluralistic ignorance. Loyalty involves changing one's attitude toward the perceived norm: A person who adopts this strategy will eventually come to internalize the norm. The Princeton freshman and the third grader can ultimately internalize drinking norms or sexual stereotyping because their private attitudes toward the norm are not well established to start with. If the perceived norm does not clash with preexisting values and beliefs, it is reasonable to assume that, after a more or less lengthy period of time, what was wrongly perceived as a norm endorsed by the majority will in fact become the majority's norm. In this case, pluralistic ignorance will disappear. To say that a norm is internalized does not necessarily mean that it becomes part of one's deepest system of values. I use internalization in a much simpler sense: An internalized norm is a norm that one is prepared to defend and rationalize as having positive value. Note that true loyalty is different from the hypocritical enforcement I discussed earlier. A person who hypocritically enforces a norm she privately dislikes may in time come to revise her beliefs about it, so that fake loyalty may become true loyalty.[10] But hypocritical enforcement, as long as it is insincere, does not count as loyalty.

Exit involves rejection of the group that upholds the norm, and voice entails an attempt to bring the norm closer to one's attitude. Yet exit is not an easy option, and, in many situations, it is not an option at all. Voice, too, is a difficult and costly choice, as it involves an attempt to change the shared norm. Exit and voice presuppose that private preferences and attitudes are well established. In this case, individuals dislike the perceived norm, and the question is whether it is feasible or it pays to leave the group or express different preferences. Take the case of corruption. In a system where corruption is the norm, there may be many reasons why denouncing corrupt transactions is a costly option. Typically in such systems the prices of public contracts are much higher than they would be in a noncorrupt system; therefore many firms have at least a short-term incentive to keep the system in place. Those who recognize

---

[10] Reduction of cognitive dissonance may play a role in such transformations.

its inefficiency may prefer to be honest but expect everyone else to be dishonest. The firm that decides not to bribe or even to denounce corrupt practices can thus expect to be an isolated case that will be excluded from future, lucrative interactions (Bicchieri and Rovelli 1995). For most firms, moving to another country or denouncing the system is just not a feasible or reasonable option.

Turnbull (1972), in his book about the Ik of Uganda, reports that they went to great lengths to avoid being caught in a situation that dictated reciprocity, or even accepting help from another person with the intent of generating a future debt. Yet norms of reciprocity were upheld, even if the situation of extreme hardship in which the Ik were living had made them ineffective, if not harmful. The very fact that everyone tried to avoid situations where such norms would have normally applied testifies to their resilience, as well as to their being privately disliked by most. The norms' resilience was apparently due to the widespread belief that they enjoined universal support (Turnbull 1972).

For the Ik as well as for the reluctant briber, exit, voice, or loyalty may not be options. Individuals may disapprove of the norm but still refrain from open dissension because they interpret others' behavior as signaling support. The unpopular norm is an equilibrium, in the sense that no individual has an incentive to try to influence other people or just reveal her true preferences by not conforming to behavior that she perceives as universally endorsed. The equilibrium is self-perpetuating, because the belief that the norm is universally endorsed generates widespread conformity, and observation of conformist behavior further confirms the expectation of universal endorsement. The equilibrium however is also fragile, because small shocks are sufficient to generate large shifts in behavior. If the huge, silent majority of 'dissenters' becomes aware that their private preferences are shared by many, they would presumably shift their behavior in the direction of their true preferences. The prescriptive force of a norm is derived by its perceived universality: If people come to recognize that support for a given norm is limited or wavering, its power to induce conformity will be greatly reduced or even nullified.

When assimilation or rejection mechanisms fail, the veil of pluralistic ignorance can be lifted through an external intervention or by an endogenous mechanism. Misperception about a norm's endorsement could be eliminated by the government or media agencies releasing public information about people's true preferences or opinions, or about some new facts that would make it easier for those who dislike the norm to openly dissent. Smoking in public places, gender-biased language, and strict sexual mores are all examples of norms that changed very quickly in response to the diffusion of public information about, say, the availability of contraception or the fact that many women consider offensive the exclusive use of male pronouns in all kinds of prose. What matters is not the quantity of information released (it may take surprisingly little) but its quality, in the sense that the source must be credible. This condition is important in all cases of pluralistic ignorance, not just those that effect the upholding of unpopular norms. In Andersen's tale, it takes a child, who is innocent and truthful, to make the emperor's nakedness common knowledge. Similarly, in a silent classroom the first question will usually generate a cascade of further questions, because it indicates to everyone that indeed the lecture was a difficult one.

Alternatively, it may just take a few vocal deviants to generate a major shift in public opinion. All revolutions were initiated by small minorities: Their visibility, as well as their ability to provide or at least present an alternative, gave voice to popular dissatisfaction, but a major political overturn would hardly have occurred had the majority of people not been already privately disappointed with the status quo. In this case, the endogenous mechanism relies exclusively on the existence of a group of individuals who for some reason refuse to conform to the established system. Though it might be true that different people have different degrees of preference for conformity, an endogenous explanation of how an established norm may suddenly break down should not be confined to the existence of a few unconventional characters. Deviant behavior is frequently the result of a momentary slip or even a mistake in processing relevant information. In the following section I show with a formal model how such actions may have a disproportionate effect, as they can lead to sudden and large shifts in collective behavior. Because my explanation of such shifts does not rely on the existence of a few nonconformists, the combination of pluralistic ignorance with the possibility of 'contravening a norm by mistake' make the collapse of unpopular norms much more likely than it would otherwise be.

Informational Cascades

To model the effects pluralistic ignorance may have on the dynamics of unpopular norms, we need to model how people may rapidly converge on a common behavioral pattern on the basis of very little information, and how even a little new information, suggesting that a different course of action is optimal, may shift collective behavior in a direction opposite to the status quo. To do so, I want to show that pluralistic ignorance is likely to generate an *informational cascade* (Bikhchandani et al. 1992). Informational cascades occur when it is optimal for an individual, having observed the actions of other individuals, to follow their behavior regardless of his own preferences or information. Once an individual acts only on the information obtained from others' actions, his decision conveys no truthful information about his private information or preferences. Because the conformity of individuals in a cascade has no informational value, cascades are fragile and could be upset by the arrival of new (truthful) public information.

In a state of pluralistic ignorance, individuals have private information about their preferences and beliefs but can only infer other people's preferences or beliefs from observing their choices. If they assume that other people's choices truthfully reveal their preferences, beliefs, or attitudes, they may find it rational to conform to patterns of behavior they privately dislike. To model the kind of situation in which the 'wrong' norms are likely to emerge, we have to modify the assumption of sequential choices made by informational cascades models. In the model presented here choices are simultaneous; moreover, I make an explicit assumption of pluralistic ignorance. The interesting conclusion to be drawn is that it takes very little to reverse a cascade. Even in a population almost entirely made of conformists, a few transgressions (wrongly interpreted as revealing true preferences) may induce a sudden change of behavior in the direction of the true majority's preferences.

The Assumptions

To avoid unnecessary complications, let us assume that people choose their own actions by observing others' actions. I model binary choices, so agents choose one action in the set $\{x_1 = 0, x_2 = 1\}$. For example, they can choose to drink either beer or soda, or they can choose to bribe a public officer or behave honestly. Individuals have a common prior belief that a certain percentage of the population is 'deviant,' but they do not know the direction of the deviance. That is, individuals have common priors on the distribution of the majority and minority. For example, if 10% of the population is 'wet' and 90% is 'dry,' individuals believe that 90% of the population is in the majority and 10% is in the minority. However, they have no idea which trait distinguishes the majority (minority). Therefore, in the absence of any background information, they put the same prior probability (50%) on two possibilities: The majority (90%)

is wet [and the minority (10%) is dry], or the majority is dry (and the minority is wet).[11]

Individuals have varying degrees of conformist preferences but believe (the majority of) others have "normal" preferences, that is, they really prefer what they choose. I am including here a crucial feature of pluralistic ignorance: Individuals assess others' reasons for action as different from their own. Thus the fact that everyone is conforming is not common knowledge. The utility (loss) function of an individual is

$$U = \{-(x_i - \hat{x})^2 - (\beta/2)(x_i - y)^2\} - \partial,$$

where y is the individual's privately preferred action, $\hat{x}$ is the perceived majority preference (which takes the value 0 if x_1 is believed to be the majority's preference, 1 if x_2, and $1/2$ if there is uncertainty as to what the majority prefers), ∂ is a discount factor (explained later), and β stands for a person's degree of nonconformism. To make the argument as simple as possible, let us assume β can take only two values, 0 and 1. When β is 0, an individual conforms no matter what. The population contains a small (relative to the whole population) number of trendsetters whose β is 1. They care about expressing their private preferences but do not want to deviate from an established norm. Their number (z) is exogenously given. The number of individuals, excluding trendsetters, is N. Individuals are rational, in that they maximize expected utility, and follow a Bayesian decision pattern whenever the use of Bayes' rule conflicts with private information.

The only difference between conformists and trendsetters is as follows: If a conformist cannot infer which is the majority on the basis of observed behaviors and his preferences, he will choose his action by flipping a coin (because in this case the probability that the majority is, say, wet, is equal to the probability that it is dry), and the conformist wants to maximize the utility of conforming to the majority, whatever it happens to be. For example, if a privately dry conformist observes only one person drink beer, he has two conflicting pieces of information: one wet person and one dry person (himself). In this case, the dry conformist will drink either beer or soda equiprobably. In the presence of conflicting

[11] These assumptions can be relaxed, however. What is crucial to the model is that individuals assign the same prior probability (50%) to the trait characterizing the majority (minority). It does not matter that people may have different beliefs about the size of the majority (minority); that is, even if some believe the majority to be 51% and others believe it is 99% of the population, we get the same results. Hence the assumption of a common prior distribution is unnecessary.

observations, the trendsetter will choose according to his true prefer-
ences. That is, if $(x_1 - \hat{x}) = (x_2 - \hat{x}) = 1/2$, a positive β will induce him
to choose on the basis of the second term $[-(\beta/2)\,(x_i - y)^2]$ of his utility function. However, in a situation in which there is a well-established
norm and the trendsetter believes the majority to prefer, say, x_1, the
trendsetter will choose x_1 irrespective of his private preference, because
$\beta/2 = 1/2 < 1$.

I am interested in modeling how an unpopular norm might emerge.
In the absence of an established norm, how will an individual choose?
Let us assume that people can choose at either time 1 or time 2, and only
these two time points exist. The discount factor, ∂, takes a small value
($\ll 1$) if the trendsetter chooses at time 2 and zero otherwise, in order
to reflect the eagerness of the trendsetters to express themselves earlier,
ceteris paribus.

At time 1, a norm has not yet been established; thus there is no information as to the majority's preference. At time 2, some information is
present, but it might not be enough to decide that a norm is in place.
At time 1, an individual has to decide whether to choose now or to defer
his choice to time 2. He will thus compare the utility of choosing now
(U_1) to his present expectation of what the utility of choosing later would
be ($E_1[U_2]$). The conformist will always wait and see because, since his
$\beta = 0$, $U_1 = -1/4 < E_1[U_2] = -\gamma/4$ (where $\gamma < 1$ is the probability
that information will be indecisive at time 2). Since his $\beta = 1$, what
will the trendsetter do? If he acts at time 1, $U_1 = -1/4$, because he
chooses according to his private preference. If he waits and acts at time
2, $E_1[U_2] = \{-1/2\,(1-\gamma)/2\} + (-1/4\,\gamma) - \partial = -1/4 - \partial$. Therefore,
$U_1 > E_1[U_2]$, and the trendsetter always acts at time 1. In a new situation,
the kind of norm that gets established will thus depend on the trendsetters, who choose first and simultaneously. Their choices may coincide, in
which case those who observe them will infer that the observed choices
represent the majority's preference. In this case, all will conform. Suppose instead that the initial trendsetters' choices are different, and thus
not decisive. In this case, a person whose $\beta = 0$ will toss a coin and act
according to the result of the toss.

Let p be the size of the majority (expressed as a percentage). Depending on the situation studied, the magnitude of the majority will make an
important difference. In corruption and elections, even a narrow majority (say, 51%) will matter, as everyone wants to bet on the winning horse.
In the case of drinking norms, it might not be reasonable to assume that
people fear being in the minority if p is close to 0.5.

The Model

Let us define π as the posterior odds of x_1 being the majority preference to x_2 being the majority preference. Let θ_i denote that x_i is the majority preference; z_i denotes the action (either x_1 or x_2) of trendsetter i, and y is a private preference. For example, $p(z_1 = x_1|\theta_1)$ is the probability that trendsetter 1 has chosen action x_1 conditional on x_1 being the majority preference. By assumption, the prior odds are 1 to 1, that is, $p(\theta_1)/p(\theta_2) = 1$. Then,

$$\pi = p(\theta_1|y, z_1, z_2, \ldots)/p(\theta_2|y, z_1, z_2, \ldots)$$
$$= [\Pi p(z_i|\theta_1)/\Pi p(z_i|\theta_2)] \cdot [p(y|\theta_1)/p(y|\theta_2)].$$

In logarithm,

$$\ln\pi = \ln[p(\theta_1|y, z_1, z_2, \ldots)/p(\theta_2|y, z_1, z_2, \ldots)]$$
$$= \Sigma\ln[p(z_i|\theta_1)/p(z_i|\theta_2)] + \ln[p(y|\theta_1)/p(y|\theta_2)].$$

All but trendsetters want to wait and see at time 1 and to conform to the expected majority at time 2. Therefore, the conformist's decision rule is

$$x = \begin{cases} \text{no action} & \text{time 1} \\ x_1 & \text{time 2 and } \pi > 1 \\ x_1 \text{ or } x_2 \text{ equiprobably} & \text{time 2 and } \pi = 1 \\ x_2 & \text{time 2 and } \pi < 1. \end{cases}$$

Trendsetters are assumed to have a relatively strong preference for expressing themselves. Therefore, they act at time 1 as shown above, while conformists defer their actions to time 2. Note that at time 1, $\pi = 1$, because we assume the common prior is $1/2$. Then,

$$x = \begin{cases} x_1 & \text{if the true preference is } x_1 \\ x_2 & \text{if the true preference is } x_2. \end{cases}$$

Results

Let us assume that the true majority (pN) prefers x_1. Suppose $z = 1$ and his (the only trendsetter's) action is x_1. After observing the trendsetter, all conformists choose simultaneously. In this case, $(1 - p)N$ people toss a fair coin, whereas pN people choose x_1. Then, the distribution of x_1 and x_2 will arbitrarily approach $[(1 + p)/2]$ and $[(1 - p)/2]$, respectively, for very large N. If the trendsetter's action is x_2, the distribution of x_1 and x_2 will approach $(p/2)$ and $[(2 - p)/2]$, respectively, for very large N. In either case, the actual distribution of actions is different from the distribution of true preferences, because those whose true preferences are different from that of the trendsetter flip a coin to choose an action. Let us call this phenomenon a *partial cascade*. Unless N is infinite, both positive and negative (complete) cascades can occur. However, even if N is small, the probability that either a positive or a negative cascade occurs is very small. For example, if $N = 9$, the probability of a negative cascade conditional on the (single) observation of x_2 is $(1/2)^9 \approx 0.002$.

If we have two trendsetters, there are three possibilities: $\{x_1, x_1\}$, $\{x_1, x_2\}$, and $\{x_2, x_2\}$. The collective behavior that follows will be, respectively:

1. N choose x_1 if $\{x_1, x_1\}$;
2. pN choose x_1 and $(1 - p)N$ choose x_2 if $\{x_1, x_2\}$;
3. N choose x_2 if $\{x_2, x_2\}$.

Only in the second case, $\{x_1, x_2\}$, will individuals reveal their true preferences; hence, p will express the true proportion of people who prefer (and choose) x_1.[12]

Although the situation looks similar to that of a sequential setting, a significant difference exists: Because the simultaneous setting does not need a sequentially specified order, which the sequential setting needs, nor does it make possible coin flipping among trendsetters, the probability that no cascade occurs is higher in the simultaneous setting than in the sequential one. For example, if $z = 4$, the probability of no cascade in a simultaneous choice setting is $_4C_2 \cdot p^2 \cdot (1 - p)^2 = 6p^2 \cdot (1 - p)^2$ instead of $p^2 \cdot (1 - p)^2$ (which is the probability of no cascade if the choices are sequential). However, if z is large (with respect to N), the probability of no cascade in the simultaneous case cannot be distinguished from that of the sequential case.

Distribution of the Trendsetters' Tastes and Simulation Results

So far, I have not specified what determines the distribution of tastes (and choices) among trendsetters. Since the distribution of trendsetters' tastes is crucial in determining the likelihood of cascades, I will now specify how it is determined and show some simulation results based on this specification. Let N be very large and represent the whole population (including trendsetters). Suppose the distribution of the entire population's tastes is given: pN are dry and $(1 - p)N$ are wet. Without loss of generality, assume that $p > 0.5 > 1 - p$. In our example, dry people belong

---

[12] In the appendix I make a simple example of what will happen with one or two trendsetters and how easily a cascade can occur.

to the majority and wet people to the minority. Nature randomly picks out of N a small number ($z \ll N$) of trendsetters. The distribution of tastes among trendsetters thus becomes

$$p \text{ (number of wet} = 0) = {}_zC_0 \cdot p^0 \cdot (1 - p)^z$$
$$p \text{ (\# of wet} = 1) \quad = {}_zC_1 \cdot p^1 \cdot (1 - p)^{z-1}$$
$$\dots\dots\dots\dots$$
$$p \text{ (\# of wet} = q) \quad = {}_zC_q \cdot p^q \cdot (1 - p)^{z-q}$$
$$\dots\dots\dots\dots$$
$$p \text{ (\# of wet} = z) \quad = {}_zC_z \cdot p^z \cdot (1 - p)^0.$$

If (# of wet – # of dry) ≥ 2, *negative cascades* occur; if (# of dry – # of wet) ≥ 2, *positive cascades* occur. In the case of an even number of trendsetters, it is possible that the number of wet is equal to the number of dry trendsetters, in which case cascades do not occur, though this possibility does not exist in the case of an odd number of trendsetters. On the other hand, it is possible that (# of wet – # of dry) $= 1$, in which case partial cascades would occur in the presence of an odd number of trendsetters but not if the number of trendsetters is even. As can be easily inferred, the actual distribution of trendsetters' tastes depends on the number of trendsetters as well as on the distribution of the entire population's tastes. Table 5.1 in the appendix shows the simulation results with the size of the (dry) majority ranging between 55 and 90% of the population and the number of trendsetters going from 2 to 20. As already mentioned, the even/odd difference matters. However, I shall focus on the even-number case because the general tendencies are the same, though we should substitute partial cascades for no cascades in the odd-number case.

Figures 5.1, 5.2, and 5.3 in the appendix graphically depict the results for the even-number case: The probability of positive cascades increases monotonically with increases in the size of the majority (as a percentage of the population) and the number of trendsetters. The probability of no cascades increases monotonically with decreases in the size of the majority and the number of trendsetters. The probability of negative cascades increases monotonically with a decrease in the size of the majority, though the relation between the probability of negative cascades and the number of trendsetters is not monotonic.

The last finding deserves a closer scrutiny. As Figure 5.3 shows, in the range of large majorities, that is, when the majority comprises 70, 80, or 90% of the population, seemingly intuitive monotonicity is preserved; that is, the smaller the number of trendsetters, the higher the probability of negative cascades. However, when the majority is just 55 or 60% of the population, monotonicity breaks down. Rather, monotonicity is reversed between 2 and 10 trendsetters, though the relation is reversed again between 10 and 20 trendsetters. In other words, if the majority as well as the number of trendsetters is small, say 55% and 10, respectively, decreasing the number of trendsetters leads to a decrease in the probability of negative cascades. Actually, in the case of a 55% majority, the probability of negative cascades is globally maximized with 10 trendsetters (26.14%). As the case of negative cascades shows, monotonicity does not hold for some combinations of parameters.

One conclusion we can draw is that, whenever a large majority of the population prefers, say, to be dry, a very small number of trendsetters can have a disproportionate effect on the probability that an unpopular drinking norm will emerge. On the contrary, if the majority of dry people is quite small, unpopular drinking norms are more likely to be established in the presence of a sizable number of trendsetters. Many social contagion phenomena like college students' alcohol consumption, binge eating, teenage smoking, and even widespread illegal behaviors such as bribing practices seem to originate from the actions of a relatively *small* group of individuals. It is always surprising to realize that many of those who adopt these behavioral patterns have a negative attitude toward them, because we have a tendency to expect consistency between attitudes and behavior. The model presented here shows that such inconsistencies are not necessarily a sign of irrationality: People in the grip of pluralistic ignorance may rationally choose to behave in ways they privately dislike. The conformists in the present model choose to conform to whatever they perceive to be the majority preference, often at the expense of neglecting their own tastes or values. Furthermore, it is important to recognize that, whenever most people share a given private preference, the presence of pluralistic ignorance makes it easy for even an extremely small "contrarian" minority to steer public behavior in the direction of their preferences. This is how unpopular norms may come into existence.

Thus far, I have not indicated whether what comes into existence is a descriptive or a social norm. A conformist wants to be in the majority and will choose whatever the majority chooses. *Why* one wants to conform is another story. Someone may be driven by a desire to coordinate with what one perceives it is 'most people do'; if one observes a frequent behavior, and expects it to occur in the future, one may just find it is in one's interest to conform to what seems to reflect the majority's opinion or preference, especially if this opinion or preference is taken to signal some valuable property of the world. This is the way some *fads* are born.

The infamous 'Tulipmania' that occurred in Holland in the first half of the seventeenth century is a case in point. It lasted a brief 3 years, but in that time people made and lost fortunes buying and selling tulip bulbs. What drove merchants, noblemen, and servants to invest their capitals and savings in such an aleatory venture? The origins of the phenomenon are uncertain, but what is clear is that, once a certain momentum was reached, everyone rushed to get a piece of the action. Observing many people buying tulip bulbs led many others to infer that bulbs must have great value, and they should thus be invested in. In fact, the increased demand for bulbs drove their price higher and higher, confirming the impression it was an excellent investment. Those who observed and imitated the buyers did not know they were imitating the imitators, and, as in a domino effect, each choice confirmed the current opinion and generated other, similar choices. The Tulipmania, like the South Sea bubble and the recent dot.com phenomenon, are fads that had a meteoric ascent and a just as swift decline.

Though imitation may have an informational component, as in the examples above, it may also have a strong normative component. Another reason to conform to what one believes to be the majority preference is the desire to fit in, or the fear of being shunned if one does not conform to what is believed to be the group's norm. The newcomer who observes other students drinking beer will infer that 'social drinking' is the norm and act accordingly. Though a student may drink beer to simply imitate what the majority does, another instead may fear being ostracized if he does not conform to what he believes to be the group's norm. The fear of ostracism may be more imaginary than real, and it may result from importing old scripts to the new situation. Small, close-knit groups often snub those who do not 'play by the rules,' and past experience with such groups would predispose a student to believe that he will be punished if he does not conform to the norms of the new group. Whereas the person who just wants to coordinate might attempt to deviate from time to time in the direction of his true preferences if the cost of deviation is perceived to be low, the person who believes he is following a social norm will be more careful in straying from it, at least insofar as he believes most others are still following it, expect him to follow it, and so on. Depending on the circumstances, past experiences, and personal dispositions, one may believe one is in the presence of a social or a descriptive norm. For example, a fad will typically be a descriptive norm, whereas the norms that emerge in small, close-knit groups may quickly become social ones. Moreover, it is worth repeating that what is a descriptive norm to some may be a social norm to others. If a majority of students believes that a social norm is in place, then deviations will be carefully avoided. However, as we shall see in the next section, when a norm is the result of pluralistic ignorance, it may take very little to subvert it.

Lifting the Veil

Once a cascade occurs, there is no incentive for anyone to deviate, even if the majority of people hates the status quo. A norm has been established, and because everyone believes other people's compliance to reveal a genuine preference, nobody wants to bear the cost of deviating from the norm. However, some may eventually deviate, because they either slip into revealing their private preferences or just make a mistake. The term 'mistake' encompasses several possible reasons why one would deviate from the norm. A 'dry' person may order beer in a bout of depression, and a manager intent on bribing a public officer might mistakenly interpret some piece of information as suggesting that in that particular moment it might be unwise to offer a bribe.

Given my assumptions, it follows that people are unlikely to consciously choose to deviate, but it is not unreasonable to assume that others believe the deviant's off-equilibrium choice to reveal his true preference. In a situation of pluralistic ignorance, this is precisely what would be presumed. Let us then assume the common belief about deviations to be as follows: The probability that a deviation from the norm reveals a true preference is taken to be $1 - \varepsilon$, and that of a simple mistake is taken to be ε ($\ll 1$). Note that ε is a function of individuals' belief about how many deviants are conformists (and hence can only make a mistake).[13] We also have to assume that people believe that some among them (the falsely perceived minority) are conformists.

It is interesting to explore under which conditions a negative cascade will be reversed, that is, when an established norm that most people privately dislike will collapse. As an example, let us consider the case of a negative cascade where the current norm is x_2 but privately the majority (pN) prefers x_1. Take $\#x_2 - \#x_1$ to be the difference between the number of type-2 and type-1 observed actions taken by trendsetters before the

---

[13] It is assumed here that ε is fixed. In this case, the mistake people make is only about who belongs to the majority, not how large the majority is. If ε is not fixed, then it must vary with p: As an agent observes, say, more and more x_1 actions, p will increase and ε will decrease. In this case, false beliefs about who is in the majority will be reinforced with time.

current cascade occurs. For example, if there are two trendsetters and both choose x_2, the difference, $\#x_2 - \#x_1$, will be 2 $(2 - 0)$. Then it will take $\#x_2 - \#x_1$ observations of 'trembled' x_1 actions to induce people who privately prefer x_1 to reveal their true preferences. The general principle is that if n $(\#x_i - \#x_j)$ actions of type i taken by trendsetters were sufficient to generate a cascade, it will take n actions of type j to reverse the cascade. The reason is simple. Once a cascade occurs, individuals' actions no longer depend on their private information (their preferences); hence their behavior is uninformative to others. Thus a cascade aggregates the information of only a few early individuals' actions. In our example, the relevant information is that provided by the actions of trendsetters. To shatter a cascade, individuals will only need to observe a number of 'deviant' actions sufficient to offset the information conveyed by the trendsetters' actions. The fact that the majority follows a norm does not therefore entail that it will take a major release of alternative public information to abandon it. Very little public information, in the form of very few observable 'deviant' actions, may be sufficient.

For example, if $\#x_2 - \#x_1 = 2$, only one observation of x_1 is not sufficient to break the equilibrium. Before observing the 'tremble' x_1, the odds of x_1-preferring people are

$$\frac{(1-p) \cdot (1-p)}{p \cdot p} \cdot \frac{p}{1-p} = \frac{1-p}{p} < 1.$$

The odds after the x_1 tremble are

$$\frac{1-p}{p} \cdot \frac{p \cdot (1-\varepsilon) + (1-p) \cdot \varepsilon}{p \cdot \varepsilon + (1-p) \cdot (1-\varepsilon)} = \frac{1-p}{p} \cdot \frac{p - (2p-1) \cdot \varepsilon}{1 - p + (2p-1) \cdot \varepsilon}$$
$$< 1 \, (\because 2p - 1 > 0).$$

But if two people tremble, the odds for x_1- and x_2-preferring people are, respectively:

$$\frac{1-p}{p} \cdot \left\{ \frac{p \cdot (1-\varepsilon) + (1-p) \cdot \varepsilon}{p \cdot \varepsilon + (1-p) \cdot (1-\varepsilon)} \right\}^2$$
$$= \frac{1-p}{p} \cdot \left\{ \frac{p - (2p-1) \cdot \varepsilon}{1 - p + (2p-1) \cdot \varepsilon} \right\}^2 > 1$$
$$\frac{(1-p)^3}{p^3} \cdot \left\{ \frac{p \cdot (1-\varepsilon) + (1-p) \cdot \varepsilon}{p \cdot \varepsilon + (1-p) \cdot (1-\varepsilon)} \right\}^2$$
$$= \frac{(1-p)^3}{p^3} \cdot \left\{ \frac{p - (2p-1) \cdot \varepsilon}{1 - p + (2p-1) \cdot \varepsilon} \right\}^2 < 1.$$

Then, everyone will be induced to truthfully reveal his preferences because x_1-preferring people switch to x_1 and x_2-preferring people stick to x_2.

It should be noted that some of the assumptions I made are important in generating a cascade. For example, I assumed that a conformist, in the absence of relevant information about what the majority is, will choose by flipping a coin. If we were to assume that people use their true preference as a tie-breaker, informational cascades would be mitigated. In the case of $z = 1$, whatever behavior this lone trendsetter takes, people would act on the basis of their true preferences. For example, if the trendsetter orders beer, wet people will order beer; dry people will choose soda because two conflicting pieces of evidence [one person is wet and one person (himself) is dry] give no clue beyond the common prior belief, and accordingly people act on their true preferences.

Actually, partial cascades, which can only occur in the case of an odd number of observations, would never occur even in the present simultaneous setting with true revelation of preferences as a tie-breaking rule. Another interesting case is that of people who are not perfect Bayesians. For example, people may take others' behavior into account more or less than predicted by Bayes' theorem, and in this case informational cascades might be amplified or mitigated. Conservative belief revision, that is, less than optimal revising from a Bayesian viewpoint, could be a useful psychological mechanism in terms of blocking the emergence of informational cascades. For example, in the strict Bayesian model presented here, only two initial observations of x_2 are sufficient to generate a cascade. But "conservative" people would need more definite pieces of evidence to conform to the perceived majority. Thus, if people were less rational in processing their information, it would be more difficult for unpopular norms to get established.

The important conclusion we can draw is that unpopular or dysfunctional norms may emerge and survive even in the presence of a huge, silent majority of dissenters. They refrain from open defiance because of social pressures they themselves help to sustain through actions that stem from pluralistic ignorance. But it may take surprisingly little new public information to reverse the original cascade. Interestingly enough, we need not assume much about the sources of such information. It would be a mistake to suppose that only the actions of a 'subversive' minority or the availability of public information about what most people really think (or like) can be expected to generate sudden and unexpected changes in well-established norms. Deviant behavior may occur for many other reasons, and it may well be unintended. What matters is that it may take very few observations to convince people to change their behavior in the direction of what they truly prefer.

Appendix to Chapter 5

To better understand how a cascade may occur, imagine a situation in which a person must decide which of the two urns below is the 'true' one. Urn 1 contains 90 'wet' balls and 10 'dry' balls, and Urn 2 contains 90 'dry' balls and 10 'wet' balls. If one is right, one gets a prize. However, one cannot directly observe the urns. What one can observe is just the result of one's extraction as well as the results of previous extractions.

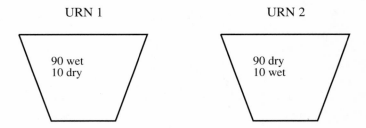

URN 1

90 wet
10 dry

URN 2

90 dry
10 wet

The prior probability that a given urn is the true one is $1/2$, so the initial odds are 1:1. Now suppose that I am told that the person before me extracted one 'wet' ball. What is the probability that the right urn is Urn 1 (i.e., that the majority of balls is of the 'wet' type)? Using Bayes's rule, we calculate

$$p(\text{Urn 1/wet ball}) = \frac{\frac{1}{2} \times \frac{9}{10}}{\frac{1}{2} \times \frac{9}{10} + \frac{1}{2} \times \frac{1}{10}} = \frac{9}{10}.$$

If I extract next a dry ball, what is the probability that Urn 1 is the right one (i.e., that I extracted a 'minority' ball)?

$$p(\text{Urn 1/wet and dry ball}) = \frac{\frac{1}{2} \times \frac{1}{10} \times \frac{9}{10}}{\frac{1}{2} \times \frac{1}{10} \times \frac{9}{10} + \frac{1}{2} \times \frac{9}{10} \times \frac{1}{10}} = \frac{9}{18} = \frac{1}{2}.$$

In this case, my model indicates the person will toss a coin, because the posterior odd of the majority of the balls being wet to the majority being dry is 1.

Suppose instead that I am told that two people before me extracted two wet balls. Now the probability that the right urn is Urn 1 (i.e., that the majority of balls is of the wet type) is

$$p(\text{Urn 1/wet, wet}) = \cfrac{\frac{1}{2} \times \frac{9}{10} \times \frac{9}{10}}{\frac{1}{2} \times \frac{9}{10} \times \frac{9}{10} + \frac{1}{2} \times \frac{1}{10} \times \frac{1}{10}} = \frac{81}{82}.$$

Suppose I next extract a dry ball. What is the posterior probability that I have extracted a 'minority' ball?

$$p(\text{Urn1/wet, wet, dry}) = \cfrac{\frac{1}{2} \times \frac{9}{10} \times \frac{9}{10} \times \frac{1}{10}}{\frac{1}{2} \times \frac{9}{10} \times \frac{9}{10} \times \frac{1}{10} + \frac{1}{2} \times \frac{1}{10} \times \frac{1}{10} \times \frac{9}{10}} = \frac{81}{90}.$$

In this case, the posterior odds of Urn 1 being the right one to Urn 2 being the right one are

$$\frac{\frac{81}{90}}{\frac{9}{90}} = \frac{81}{9} \text{ or } 9:1.$$

In this case, because $\pi > 1$, I decide that Urn 1 is the right one.

Note that in this case a cascade has occurred. I discount my private information and declare Urn 1 to be the right one, and so will anyone following me, irrespective of the type of ball they observe.

TABLE 5.1. *Simulation results (even)*

Number of Trendsetters	20	20	20	20	20
Size of Majority	0,90	0,80	0,70	0,60	0,55
Size of Minority	0,10	0,20	0,30	0,40	0,45
Prob. of Negative Cascades	0,00	0,00	0,02	0,13	0,25
Prob. of Positive Cascades	1,00	1,00	0,95	0,76	0,59
Prob. of Partial Cascades	–	–	–	–	–
Prob. of No Cascades	0,00	0,00	0,03	0,12	0,16
Number of Trendsetters	**10**	**10**	**10**	**10**	**10**
Size of Majority	0,90	0,80	0,70	0,60	0,55
Size of Minority	0,10	0,20	0,30	0,40	0,45
Prob. of Negative Cascades	0,00	0,01	0,05	0,17	0,26
Prob. of Positive Cascades	1,00	0,97	0,85	0,63	0,50
Prob. of Partial Cascades	–	–	–	–	–
Prob. of No Cascades	0,00	0,03	0,10	0,20	0,23
Number of Trendsetters	**8**	**8**	**8**	**8**	**8**
Size of Majority	0,90	0,80	0,70	0,60	0,55
Size of Minority	0,10	0,20	0,30	0,40	0,45
Prob. of Negative Cascades	0,00	0,01	0,06	0,17	0,26
Prob. of Positive Cascades	0,99	0,94	0,81	0,59	0,48
Prob. of Partial Cascades	–	–	–	–	–
Prob. of No Cascades	0,00	0,05	0,14	0,23	0,26
Number of Trendsetters	**6**	**6**	**6**	**6**	**6**
Size of Majority	0,90	0,80	0,70	0,60	0,55
Size of Minority	0,10	0,20	0,30	0,40	0,45
Prob. of Negative Cascades	0,00	0,02	0,07	0,18	0,26
Prob. of Positive Cascades	0,98	0,90	0,74	0,54	0,44
Prob. of Partial Cascades	–	–	–	–	–
Prob. of No Cascades	0,01	0,08	0,19	0,28	0,30
Number of Trendsetters	**4**	**4**	**4**	**4**	**4**
Size of Majority	0,90	0,80	0,70	0,60	0,55
Size of Minority	0,10	0,20	0,30	0,40	0,45
Prob. of Negative Cascades	0,00	0,03	0,08	0,18	0,24
Prob. of Positive Cascades	0,95	0,82	0,65	0,48	0,39
Prob. of Partial Cascades	–	–	–	–	–
Prob. of No Cascades	0,05	0,15	0,26	0,35	0,37
Number of Trendsetters	**2**	**2**	**2**	**2**	**2**
Size of Majority	0,90	0,80	0,70	0,60	0,55
Size of Minority	0,10	0,20	0,30	0,40	0,45
Prob. of Negative Cascades	0,01	0,04	0,09	0,16	0,20
Prob. of Positive Cascades	0,81	0,64	0,49	0,36	0,30
Prob. of Partial Cascades	–	–	–	–	–
Prob. of No Cascades	0,18	0,32	0,42	0,48	0,50

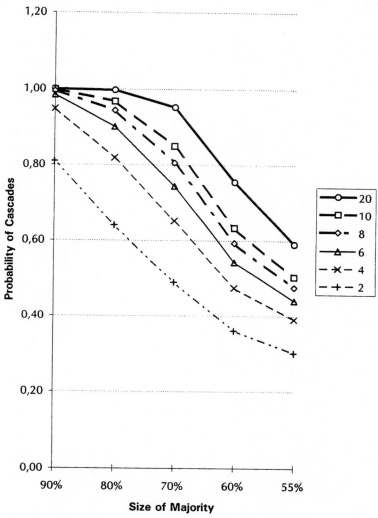

FIGURE 5.1. Probabilities of positive cascades

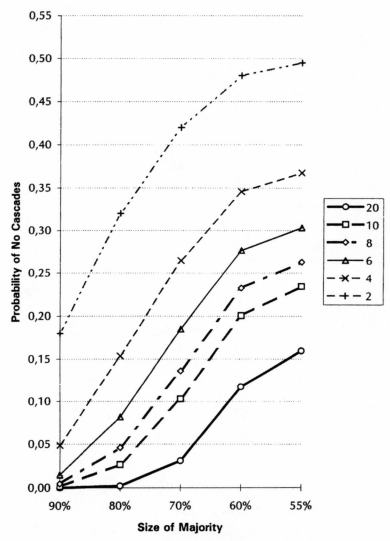

FIGURE 5.2. Probabilities of no cascades

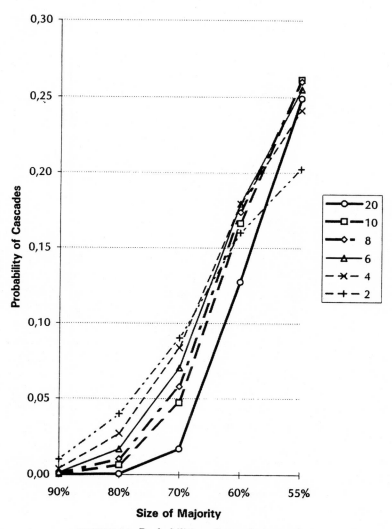

FIGURE 5.3. Probabilities of negative cascades

6

The Evolution of a Fairness Norm

Introduction

The example I used in the previous chapter is that of the emergence of a drinking norm. Such a norm is typically descriptive, though in some situations even such an irrelevant behavior may come to signify allegiance to a particular group, not unlike the rules of etiquette I described in Chapter 1. When what started as a descriptive norm acquires some ulterior significance, when people start attributing value to it and believe they are expected by others to follow the group norm, it becomes a social norm. Probably many group norms that fulfill a signaling or exclusionary function were born as descriptive norms. Teenage groups are an example: Their dress codes may have emerged by chance, but soon enough they become imbued with meaning and value.

Not all social norms, however, stem from descriptive norms. In particular, the pro-social norms I am interested in seem to partake of a very different origin. Norms of cooperation, promise-keeping, reciprocity, or fairness are some of the institutions that allow a society to function smoothly, if not exist. The problem of social order, its origin and maintenance, has traditionally been associated with the existence of pro-social behaviors. If, as I am, one is interested in the spontaneous emergence of such order, then a central question becomes how to model the emergence of those behavioral patterns that keep a society together. There is, however, a difference in pro-social norms as to their importance for society's survival. Whereas a society cannot survive without some cooperation, some trusting and reciprocating, and a measure of honesty in its members' dealing with each other, fairness as we usually understand it does not seem as necessary. We can easily imagine a society where goods and privileges are distributed unequally according to rank, seniority, or gender. Yet we cannot imagine a society worthy of its name in which people constantly cheat each other. This difference between pro-social norms becomes very clear when we study their emergence. To understand this point, imagine being an observer in a society in which you soon enough come to realize that almost everyone engages in acts of trust and, when trusted, reciprocates. You might come to the conclusion that almost everyone is adopting the same unconditional strategy of "always trust/always reciprocate." On second thought, however, you would also recognize that such a nice, unconditional strategy could not have survived for long. In a society in which most people are unconditional trusters, cheaters would thrive, and, soon enough, they would 'take over' the population. What you observe is a nice, cooperative behavioral pattern that is supported by many different strategies (Bicchieri et al. 2004). Some people may be harsh punishers of transgressors, and others may be more lenient, but all are conditional trusters/reciprocators. Trusting, reciprocating, and, in general, any cooperative behaviors, when widespread and thriving, are supported by several conditional strategies, all observationally equivalent. A norm of cooperation, as well as a norm of trust/reciprocity, should never be identified with the strategies that support it.

Things are quite different with fairness norms. Suppose observing a society in which, whenever two members are engaged in some sort of 'divide the pie' activity, they consistently choose an equal share. Does this mean that the 50/50 rule is supported by several different strategies, as in the case of trust? Is it possible that some agent adopts a strategy of proposing a 70/30 share and rejects offers of less that 50%, whereas another agent offers only 50/50 shares and rejects any offer less that 30%? A brief reflection tells us that, if we observe 50/50 divisions, it is exactly what people offer and accept. The interesting question then is to determine how such a rule could have emerged from what is likely to have been a trial-and-error period in which many different offer types were present.

Many experimental results tell us that, in the absence of other considerations (such as focusing subjects on need, merit, etc.) people gravitate toward a 50/50 share. I discussed in Chapter 3 how the results of experimental games point to the importance of fairness considerations in shaping players' behavior. The pioneering work of Guth et al. (1982) on Ultimatum bargaining, along with many other recent variations of the Ultimatum game (Camerer 2003), reveal that the subjects' payoff values do not reflect just their own monetary gains. Experiments consistently show that subjects seem to have a shared idea of a fair outcome, as well as a tendency to enact it. Several models have been advanced to explain the data, all of them introducing modified utility functions that assume either an individual's preference for fair outcomes (Fehr and Schmidt 1999), a sensitivity to the intentions of other players (Rabin 1993), or a player's propensity to recognize and follow established norms.[1] In what follows, I build on my social norms approach and assume that, whenever a social norm exists (or is believed to exist), individuals who are aware of it and believe that a sufficiently high proportion of the population follows it and expects them to comply, too, have an incentive to obey the norm. In my model, most individuals who behave in a "fair" or "decent" way do so simply because they have certain kinds of expectations.

The role expectations play in supporting a norm and motivating compliance has only recently been fully recognized and formally assessed (see Chapter 3). A crucial step, however, remains to be taken, namely, providing an account of how individuals *come to form the right kinds of expectations.* Knowing how a norm emerges means knowing how individuals come to believe that it exists and then act on those beliefs. The emergence of a social norm thus involves two distinct but related psychological processes. The first is the process by which individuals come to believe that a social norm exists, and the second is the process through which an individual's belief about the social norm affects his decisions.

Instead of taking social norms as given, I will now explore their emergence as the outcome of independent individual decisions made in the context of a repeated game. Focusing on the norm of fair division in the Ultimatum game, I want to show that this norm can emerge and survive even if it is not particularly efficient or morally sound. The reasons for the norm's emergence lie in particular facts of individuals' psychology, crucially, the fact that individuals display "herding behavior."[2] A vast psychological literature, supported by experimental data, shows that when individuals are faced with new tasks or an uncertain situation they will, whenever possible, look to behavioral regularities for guidance in making choices. In our case, this means that an individual faced with a monetary

---

[1] For a comparison of three alternative models of 'social preference,' see Chapter 3.

[2] By "herding behavior" is meant the tendency of rational individuals to conform to the actions or opinions of other individuals in ambiguous or uncertain situations. If deviating from what one believes to be public opinion or a shared norm involves some costs, it may be rational for an individual to conform, even if she disagrees with the opinion or dislikes the norm. I discussed such behavior in the previous chapter.

division task will almost certainly try to discover what behavioral regularity, or 'norm,' exists before acting, because by following the norm he can legitimately expect his offer not to be rejected. Once an individual believes he has identified a norm, he will tend to follow it, provided he believes a sufficient proportion of the population to follow it, and also believes that this proportion of the population also expects him to conform to the norm. In the Ultimatum games we are considering, not following the norm may mean that one's offer is rejected, and hence one receives a payoff of zero.

A norm of fair division is thus the 'natural' outcome of the interaction of individuals who display what I believe are quite common and well-documented psychological propensities. My conclusion is quite different from explanations of the emergence of norms found previously in the literature. For example, although Axelrod (1992) attempts to show how norms can emerge by considering evolutionarily successful strategies in the so-called norms game, what we ultimately get is only an account of why any action that is behaviorally equivalent to "following a norm" would emerge. Objections similar in spirit have been raised against Skyrms's (1996) account of the origin of the 50/50 split in the game of divide-the-cake. Kitcher (1996) notes that, although "it's important to demonstrate that the forms of behavior that accord with our sense of justice and morality can originate and be maintained under natural selection . . . we should also be aware that the demonstration doesn't necessarily account for the superstructure of concepts and principles in terms of which we appraise those forms of behavior." Any account of the evolution of social norms that truly provides a model of the evolution of *social norms* as opposed to simple behavioral regularities must then move beyond mere descriptions of behavior and attempt to show how various psychological aspects of norm-following might emerge. One virtue of the proposed model is that it provides a psychological rather than a behavioral account of norms of fair division.

The Ultimatum Game

As we saw in Chapter 3, the Ultimatum game has a simple structure. For the sake of readers' convenience, I will repeat here some of the basic facts about such game and reproduce here the game of Figure 3.1. As always, the subjects form pairs, one person being identified as the Proposer and the other as the Responder. The Proposer is awarded a given amount M (usually $10) to be divided between the Proposer and the Responder.

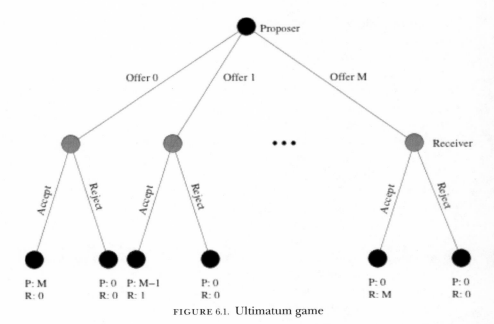

FIGURE 6.1. Ultimatum game

The Proposer's offer can range between M and zero, and the Responder has a binary choice in each case: to accept the offer or to reject it.
If the offer is accepted, the Proposer receives $M - x$ and the Responder
receives x, where x is the offer amount. If the offer is rejected, each player
receives nothing. The Ultimatum choice situation can be represented as
the extensive form game of perfect information shown in Figure 6.1. If
we use a classic utility function, which presupposes that players only care
about their own monetary payoff, and assume such functions to be common knowledge among the players, then the Proposer should offer the
minimum amount x guaranteed to be accepted. The Responder, in turn,
will accept anything greater than zero. For example, if the minimum
available amount is 1¢, the Proposer should offer it and the offer should
be accepted, leaving the Proposer with $9.99.

   In Chapter 3 I discussed the results of experiments that show that
nobody offers 1¢ or even $1. It is worth repeating that in most countries
the modal and median offers in experimental games are 40 to 50% of
the total amount, and the mean offers are 30 to 40%. Offers below 20%
are rejected about half the time (Camerer 2003). Are subjects irrational?
Clearly if by rationality we mean that subjects maximize expected utility

and that they only value monetary outcomes, then subjects who reject nonzero offers *are* acting irrationally. However, individuals' behavior across games suggests that there is a concern for fairness, so much so that subjects are prepared to punish those who behave in inequitable ways at a cost to themselves.[3]

Though several alternative utility functions have been proposed to explain pro-social behavior in Ultimatum games, virtually no explanation has considered the possibility that players may be responding to what they perceive to be widely accepted social norms. The absence of social norms in economists' explanations was in part due to the lack of a good operational, testable definition of social norms as well as to the (related) difficulty of constructing a testable utility function that includes social norms. I hope I have remedied this situation with the norm-based utility function I introduced in this book. Such a function, we have seen, incorporates norms in the calculation of payoffs.

Though I have already provided a formal definition of a social norm in the appendix to Chapter 1, it is worth repeating at least some of the crucial features here. Consider a typical N-person (normal-form) game. For ease of formal treatment, I conceive a norm as a function that maps one's expectations concerning the behavior of others into what one "ought to do." In other words, a norm regulates behavior conditional on other people's behaviors. Denote the strategy set of player i by S_i, and let $S_{-i} = \prod_{j \neq i} S_j$ be the set of strategy profiles of players other than i. Then a norm for player i may be formally represented by a function $N_i : L_{-i} \rightarrow S_i$, where $L_{-i} \subseteq S_{-i}$. In an Ultimatum game, for example, a shared norm may be a 50/50 division of the money. In that case, L_{-i} includes all the strategies of all players (excluding player i) that prescribe a 50/50 division.

A feature of this definition is particularly important for what follows. Given the other players' strategies, there may or may not be a norm that prescribes how player i ought to behave. So L_{-i} need not be, and usually is not, equal to S_{-i}. In particular, L_{-i} could be empty in the situation where there is no norm whatsoever to regulate player i's behavior, and in the model that follows we handle this case by having individuals look at the distribution of strategies in the population.

---

[3] We know that Responders reject unfair offers even when the stakes are as high as three months' earnings (Cameron 1995). Furthermore, experiments in which third parties have a chance to punish an 'unfair' Proposer at a monetary cost to themselves show that costly punishment is frequent (Fehr and Fischbacher 2004).

A strategy profile $s = (s, \ldots, s_n)$ *instantiates* a norm for j if $s_{-j} \in L_{-j}$, that is, if N_j is defined at s_{-j}. It *violates* a norm if, for some j, it instantiates a norm for j but $s_j \neq N_j(s_{-j})$. Let π_i be the payoff function for player i. The norm-based utility function of player i depends on the strategy profile s and is given by

$$U_i(s) = \pi_i(s) - k_i \max_{s_{-j} \in L_{-j}} \max_{m \neq j}\{\pi_m(s_{-j}, N_j(s_{-j})) - \pi_m(s), 0\},$$

where $k_i \geq 0$ is a constant representing a player's sensitivity to the relevant norm.[4] Recall that the second maximum operator ranges over all the players other than the norm violator. Hence the discounting term (multiplied by k_i) is the maximum payoff deduction resulting from all norm violations.

In what follows I apply the norm-based utility function to the Ultimatum game. In a typical Ultimatum game, the norm usually prescribes a 'fair' amount the Proposer ought to offer. The norm functions that represent this norm are the following: N_1 is a constant N function, where N denotes the "fair" amount in the situation, and N_2 is nowhere defined.[5] The norm-based utility functions for the Ultimatum game are then the following:

$$U_{1,\text{reject}}(x) = U_{2,\text{reject}}(x) = 0$$
$$U_{1,\text{accept}}(x) = (M - x) - k_1 \max(N - x, 0)$$
$$U_{2,\text{accept}}(x) = x - k_2 \max(N - x, 0).$$

Note that if the Responder is offered $x \geq N$, then $U_{2,\text{accept}}(x) = x - k_2 \max(N - x, 0) = x$, and similarly the Proposer's payoff is $M - x$. If the Responder rejects, the utilities of both players correspond to a payoff of zero. If the Proposer offers x and the Responder accepts, the utilities are as above. In the general utility function, N_i denotes the amount player i thinks he should get/offer according to some social norm applicable to the situation, and k_i is nonnegative. For the moment, let me assume it is common knowledge that $N_1 = N_2 = N$, which is not too unreasonable in a typical Ultimatum game. I shall relax this assumption in the next section, when players are trying to 'guess' what the norm is from observing other players' actions. In that case, I allow N to range over $(0, 1, \ldots, M)$, because the social norm that emerges may in principle be *any* value.

---

[4] Recall that k_i is only unique up to some positive factor that varies according to the players' payoff functions.

[5] Intuitively, N_2 should proscribe rejection of fair (or hyperfair) offers.

The Responder should accept the offer if and only if $U_{2,\text{accept}}(x) \geq U_{2,\text{reject}}(x) = 0$, which implies the following *threshold for acceptance*: $k_2 < (x/N - x)$. Notice that an offer greater than the norm dictates is not necessary for the sake of acceptance. For the Proposer, the utility function is decreasing in x when $x \geq N$; hence a rational Proposer will not offer more than N. Suppose $x \leq N$. If $k_1 > 1$, the utility function is increasing in x, which means that the best choice for the Proposer is to offer N. If $k_1 < 1$, the utility function is decreasing in x, which implies that the best strategy for the Proposer is to offer the least amount that would result in acceptance, that is, (a little bit more than) the threshold $k_2(N - x)$. If $k_1 = 1$, between $k_2(N - x)$ and N, it does not matter how much the Proposer offers.[6]

It is also the case that the Proposer's belief about the Responder's type figures in her decision when $k_1 < 1$. The belief can be represented by a joint probability over k_2 and N_2, if the value of N_2 is not common knowledge.[7] The Proposer should choose an offer that maximizes the expected utility

$$EU(x) = P(k_2(N_2 - x) < x) \times (M - x - k_1(N_1 - x)).$$

Emerging Norms

The following model aims to show how a social norm can emerge as an artifact of independent individual decisions made in the context of a repeated game.[8] Because a "social norm," as used here, refers to motivating beliefs of individual agents, the following model needs to represent two different psychological processes. The first is the process by which individuals come to believe a social norm exists, and the second is the process through which an individual's subjective beliefs regarding the social norm affect or influence the decisions that individual makes. As a consequence, this approach requires more complex initial assumptions

---

[6] It is also possible to have $k_1 < 0$. In that case, the Proposer would receive positive utility from a norm deviation in his favor. Such a Proposer would make an offer as low as the expected Responder's threshold for acceptance permits.

[7] As an example in which the norm may be ambiguous, think of an Ultimatum game in which it is common knowledge that the Proposer solved a difficult task before playing the game. In that case, some players may shift from an equal share to an equitable one, in which the "deserving" Proposer offers less than half, and the Responder accepts (Hoffman et al. 1994; Frey and Bohnet 1995).

[8] Jason Alexander and I have been working at running simulations of a model based on my utility function. The results presented here are the outcome of our joint project.

than those typically used in evolutionary models based on the replicator dynamics or local interaction models.[9] However, I believe that the overall flexibility and power of this modeling approach more than compensates for the additional increase in complexity.

Let us consider a population $P = \{1, \ldots, N\}$ of individuals who pair at random and play the Ultimatum game. Each individual i has a *strategy* s_i, an integer from the set $\{0, 1, \ldots, M\}$, where M is the amount of dollars to be divided among the players. A strategy s_i denotes the amount of M that i will offer when in the role of Proposer. Initially, the strategies s_i are assigned to individuals at random according to a uniform distribution over the set $\{0, 1, \ldots, M\}$.[10] In later generations, individuals adopt new strategies according to *a best-response calculation* based upon incomplete information about the state of the population (I describe later on the precise way in which this occurs). In particular, individuals will form a subjective assessment of what the norm might be and choose a strategy that maximizes their expected utility with respect to the 'putative' norm.

In addition to the agent's strategy, each individual i has two parameters, denoted k_i and k_i', both measuring the extent to which the perceived social norm influences their behavior, or their sensitivity to the norm. The first parameter, k_i, lies in the range $[0, k_{\max}]$ and represents how sensitive a person in the role of Responder is to the perceived social norm. Individuals with a low k_i parameter are less likely to reject low offers in the ultimatum game (where a "low offer" means one falling below the perceived social norm), as they feel no strong inclination to enforce conformity to the social norm, especially when enforcement requires rejection of the offer, meaning that the punisher receives a payoff of zero. Individuals with a high k_i parameter are more likely to reject low offers, because they may feel 'outraged' at being treated unfairly. Note that I assume each player to start the game with a subjective probability distribution over k, the Responder's parameter. In the course of play, such an estimate will change in accordance with what a player observes when in the role of Proposer.

The second parameter, k_i', is selected from a normal distribution with mean 0 and a standard deviation of 0.2.[11] The k_i' parameter measures

---

[9] See, e.g., Nowak and May (2000), Binmore (1994), Alexander (2003), and Bicchieri et al. (2004)

[10] The uniform distribution assumption can easily be relaxed.

[11] Mean 0 means that there will be people who are neutral with respect to the norm, and the standard deviation value was chosen so that we do not have wild fluctuations in the

the extent to which i is willing to conform to the perceived social norm when in the role of Proposer. It essentially gauges the disutility or utility felt by individuals when they deviate from the social norm governing offers in the game. Individuals with a low but positive k'_i parameter feel little "remorse" at offering less than the social norm and hence will be inclined to make low offers if they believe that low offers are likely to be accepted. Individuals with a high, positive k'_i parameter are more likely to conform to the perceived social norm as deviations from it will tend to produce greater disutility. I did not consider negative values for the k'_i parameter, as they would mean that the individual benefits from deviating from the perceived social norm, with the amount of "benefit" increasing according to the absolute value of the k'_i parameter. For example, a 'difference maximizer' might actually enjoy offering as little as he expects to be accepted by the Responder, because his utility increases with the difference between $M - x$ and x.

In the previous paragraphs, I have made several references to the "perceived social norm." Because the social norm arises endogenously, we must model the process by which actors come to believe that a social norm exists. To begin, since the population of actors in the model is small (typically on the order of 100 individuals or less), it is assumed that the distribution of strategies over the population is public knowledge. That is, every individual knows the proportion of offers of $0, 1, \ldots, M$ in the population. Each individual also possesses a *threshold* $t_i \in [0, 1]$ representing the proportion of the population that must adopt a common strategy before that individual considers the common strategy to be a "social norm." Thus, two individuals with different thresholds can have differing opinions as to what the current social norm is or, indeed, on *whether* a social norm exists at all. Social norms, in the sense adopted here, are entirely subjective phenomena that depend only on the particular beliefs of individuals. This is the reason why conditions (a), (b), and (b') of my definition of social norms (Chapter 1) refer to a "sufficiently large subset of the population," where the meaning of 'sufficiently large' may vary for different individuals.

Let $S = \{0, 1, \ldots, M\}$ denote the common set of strategies for each member of the population, and let P denote the distribution of strategies across the population at a given time (the time index is suppressed for clarity of notation). Note, again, that P is assumed to be common

---

value of k'_i. If we only admit 'reasonable' variations in k'_i, the effect of k'_i is unlikely to swamp the effect of k_i.

knowledge. In each iteration of the model, every individual calculates the following:

$$n_i = \{s \in S : P(s) > t_i\},$$

where n_i denotes the set of all strategies with more than t_i of the population following them. In other words, n_i is the set of strategies that are considered by a given player i as 'candidate' social norms. If $n_i \neq \varnothing$, then let P_{n_i} denote the probability distribution P restricted to the set n_i, "trimmed" at the threshold, and renormalized. More precisely,

$$P_{n_i}(s) = \begin{cases} \kappa(P(s) - t_i) & \text{if } s \in n_i \\ 0 & \text{otherwise,} \end{cases}$$

where κ is a suitably chosen renormalization constant.[12] P_{n_i} thus represents individual i's beliefs regarding the current social norm. If $n_i = \varnothing$, then no single offer type is sufficiently frequent in the population to be considered a possible candidate for a social norm by i. Finally, let

$$P_i = \begin{cases} P_{n_i} & \text{if } n_i \neq \varnothing \\ P & \text{otherwise,} \end{cases}$$

where P_i is a probability distribution over (possible) social norms, given completely accurate information about the state of the population and individual i's beliefs about how much agreement is necessary for a social norm to exist. Using this information, i then takes the following as his or her best estimate of the social norm:

$$N_i = \sum_{j=0}^{M} j P_i(j).$$

Note that N_i is a real number. That is, an individual will always be able to give a precise value to what he believes is the social norm that is in place.

Figures 6.2 and 6.3 illustrate this process of estimating the social norm for two different agents. In the example, $M = 10$ dollars, and agents can offer any integer amount of dollars. In both figures, the leftmost chart represents the distribution of strategies in the population. The horizontal axis represents the possible offers (from zero to 10 dollars), and the vertical axis shows the proportion of the population playing each strategy.

---

[12] For example, if only three strategies ('give 1,' 'give 2,' and 'give 3') 'make the cut' for player i, then we take **k** to be equal to $1/(P(1) - t_i) + (P(2) - t_i) + (P(3) - t_i)$.

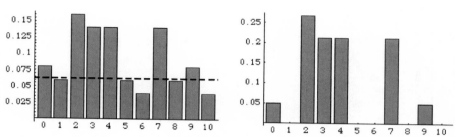

FIGURE 6.2. The adjusted probability distribution P_i for an agent with a low threshold

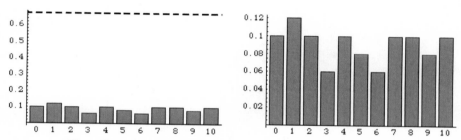

FIGURE 6.3. The adjusted probability distribution P_i for an agent with a high threshold

The dashed horizontal line on the left chart illustrates the threshold for a particular agent. In Figure 6.2, the agent has a relatively low threshold with $t_i = 0.06$. As the proportion of the population offering 0, 2, 3, 4, 7, and 9 dollars exceeds this threshold, this particular agent believes that all of these strategies (and *only* these strategies) are likely candidates for the social norm. The adjusted probability distribution P_i for this agent is displayed to the right of Figure 6.2, where all the strategies below the threshold have been eliminated.

In contrast, Figure 6.3 shows the adjusted probability distribution P_i for an agent with a high threshold. In this case, no strategy has sufficient mass on the distribution to exceed the agent's threshold. Hence, the agent will simply use the actual strategy distribution in the population when estimating the social norm.

It is also possible for an agent to have such a low threshold that every strategy exceeds it. In this case, the adjusted probability distribution very closely resembles the actual distribution of strategies in the population. However, the adjusted distribution does not exactly equal the actual distribution; due to the "trimming" taking place in the definition of P_{n_i},

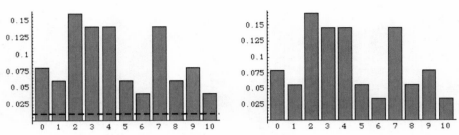

FIGURE 6.4. The adjusted probability distribution P_i for an agent with an extremely low threshold

some distortion is introduced. Figure 6.4 illustrates a case where every strategy exceeds the low threshold of a particular agent.

Once each agent's estimate of the social norm is formed, every person is paired at random with I other players and plays the Ultimatum game. In the simulations we ran, we assumed $I < P$ (agents are paired only with a subset of the population), so that the information a player gets is incomplete. This is equivalent to introducing noise in the system. If on the contrary we were to set $I = P$, we could predict how agents learn because we would know the information they have. An agent may thus be paired with, say, five other agents and play simultaneously with each of them. For each pairwise interaction, the roles of Proposer and Responder are assigned at random.[13] The Proposer i offers an amount x_i to the Responder, who then decides whether to accept the offer. The Responder accepts the offer if it confers positive utility and rejects the offer if it gives negative or zero utility. We assume that the utility functions employed by Proposers and Responders have the following forms:

$$U_{R,\text{accept}}^i(x) = \begin{cases} x & \text{if } x \geq N_i \\ x - k_i(N_i - x) & \text{otherwise} \end{cases}$$

$$U_{P,\text{accept}}^i(x) = \begin{cases} M - x & \text{if } x \geq N_i \\ (M - x) - k'_i(N_i - x) & \text{otherwise} \end{cases}$$

$$U_{P,\text{reject}}^i(x) = U_{R,\text{reject}}^i(x) = 0.$$

The role of the k_i parameter should now be clear. If the Responder is offered an amount exceeding or equal to the Responder's subjective estimate of the social norm, then the utility conferred to the Responder

---

[13] This randomization, too, makes the system nondeterministic, in that we cannot predict how agents will learn.

exactly equals the amount offered. However, if the offer is lower than the Responder's subjective perception of the social norm, the utility conferred equals the amount offered *decreased* in proportion to the amount that the offer falls short of the perceived social norm, with the k_i parameter being the constant of proportionality. As rejecting an offer always confers a payoff of zero, the Responder accepts the offer if and only if $U^i_{R,\text{accept}}(x)$ is greater than zero.

Notice that the Responder gets no new information from this interaction, because the distribution P of strategies (offer types) among the population is (by assumption) public knowledge. However, the Proposer obtains information about the distribution of the k_i parameter in the population (which is not public knowledge): Since the offer is accepted if and only if $U^i_{R,\text{accept}}(x) > U^i_{R,\text{reject}}(x)$, the Proposer can infer that the value of the k_i parameter must fall in the range $[0, \frac{x}{N_i - x}]$.

This information is consolidated by the Proposer at the end of each round of interaction and is used to adjust the Proposer's beliefs about the distribution of the k_i parameter in the population. The adjustment procedure occurs in the following way: Because a proposal x_i is accepted by individual j if and only if $k_j < (x_i/N_j - x_i)$, where N_j is j's subjective estimate of the social norm, the fact that x_i was accepted gives i evidence for thinking that each Responder who accepted the offer had a value of their k parameter bounded above by $x_i/N_i - x_i$. Note that N_j and N_i have different subscripts. Though N_j is the norm estimated by player j, player i has no way of knowing it. Because each individual's subjective perception of the social norm is private and inaccessible to others, the only reasonable way i may estimate j's perceived social norm is by *projection*. That is, i assumes that all *other* individuals in the population are using the same social norm as the one perceived by i. This assumption becomes plausible if we attribute to each individual two beliefs: first, the belief that there is, in fact, a *real* social norm that she is attempting to discover, and second, that, as each person is a competent cognitive agent, each person's subjective perception of the social norm is likely to be relatively close to the real social norm. Under these two assumptions, in the absence of any other information, it becomes reasonable for i to ascribe his perceived social norm to other individuals in the population.[14]

---

[14] There is ample evidence in the psychological literature that, in the absence of information about other people's preferences, beliefs, and dispositions, individuals will use their own beliefs, etc., as a reliable estimate of what others believe, what their attitudes are, etc. (Dawes 2001).

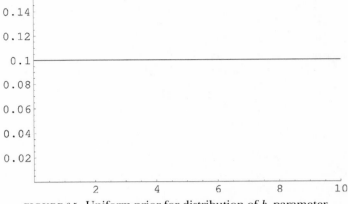

FIGURE 6.5. Uniform prior for distribution of k_i parameter

Updating Beliefs and Strategies

Given that i can (plausibly) infer that the k parameter for Responder who accept i's offer is bounded above by $x_i/N_i - x_i$, this information can be used to refine i's distribution for the k parameter in the population. Let Δ denote the amount of reinforcement given to a single accepted offer, and let $f_i(k)$ be i's current distribution function for the k parameter in the population. Δ measures how much the new information he gets matters to a player, or his *prudence* in updating. A large Δ thus means that the player discounts the past quite a bit, in the sense that past information decays very quickly for him. I assume here that Δ is constant in the population. If we instead allow for individual Δ's, then, depending on the proportions of 'quick' and 'slow' updaters, we will observe slow or quick convergence to a norm.

If Q people have accepted i's offer in the current round of interactions, i's new distribution function $f'_i(k)$ is then given by

$$f'_i(k) = f_i(k) + \begin{cases} Q\Delta & \text{if } k < \dfrac{x_i}{N_i - x_i} \\ 0 & \text{otherwise,} \end{cases}$$

suitably renormalized.[15] Note that the updating is non-Bayesian, because a player in the Proposer's role has only an upper bound, $x_i/N_i - x_i$, and does not know a Responder's k value.

---

[15] If we take c to be equal to $\int_0^{k\,\max} f'_i(k)\,dk$, then $f''_i(k) = (1/c)\, f_j{}'(k)$.

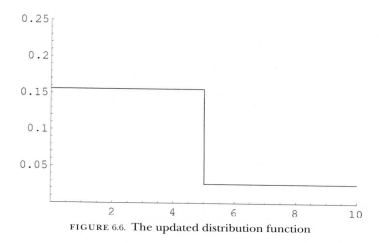

FIGURE 6.6. The updated distribution function

Consider the following example. Assume that i begins with a uniform prior for the distribution of the k parameter, as shown in Figure 6.5.[16] Suppose that the amount to be divided is \$10 and that $k_{max} = 10$.

Suppose that, in the last round of interaction, i interacts with eight people and that five receivers accept his offer. If i offers \$5 and his subjective social norm is $N_i = \$6$, the renormalized updated distribution function is as portrayed in Figure 6.6 (i.e., the new distribution function is $(1/k_{max}) + 5\Delta$).

Suppose that, after updating his strategy, in the next round of interactions i continues to offer \$5, has a subjective social norm of $N_i = \$5.70$, and has three accept offers. The new, updated, normalized distribution function in this case is that of Figure 6.7.

If i now switches his strategy to offer \$3, calculates a new subjective social norm of \$4.70, and has three people accept his offer, the third updated distribution function for the k parameter is as shown in Figure 6.8.

The last part of the model concerns the updating of strategies. After every individual plays the Ultimatum game with their selected partners and updates their distribution functions for the k parameter, they engage in strategic updating. Strategic updating involves each person calculating the *best-response* offer based on their estimate of the k parameter distribution and their subjective social norm (recall that the current distribution of offers in the population is public knowledge). Note that the

---

[16] I am assuming here that the initial distribution of the k parameter is $1/k_{max}$.

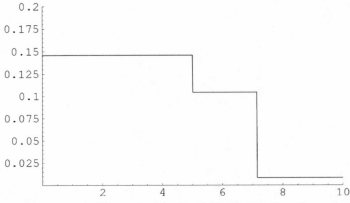

FIGURE 6.7. The second updated distribution function

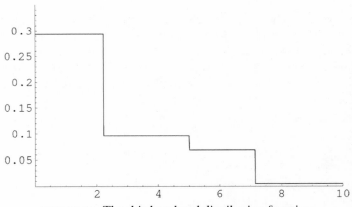

FIGURE 6.8. The third updated distribution function

distribution of offers in the population may change after a round of interactions, and therefore the subjective social norms will also take different values.

The relevant utility functions are the following. For the Responder, the acceptance criteria that determines whether the offer is accepted or not is the sign on the following function:

$$U_{R,\text{accept}}(x, N_i) - U_{R,\text{reject}}(x, N_i) = x + \begin{cases} 0 & \text{if } x \geq N_i \\ -k(N_i - x) & \text{otherwise.} \end{cases}$$

If the above difference is nonnegative, the Responder accepts the offer. If the difference is negative, the Responder rejects the offer. For the Proposer, the following utility function gives his utility:

$$U_{P,\text{accept}}(M - x, N_i) = (M - x) + \begin{cases} 0 & \text{if } x \geq N_i \\ -k'(N_i - x) & \text{otherwise.} \end{cases}$$

The best-response offer is the offer x that maximizes $U_{P,\text{accept}}$ $(M - x, N_i)$, where N_i denotes the current subjective social norm held by the individual, and also gives a *nonnegative* value to the difference $U_{R,\text{accept}}(x, N_i) - U_{R,\text{reject}}(x, N_i)$. The estimated value of k in the population used by i in calculating values for the above utility difference for Responder is simply the expected value of k, according to i's current k parameter distribution: $\int_0^{k_{\max}} k f(k) \, dk$.

To summarize, the dynamics in each round of interaction are

1. For each $i \in P$, determine N_i.
2. For each $i \in P$, pair with a group drawn at random from $P - \{i\}$. Play the Ultimatum game with each of these individuals, keeping track of the number of offers that one makes which are accepted.
3. For each $i \in P$, update i's estimate of the k parameter distribution.
4. For each $i \in P$, adopt a best-response offer for the next round, using the value of N_i previously calculated and the expected value of k as determined from the updated k parameter distribution.

My colleague Jason Alexander and I ran a number of simulations using this model, and the results were encouraging: If we take 50 individuals and let each interact with 5 others in each round, we obtain convergence to an 'equal division' or 'quasi-equal division' norm in each simulation, where the time to convergence is quite rapid at less that 20 interactions.

For example, consider the initial distribution of strategies (offers) in Figure 6.9. After less than 20 iterations of the Ultimatum game, the final strategy distribution looks like the one in Figure 6.10. In this case, the population converged to a 50/50 norm of fair division. Take instead a very different initial distribution (Figure 6.11). In that case, after less than 20 iterations of the Ultimatum game, the distribution of offers converges to a distribution in which half of the population offers 50% of the money, and the rest is spread between 40 and 60% (Figure 6.12).

It thus seems that the simple model proposed here, based on some well-established psychological characteristics of individuals such as their

The Evolution of a Fairness Norm

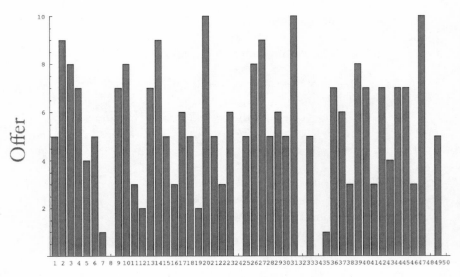

FIGURE 6.9. Initial distribution of offers

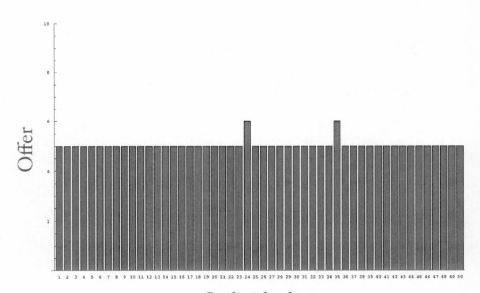

FIGURE 6.10. Final distribution of offers

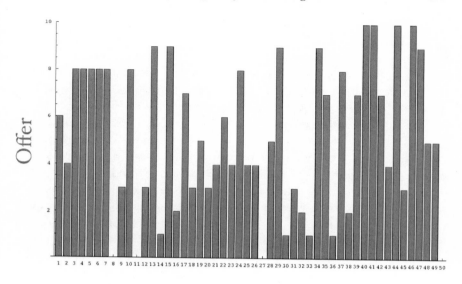

FIGURE 6.11. Initial distribution of offers

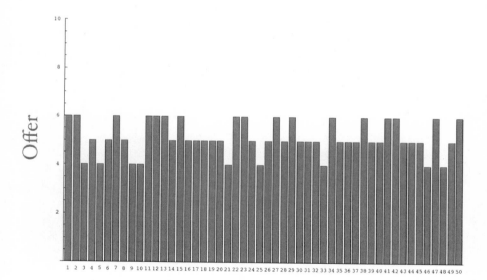

FIGURE 6.12. Final distribution of offers

propensity to display herding behavior in uncertain or ambiguous situations as well as their conditional preferences for following what is believed to be a shared norm, leads to the emergence of a social norm of fair sharing in repeated Ultimatum games under a variety of initial conditions. Note that the distribution of k's is what drives compliance with a social norm. In the model I presented here, the distribution of k's, that is, the distribution of various types in the population, was taken as given. What really needs to be explained is how such a distribution of types has evolved. I believe our sensitivity to social norms, and the accompanying disposition to punish transgressors, has evolved out of social dilemma-type situations. The propensity to recognize and conform to norms, as well as to be prepared to punish defectors, is evolutionarily necessary to the production and maintenance of any public good. Societies produced public goods (including the society itself) well before the founding of institutions devoted to monitor compliance and punish transgression. I would venture that a norm-complying distribution of k-types has evolved only in social dilemma-type situations and then has been extended to all sorts of social norms, some of them clearly unnecessary to the survival of society.

References

Alexander, J. M. (2003). "Random Boolean Networks and Evolutionary Game Theory." *Philosophy of Science* **70**: 1289–1304.

Allison, S. T. and N. L. Kerr (1994). "Group Corespondence Biases and the Provision of Public Goods." *Journal of Personality and Social Psychology* **21**: 563–579.

Allport, E. H. (1924). *Social Pyschology*. Boston, Houghton Mifflin.

Andersen, H. C. (2000). *The Emperor's New Suit (1837)*. Zurich, North-South Books.

Andreoni, J. (1990). "Impure Altruism and Donations to Public Goods: A Theory of Warm-Glow Giving." *The Economic Journal* **100**: 464–477.

Andreoni, J. (1995). "Cooperation in Public-Goods Experiments: Kindness or Confusion?" *American Economic Review* **90**: 166–193.

Asch, S. E. (1955). "Opinions and Social Pressure." *Scientific American*, 31–35.

Axelrod, R. (1992). "Citation Classic: How to Promote Cooperation." *Social and Behavioral Sciences* **44**: 10.

Banerjee, A. V. (1992). "A Simple Model of Herd Behavior." *Quarterly Journal of Economics* **107**: 797–818.

Bargh, J. A. (1994). "The Four Horsemen of Automaticity: Awareness, Intention, Effciency, and Control in Social Cognition." In *Handbook of Social Cognition*. R. S. Wyer and T. K. Srull, Eds. Hillsdale, NJ, Lawrence Erlbaum Associates.

Bargh, J. A., S. Chaiken, P. Raymond, and C. Hymes (1996). "The Automatic Evaluation Effect: Unconditional Automatic Attitude Activation with a Pronunciation Task." *Journal of Experimental Social Psychology* **32**: 104–128.

Barsalou, L. (1982). "Context-Independent and Context-Dependent Information in Concepts." *Memory and Cognition* **10**(1): 82–93.

Bartlett, F. C. (1932). *Remembering: A Study in Experimental and Social Psychology*. New York, Cambridge University Press.

Bernstein, L. (1992). "Opting Out of the Legal System: Extralegal Contractual Relations in the Diamond Industry." *Journal of Legal Studies* **21**: 115–157.

Bettenhausen, K. and K. Murnighan (1985). "The Emergence of Norms in Competitive Decision-Making Groups." *Administrative Science Quarterly* **30**: 350–372.

———— (1991). "The Development of an Intragroup Norm and the Effecs of Interpersonal and Structural Challenges." *Administrative Science Quarterly* **36**: 20–35.

Bicchieri, C. (1990). "Norms of Cooperation." *Ethics* **100**: 838–861.

Bicchieri, C. (1993). *Rationality and Coordination.* Cambridge, Cambridge University Press.

Bicchieri, C. (1997). "Learning to Cooperate." *In The Dynamics of Norms.* C. Bicchieri, R. Jeffrey, and B. Skyrms, Eds. Cambridge, Cambridge University Press.

Bicchieri, C. (1999). "Local Fairness." *Philosophy and Phenomenological Research* **LIX**(1): 229–236.

Bicchieri, C. (2000). "Words and Deeds: A Focus Theory of Norms." In *Rationality, Rules and Structure.* J. Nida-Rumelin and W. Spohn, Eds. Dordecht, Kluwer Academic Publishers.

Bicchieri, C. and J. Duffy (1997). "Corruption Cycles." *Political Studies* **3**(45): 61–79.

Bicchieri, C. and Y. Fukui (1999). "The Great Illusion: Ignorance, Informational Cascades and the Persistence of Unpopular Norms." *Business Ethics Quarterly* **9**: 127–155.

Bicchieri, C. and C. Rovelli (1995). "Evolution and Revolution: Catastrophe Theory and the Dynamics of Norms." *Rationality and Society* **7**: 201.

Bicchieri, C. and J. Zhang (2004). "A Note on Fairness Preferences" mimeo, Carnegie Mellon University, Pittsburgh, PA.

Bicchieri, C., J. Duffy, et al. (2004). "Trust Among Strangers." *Philosophy of Science* **71**: 286–319.

Bikchandani, S., D. Hirshleifer, and I. Walsh (1992). "A Theory of Fads, Fashions, Customs, and Cultural Change as Information Cascades." *Journal of Political Economy* **100**: 992–1026.

Binmore, K. G. (1994). *Playing Fair: Game Theory and the Social Contract.* Cambridge, MA, MIT Press.

Blount, S. (1995). "When Social Outcomes Aren't Fair: The Effect of Causal Attributions on Preferences." *Organizational Behavior and Human Decision Processes* **63**: 131–144.

Bornstein, G. (1992). "The Free Rider Problem in Intergroup Conflicts Over Step-Level and Continuous Public Goods." *Journal of Personality and Social Psychology* **62**: 597–602.

Bouas, K. S. and S. S. Komorita (1996). "Group Discussion and Cooperation in Social Dilemmas." *Personality and Social Psychology Bulletin* **22**: 1144–1150.

Brewer, M. B. (1979). "Ingroup Bias in the Minimal Intergroup Situation: A Cognitive Motivational Analysis." *Psychological Bulletin* **86**: 307–324.

Brewer, M. B. and R. M. Kramer (1986). "Choice Behavior in Social Dilemmas: Effects of Social Identity, Group Size and Decision Framing." *Journal of Personality and Social Psychology* **3**: 543–549.

Brewer, M. B. (1991). "The Social Self: On Being the Same and Different at the Same Time." *Personality and Social Psychology Bulletin* **17**: 475–482.

Bruner, J. S. (1957). "Going Beyond the Information Given." In *Contemporary Approaches to Cognition.* J. S. Bruner, E. Brunswik, and L. Festinger, Eds. Cambridge, MA, Harvard University Press, pp. 41–69.

Calvino, I. (1951). *The Nonexistent Knight and the Cloven Viscount.* Italy, Giulio Einaudi Editore.

Camerer, C. (2003). *Behavioral Game Theory: Experiments on Strategic Interaction.* Princeton, NJ, Princeton University Press.

Camerer, C. and R. H. Thaler (1995). "Anomalies: Ultimatums, Dictators, and Manners." *Journal of Economic Perspectives* **9**(2): 209–219.

Camerer, C., G. Loewenstein, and M. Rabin (2004). *Advances in Behavioral Economics.* Princeton, NJ, Princeton University Press.

Cameron, L. (1995). "Raising the Stakes in the Ultimatum Game: Experimental Evidence from Indonesia." Working paper, *Princeton Department of Economics–Industrial Relations Sections*, Princeton University, Princeton, NJ.

Cialdini, R., C. Kallgren, and R. Reno (1990). "A Focus Theory of Normative Conduct: A Theoretical Refinement and Reevaluation of the Role of Norms in Human Behavior." *Advances in Experimental Social Psychology* **24**: 201–234.

Collins, A. M. and E. F. Loftus (1975). "A Spreading Activation Theory of Semantic Memory." *Psychological Review* **82**: 407–428.

Collins, A. M. and M. R. Quillian (1969). "Retrieval Time from Semantic Memory." *Journal of Verbal Learning and Verbal Behavior* **8**: 240–248.

Cooke, N. M., F. T. Durso, and R. W. Schvaneveldt (1986). "Recall and Measures of Memory Organization." *Journal of Experimental Psychology: Learning, Memory, and Cognition* **12**: 538–549.

Dana, J., R. Weber, and J. X. Kuang (2003). "Exploiting Moral Wriggle Room: Behavior Inconsistent with a Preference for Fair Outcomes." *Carnegie Mellon Behavioral Decision Research Working Paper* **349**.

Dawes, R. (1972) *Fundamentals of Attitude Measurement.* New York, Wiley.

Dawes, R. (1980). "Social Dilemmas." *Annual Review of Psychology* **31**: 169–193.

Dawes, R. and R. H. Thaler (1988). "Anomalies: Cooperation." *Journal of Economic Perspectives* **2**(3): 187–197.

Dawes, R., J. McTavish, and H. Shaklee (1977). "Behavior, Communication, and Assumptions About Other Peoples' Behavior in a Commons Dilemma Situation." *Journal of Personality and Social Psychology* **35**: 1–11.

Dawes, R., J. Orbell, R. Simmons, and A. van de Kragt (1986). "Organizing Groups for Collective Action." *American Political Science Review* **80**: 1171–1185.

Dawes, R., J. Orbell, and A. van de Kragt (1988). "Not Me or Thee But We: The Importance of Group Identity in Eliciting Cooperation in Dilemma Situations." *Acta Psychologica* **68**: 83–97.

Dawes, R., A. van de Kragt, and J. Orbell (1990). "Cooperation for the Benefit of Us, Not Me, or My Conscience." In *Beyond Self-Interest*, J. Mansbridge, Ed. Chicago, University of Chicago Press.

de Tocqueville, A. (1856). *L'Ancien Regime.* Paris, Michael Levy.

Deutsch, M. and H. B. Gerard (1955). "A Study of Normative and Information Social Influences Upon Individual Judgment." *Journal of Abnormal and Social Psychology* **51**: 629–636.

Elias, N. (1978). *The History of Manners.* New York, Pantheon.

Elio, R. and J. R. Anderson (1981). "The Effects of Category Generalizations and Instance Similarity on Schema Abstraction." *Journal of Experimental Psychology: Learning, Memory, and Cognition* **7**: 397–417.

References

Elster, J. (1989). *The Cement of Society.* Cambridge, Cambridge University Press.

Epley, N. and T. Gilovich (1999). "Just Going Along: Nonconscious Priming and Conformity to Social Pressure." *Journal of Experimental Social Psychology* **35**: 578–589.

Estes, W. K. (1986). "Memory Storage and Retrieval Processes in Category Learning." *Journal of Experimental Psychology* **115**: 155–174.

Falk, A., E. Fehr, et al. (2000). "Informal Sanctions." IEER Working Paper No. 59.

Fehr, E. and S. Gachter (2000a). "Fairness and Retaliation: The Economics of Reciprocity." *Journal of Economic Perspectives* **14**(3): 159–181.

Fehr, E. and S. Gachter (2000b). "Cooperation and Punishment in Public Goods Experiments." *American Economic Review* **90**(4): 980–994.

Fehr, E. and K. Schmidt (1999). "A Theory of Fairness, Competition, and Cooperation." *The Quarterly Journal of Economics* **114**(3): 817–868.

Fehr, E., A. Falk, and U. Fischbacher (2003). "Testing Theories of Fairness – Intentions Matter." Working Paper No. 63, Institute for Empirical Research in Economics, University of Zürich.

Fehr, E. and U. Fischbacher (2004). "Third Party Punishment and Social Norms." *Evolution and Human Behavior* **25**: 63–87.

Fiske, S. T. and S. E. Taylor (1991). *Social Cognition.* New York, McGraw-Hill.

Fiske, S. T. (1980). "Attention and Weight in Person Perception: The Impact of Negative and Extreme Behavior." *Journal of Personality and Social Psychology* **37**: 1758–1768.

Fiske, S. T. and S. L. Neuberg (1990). "A Continuum of Impression Formation, From Category-Based to Individuating Processes: Influences of Information and Motivation on Attention and Interpretation." In *Advances in Experimental Social Psychology.* L. Berkowitz, Ed. New York, Academic Press. **23**.

Fiske, A. (1992). "The Four Elementary Forms of Sociality: Framework for a Unified Theory of Social Relations." *Psychological Review* **99**: 689–723.

Forsythe, R., J. L. Horowitz, N. E. Savin, and M. Sefton (1994). "Fairness in Simple Bargaining Experiments." *Games and Economic Behavior* **6**(3): 347–369.

Frey, B. and I. Bohnet (1995). "Institutions Affect Fairness: Experimental Investigations." *Journal of Institutional and Theoretical Economics* **151**(2): 286–303.

Frey, B. and I. Bohnet (1997). "Identification in Democratic Society." *Journal of Socio-Economics* **XXVI**: 25–38.

Gaertner, S. L. and J. F. Dovidio (1996). "Revisiting the Contact Hypothesis: The Induction of a Common Ingroup Identity." *International Journal of Intercultural Relations* **20**: 271–290.

Geanakoplos, J., D. Pearce, and E. Stacchetti (1989). "Psychological Games and Sequential Rationality." *Games and Economic Behavior* **1**: 60–79.

Gelman, S. (1988). "The Development of Induction Within Natural Kind and Artifact Categories." *Cognitive Psychology* **20**: 65–95.

Goffman, E. (1959). *The Presentation of Self in Everyday Life.* Garden City, NY, Doubleday.

Goodman, N. (1972). "Seven Strictures on Similarity." In *Problems and Projects.* N. Goodman, Ed. New York, The Bobbs-Merrill Co.

Graf, P. and D. L. Schacter (1985). "Implicit and Explicit Memory for New Associations in Normal and Amnesic Subjects." *Journal of Abnormal and Social Psychology: Learning, Memory, and Cognition* 11: 501–518.

Greenwald, A. G. and M. R. Banaji (1995). "Implicit Social Cognition: Attitudes, Self-Esteem, and Stereotypes." *Psychological Review* 102: 4–27.

Guth, W., R. Schmittberger, and B. Schwarze (1982). "An Experimental Analysis of Ultimatum Games." *Journal of Economic Behavior and Organization* 3: 367–388.

Guth, W. (1995). "On Ultimatum Bargaining Experiments: A Personal Review." *Journal of Economic Behavior and Organization* 27: 329–344.

Harsanyi, J. (1967–8). "Games with Incomplete Information Played by 'Bayesian' Players." Parts 1, 2, and 3. *Management Science* 14: 159–182, 320–332, 468–502.

Harsanyi, J. and Selten, R. (1988). *A General Theory of Equilibrium Selection in Games.* Cambridge, MA: MIT Press.

Harvey, M. D. and M. E. Enzle (1981). "A Cognitive Model of Social Norms for Understanding the Transgression-Helping Effect." *Journal of Personality and Social Psychology* 41: 866–875.

Henrich, J. (2000). "Does Culture Matter in Economic Behavior? Ultimatum Game Bargaining Among the Machiguenga." *American Economic Review* 90(4): 973–979.

Henrich, J., R. Boyd, S. Bowles, H. Gintis, C. Camerer, E. Fehr, Eds. (2004). *Foundations of Human Sociality: Ethnography and Experiments in 15 Small-Scale Societies.* Oxford, Oxford University Press.

Hertel, G. and N. L. Kerr (2001). "Priming Ingroup Favoritism: The Impact of Normative Scripts in the Minimal Group Paradigm." *Journal of Experimental Social Psychology* 37: 316–324.

Hinkle, S., L. Taylor, D. Fox-Cardamone, and K. Crook (1989). "Intragroup Identification and Intergroup Differentiation: A Multi-Component Approach." *British Journal of Social Psychology* 28: 305–317.

Hirschman, A. O. (1970). *Exit, Voice, and Loyalty: Reponses to Decline in Firms, Organizations, and States.* Cambridge, MA, Harvard University Press.

Hoffman, E. and M. Spitzer (1985). "Entitlements, Rights, and Fairness: An Experimental Examination of Subjects' Concept of Distributive Justice." *Journal of Legal Studies* 2: 259–297.

Hoffman, E., K. A. McCabe, K. Shachat, and V. L. Smith (1994). "Preferences, Property Rights, and Anonymity in Bargaining Games." *Games and Economic Behavior* 7: 346–380.

Hoffman, E., K. A. McCabe, and V. L. Smith (1998). "Behavioral Foundations of Reciprocity: Experimental Economics and Evolutionary Psychology." *Economic Inquiry* 36: 335–352.

Hogg, M. A. and J. C. Turner (1987). "Social Identity and Conformity: A Theory of Referent Informational Influence." In *Current Issues in European Social Psychology.* W. Doise and S. Moscovici, Eds. Cambridge, Cambridge University Press.

Hume, D. (1966). *An Enquiry Concerning the Principles of Morals* (1751). London, Free Press.

Hume, D. (1978). *A Treatise of Human Nature (1739).* Oxford, Oxford University Press.

Insko, C. A. and J. Schopler (1987). "Categorization, Competition, and Collectivity." In *Review of Personality and Social Psychology: Group Processes*. C. Hendrick, Ed. Beverly Hills, Sage.

Isaac, R. and J. Walker (1988). "Communication and Free-Riding Behavior: The Voluntary Contribution Mechanism." *Economic Inquiry* **26**: 585–608.

Jacoby, L. L. (1983). "Perceptual Enhancement: Persistent Effects of an Experience." *Journal of Experimental Psychology: Learning, Memory, and Cognition* **9**(1): 21–38.

Jetten, J., R. Spears, and A. S. R. Manstead (1996). "Intergroup Norms and Intergroup Discrimination: Disctinctive Self-Categorization and Social Identity Effects." *Journal of Personality and Social Psychology* **71**: 1222–1233.

Jin, N., T. Yamagishi, and T. Kiyonari (1996). "Bilateral Dependency and the Minimal Group Paradigm." *Japanese Journal of Psychology* **67**: 77–85.

Jones, E. E. and R. Nisbett (1972). "The Actor and the Observer: Divergent Perceptions of the Causes of Behavior." In *Attribution: Perceiving the Causes of Behavior*. E. E. Jones, H. H. Kanouse, R. E. Kelley et al., Eds. Morristown, NJ, General Learning Press.

Kagel, J. H., C. Kim, and D. Moser (1996). "Fairness in Ultimatum Games with Asymmetric Information and Asymmetric Payoffs." *Games and Economic Behavior* **13**: 100–110.

Kahneman, D. and A. Tversky (1972). "Subjective Probability: A Judgment of Representativeness." *Cognitive Psychology* **3**: 430–454.

——— (1973). "Availability: A Heuristic for Judging Frequency and Probability." *Cognitive Psychology* **5**: 207–232.

——— (1982). "The Simulation Heuristic." *In Judgement Under Uncertainty: Heuristics and Biases*. D. Kahneman, P. Slovic, and A. Tversky, Eds. New York, Cambridge University Press, pp. 201–208.

Kahneman, D., J. Knetsch, and R. Thaler (1986). "Fairness as Constraint on Profit Seeking: Entitlements in the Market." *American Economic Review* **76**(4): 728–741.

Kauffman, K. (1988). *Prison Officers and Their World*. Cambridge, MA, Harvard University Press.

Kerr, N. L. and C. Kaufman-Gilliland (1994). "Communication, Commitment, and Cooperation in Social Dilemmas." *Journal of Personality and Social Psychology* **66**: 513–529.

Kerr, N. L., J. Garst, D. A. Lewandowski, and S. E. Harris (1997). "The Still, Small Voice: Commitment to Cooperate as an Internalized versus a Social Norm." *Personality and Social Psychology Bulletin* **23**: 1300–1311.

Kiesler, S., L. Sproull, and K. Waters (1996). "A Prisoner's Dilemma Experiment on Cooperation with People and Human-Like Computers." *Journal of Personality and Social Psychology* **70**: 47–65.

Kitcher, P. (1996). *The Lives to Come: The Genetic Revolution and Human Possibilities*. London, Penguin Books.

Klofas, J. M. and H. Toch (1982). "The Guard Subculture Myth." *Journal of Research in Crime and Delinquency* **19**: 238–254.

Kramer, R. M. and M. B. Brewer (1984). "Effects of Group Identity on Resource Use in a Simulated Commons Dilemma." *Journal of Personality and Social Psychology* **46**: 1044–1057.

————(1986). "Social Group Identity and the Emergence of Cooperation in Resource Conservation Dilemmas." In *Psychology of Decisions and Conflict: Experimental Social Dilemmas.* H. A. Wilke, Ed. Frankfurt: Verlag Peter Lang.

Kreps, D., Milgrom, P., Roberts, J., and Wilson, R. (1982). "Rational Cooperation in the Finitely Repeated Prisoner's Dilemma." *Journal of Economic Theory* **27**: 245–52.

Kripke, S. (1982). *Naming and Necessity.* Cambridge, MA, Harvard University Press.

Kuran, T. (1995). *Private Truths, Public Lies.* Cambridge, MA, Harvard University Press.

Lamberts, K. (1994). "Flexible Tuning of Similarity in Exemplar-Based Categorization." *Journal of Experimental Psychology: Learning, Memory, and Cognition* **20**(5): 1003–1021.

Lamberts, K. and D. Shanks, Eds. (1997). *Knowledge, Concepts, and Categories,* Hove: Psychology Press.

Latane, B. and J. M. Darley (1968). "Group Inhibition of Bystander Intervention." *Journal of Personality and Social Psychology* **10**(3): 215–221.

Lewis, D. (1969). *Convention: A Philosophical Study.* Cambridge, MA, Cambridge University Press.

———— (1975). "Languages and Language." In *Minnesota Studies in the Philosophy of Science.* K. Gunderson, Ed. Minneapolis, University of Minnesota Press. pp. 3–35.

Lieberman, M. D. (2000). "Intuition: A Social Cognitive Neuroscience Aproach." *Psychological Bulletin* **126**: 109–137.

Macauley, J. A. (1970). "A Shill for Charity." In *Altruism and Helping Behavior.* J. A. Macauley and L. Berkowitz, Eds. New York, Academic Press.

Macaulay, S. (1963). "Non-Contractual Relations in Business: A Preliminary Study." *American Sociological Review* **28**: 55–67.

Mackie, G. (1996). "Ending Footbinding and Infibulation: A Convention Account." *American Sociological Review* **61**(6): 999–1017.

———— (1997). "Noncredible Social Contracts Are Credible: Communication and Commitment in Social Dilemma Experiments." Unpublished Paper, Mimeo.

Markus, H. and R. B. Zajonc (1985). "The Cognitive Perspective in Social Psychology." In *Handbook of Social Psychology.* G. Lindzey and E. Aronson, Eds. New York, Random House. pp. 137–230.

Matza, D. (1964). *Delinquincy and Drift.* New York, Wiley.

McClelland, J. (1979). "On the Time Relations of Mental Processes: An Examination of Systems of Processes in Cascade." *Psychological Review* **86**: 287–330.

McFarland, C., and D. T. Miller (1990). "Judgments of Self-Other Similiarity: Just Like Others Only More So." *Personality and Social Psychology Bulletin* **16**: 475–484.

Medin, D. and A. Ortony (1989). "Psychological Essentialism." In *Similarity and Analogical Reasoning.* S. Vosniadou and A. Ortony, Eds. Cambridge, Cambridge University Press.

Messick, D. M. and K. Sentis (1983). "Psychological and Sociological Perspectives on Distributive Justice: Convergent, Divergent, and Parallel Lines." In *Equity Theory: Psychological and Sociological Perspectives.* D. M. Messick and K. Cook, Eds. New York, Praeger. pp. 61–94.

Meyer, D. E. and R. W. Schvaneveldt (1971). "Facilitation in Recognizing Pairs of Words: Evidence of a Dependence Between Retrieval Operations." *Journal of Experimental Psychology* **90**: 227–234.

Miller, D. and C. McFarland (1987). "Pluralistic Ignorance: When Similarity Is Interpreted as Dissimilarity." *Journal of Personality and Social Psychology* **53**: 298–305.

Miller, D. and C. McFarland (1991). When Social Comparison Goes Awry: The Case of Pluralistic Ignorance." In *Social Comparison: Contemporary Theory and Research.* J. Suls and T. A. Wills, Eds. Hillsdale, NJ, Erlbaum. pp. 115–133.

Miller, D. and D. A. Prentice (1994). "Collective Errors and Errors About the Collective." *Personality and Social Psychology Bulletin* **20**: 541–550.

Miller, D. and R. Ratner (1998). "The Disparity Between the Actual and Assumed Power of Self-Interest." *Journal of Personality and Social Psychology* **74**: 53–62.

Nisbett, R. and T. Wilson (1977). "Telling More Than We Can Know: Verbal Reports on Mental Processes." *Psychological Review* **84**(3): 231–259.

Nowak, M. A. and R. M. May (2000). *Virus Dynamics.* Oxford, Oxford University Press.

O'Gorman, H. J. (1975). "Pluralistic Ignorance and White Estimates of White Support for Racial Segregation." *Public Opinion Quarterly* **39**: 313–330.

Orbell, J. and R. Dawes (1993). "Social Welfare, Cooperators' Advantage, and the Option of Not Playing the Game." *American Sociological Review* **58**: 787–800.

Orbell, J., A. van de Kragt, and R. Dawes (1988). "Explaining Discussion-Induced Cooperation." *Journal of Personality and Social Psychology* **54**: 811–819.

Orbell, J., A. van de Kragt, and R. Dawes (1991). "Convenants Without the Sword: The Role of Promises in Social Dilemma Circumstances." In *Social Norms and Economic Institutions.* I. K. Koford and D. Miller, Eds. Ann Arbor, University of Michigan Press.

Packard, J. S. and D. J. Willower (1972). "Pluralistic Ignoranc and Pupil Control Ideology." *Journal of Education Administration* **10**: 78–87.

Piliavin, I. M., J. Rodin, et al. (1969). "Good Samaritanism: An Underground Phenomenon?" *Journal of Personality and Social Psychology* **13**: 289–299.

Pillutla, M. and X. P. Chen (1999). "Social Norms and Cooperation in Social Dilemmas." Organizational Behavior and Human Decision Processes **78**: 81–103.

Pratto, F. (1994). "Consciousness and Automatic Evaluation." In *The Heart's Eye: Emotional Influences on Perception and Attention.* P. Niedenthal and S. Kitayama, Eds. San Diego, CA, Academic Press. pp. 115–143.

Prentice, D. A. and D. Miller (1996). "Pluralistic Ignorance and the Perpetuation of Social Norms by Unwitting Actors." *In Advances in Experimental Social Psychology.* M. P. Zanna, Ed. San Diego, CA, Academic Press. pp. 161–209.

Putnam, H. (1988). *Representation and Reality.* Cambridge, MA, MIT Press.

Quine, W. v. O. (1974). *The Roots of Reference.* La Salle, IL, Open Court.

Rabin, M. (1993). "Incorporating Fairness Into Game Theory and Economics." *American Economic Review* **83**: 1281–1302.

Rabin, M. (1995). "Moral Preferences, Moral Constraints, and Self-Serving Biases." Berkeley Dept. of Economics Working Paper No. 95–241.

Ratner, R. and D. Miller (2001). "The Norm of Self-Interest and Its Effects on Social Action." *Journal of Personality and Social Psychology* **81**: 5–16.

Rosch, E., C. B. Mervis, W. D. Gray, D. M. Johnson, and P. Boyes-Braem (1976). "Basic Objects in Natural Categories." *Cognitive Psychology* **8**: 382–439.

Rosch, E. (1978). "Principles of Categorization." In *Cognition and Categorization.* E. Rosch and B. Lloyd, Eds. Hillsdale, NJ, Lawrence Erlbaum Associates.

Ross, L. (1977). "The Intuitive Psychologist and His Shortcomings: Distortions in the Attribution Process." In *Advances in Experimental Social Psychology.* L. Berkowitz, Ed. New York, Academic Press.

Roth, E. M. and E. J. Shoben (1983). "The Effect of Context on the Structure of Categories." *Cognitive Psychology* **15**: 346–378.

Roth, A. E., V. Prasnikar, M. Okuna-Fujiwara, and S. Zamir (1991). "Bargaining and Market Behavior in Jerusalem, Ljubljana, Pittsburgh, and Tokyo: An Experimental Study." *American Economic Review* **81**(5): 1068–1095.

Rothbart, M. and M. Taylor (1992). "Category Labels and Social Reality: Do We View Social Categories as Natural Kinds?" In *Language, Interaction and Social Cognition,* G. R. Semin and K. Fiedler, Eds. London, Sage. pp. 11–36.

Rumelhart, D. E. (1997). "The Architecture of Mind: A Connectionist Approach." In *Mind Design II.* J. Haugeland, Ed. Cambridge, MA, MIT Press. pp. 205–232.

Runciman, W. G. (1966). *Relative Deprivation and Social Justice.* London, Routledge.

Sally, D. (1995). "Conversation and Cooperation in Social Dilemmas." *Rationality and Society* **7**: 58–92.

Schanck, R. L. (1932). "A Study of a Community and Its Groups and Institutions Conceived as Behaviors of Individuals." *Psychological Monographs* **43**(195).

Schank, R. and R. Abelson (1977). *Scripts, Plans, Goals, and Understanding: An Inquiry Into Human Knowledge Structures.* Hillsdale, NJ, Lawrence Erlbaum.

Schelling, T. (1960). *The Strategy of Conflict.* Cambridge, MA, Harvard University Press.

Schelling, T. (1961). "Experimental Games and Bargaining Theory." *World Politics* **14**(1): 47–68.

Schopler, J. and C. A. Insko (1992). "The Discontinuity Effect in Interpersonal and Intergroup Relations: Generality and Mediation." In *European Review of Social Psychology, Vol. 3.* W. Stroebe and M. Hewstone, Eds., New York, John Wiley. pp. 121–151.

Schroeder, D. A., T. D. Jensen, J. Reed, D. K. Sullivan, and M. Schwab (1983). "The Actions of Others as Determinants of Behavior in Social Trap Situations." *Journal of Experimental Social Psychology* **19**: 522–539.

Schwartz, S. H. and G. T. Clausen (1970). "Responsibility, Norms, and Helping in an Emergency." *Journal of Personality and Social Psychology* **16**: 299–310.

Shanks, D. (2005). "Implicit Learning." In *Handbook of Cognition.* K. Lamberts and R. L. Goldstone, Eds. London: Sage.

Sherif, M. (1966). *In Common Predicament.* Boston, MA, Houghton Mifflin.

Simmel, G. (1950). *The Sociology of Georg Simmel.* New York, Free Press.

Skyrms, B. (1996). *Evolution of the Social Contract.* Cambridge, Cambridge University Press.

Sugden, R. (2000). "The Motivating Power of Expectations." In *Rationality, Rule and Structure*. J. Nida-Rumelin and W. Spohu, Eds., The Netherlands: Kluwer.

Sugden, R., and R. Cubitt (2003). "Common Knowledge, Salience and Convention: A Reconstruction of David Lewis's Game Theory." *Economics and Philosophy* **19**: 175–210.

Tajfel, H. (1970). "Experiments in Intergroup Discrimination." *Scientific American* **5**(223): 79–97.

——— (1973). "The Roots of Prejudice: Cognitive Aspects." In *Psychology and Race*. P. Watson, Ed. Harmondsworth, Penguin.

——— (1981). *Human Groups and Social Categories*. Cambridge, Cambridge University Press.

——— (1982). "Social Psychology of Intergroup Relations." *Annual Review of Psychology* **33**: 1–30.

Tajfel, H., M. Billig, R. Bundy, and C. Flament (1971). "Social Categorization in Intergroup Behavior." *European Journal of Social Psychology* **1**: 149–178.

Tetlock, P. E. and R. Boettger (1989). "Accountability: a Social Magnifier of the Dilution Effect." *Journal of Personality and Social Psychology* **57**: 388–398.

Thaler, R. H. (1992). *The Winner's Curse: Paradoxes and Anomalies in Economic Life*. New York, Free Press.

Turnbull (1972). *The Mountain People*. New York, Simon and Schuster.

Turner, J. C., M. A. Hogg, P. J. Oakes, S. D. Reicher, and M. S. Wetherell (1987). *Rediscovering the Social Group: A Self-Categorization Theory*. Oxford, Blackwell.

Tversky, A. and D. Kahneman (1981). "The Framing of Decisions and the Psychology of Choice." *Science* **211**: 453–458.

Ullmann-Margalit, E. (1977). *The Emergence of Norms*. Oxford, Oxford University Press.

Van Avermaet, E. (1974). "Equity: A Theoretical and Empirical Analysis." In *Psychology*. Santa Barbara, University of California, Press.

Vanderschraaf, P. and B. Skyrms (1994). "Deliberational Correlated Equilibrium." *Philosophy Topics* **21**: 191–227.

Wason, P. and P. Johnson-Laird (1972). *Psychology of Reasoning: Structure and Content*. Cambridge, MA, Harvard University Press.

Wheeler, S. (1961). "Socialization in Correctional Communities." *American Sociological Review* **26**: 697–712.

Wuthnow, R. (1991). *Acts of Compassion: Caring for Others and Helping Ourselves*. Princeton, Princeton University Press.

Yamagishi, T. (1998). *Structure of Trust*. Tokyo, Tokyo University Press.

Yamagishi, T. and K. Cook (1993). "Generalized Exchange and Social Dilemmas." *Social Psychology Quarterly* **56**(4): 235–248.

Yamagishi, T., N. Jin, and T. Kiyonari (1999). "Bounded Generalized Reciprocity: In-Group Boasting and In-Group Favoritism." *Advances in Group Processes* **16**: 161–197.

Index

abstract concepts, difficulty defining, 95

activation, 57
    experimentation's role in understanding of, 59
    focus on norm required for, 58
    network structure, organization of concepts in, 72, 73
    schemata and scripts activated by categorization, 81
    situation and context, specificity to, 80
    spreading activation process, 70–76, 83

Alexander, Jason, 221, 231

Allison, S. T., 173

altruism, 16–20, 105, 106, 189

ambiguous situations leading to conflicting interpretations of applicable norms, 78

Andersen, Hans Christian, 185, 196

anti-social and pro-social behavior. *See also* unpopular norms
    descriptive *vs.* social norms used to control, 64–68, 70
    evolution of norms controlling, 214
    external interventions affecting, 195
    group communication creating negative norms, 177
    manipulation of norms to control, 7
    "preaching to the converted," problem of, 75
    transgressions of social norms, effect of, 72
    zero tolerance policies, effectiveness of, 67, 73

AR (Authority Ranking), 92

Ash, C., 193

asymmetric information and payoffs, Ultimatum games with, 118–121

attention to cues leading to categorization, 85–88

attribution error, 189

Authority Ranking (AR), 92

awareness and choice, 47

Axelrod, R., 217

Bayesian games
    awareness and choice in following social norms, 48
    fairness norms and Ultimatum games, 121
    prisoner's dilemma games transformed into coordination games by cooperative norms, 27, 28

245

Made in United States
North Haven, CT
24 February 2024

49068612R00167